AF886777

FERTILIZERS

FERTILIZERS: OLIN/EISENMAN

JULIA CZERNIAK
FOREWORD BY CLAUDIA GOULD

INSTITUTE OF CONTEMPORARY ART / UNIVERSITY OF PENNSYLVANIA

FERTILIZERS: OLIN/EISENMAN

Published on the occasion of the exhibition at Institute of Contemporary Art,
September 9 – December 17, 2006.

ISBN 0-88454-109-6

Institute of Contemporary Art
University of Pennsylvania
118 South 36th Street
Philadelphia PA 19104
www.icaphila.org

EDITOR: JENELLE PORTER, ICA ASSOCIATE CURATOR
DESIGN: PURTILL FAMILY BUSINESS
PRINTED BY SHAPCO PRINTING, INC., MINNEAPOLIS

PHOTOGRAPHY CREDITS:
ALL OLIN IMAGES COURTESY OLIN PARTNERSHIP
ALL EISENMAN IMAGES COURTESY EISENMAN ARCHITECTS
FERTILIZERS INSTALLATION: AARON IGLER

COVER IMAGE: FERTILIZERS, INSTALLATION VIEW

CONTENTS

THE OLIN/EISENMAN AFFAIR

I have always visualized relationships as beginning with a strand of string that over time forms knots, where additional pieces are linked, interlacing one another—sometimes they become infinite, other times not. This ever-forming constellation becomes the basis for all relationships. Here, we have one knot composed of architect Peter Eisenman and landscape architect Laurie Olin. And then we have the growing constellation of their twenty-five-year collaborative practice, the people they've met along the way, the stories that follow, the projects they built, and the ones that were lost. This on-again, off-again affair of built and unbuilt projects of Olin and Eisenman is the reason for this project at the Institute of Contemporary Art.

On a more personal note, the Eisenman/Olin affair has also formed an endless series of interconnections for me; some immediate, some remote, unbeknownst to either of the parties and most of all to myself. In late fall of 1988, a year before the Wexner Center for the Arts opened, I was hired as Curator of Exhibitions. The building was Peter Eisenman's first, as well as the first realized collaboration between Eisenman and Olin. The landscape as extension of the building was as controversial as the building itself and has subsequently informed many of their future collaborations. It was there that I met both men. Working and living with the building changed the way I look and see, and began my long affair with architecture. When I became director at Artists Space in 1994, we reinvigorated a dormant architecture series. The first person I contacted in this endeavor was Peter Eisenman, inviting him to select a younger architect to create a project. He invited Greg Lynn. A year later Lynn selected Dutch architectural team Ben van Berkel and art historian Caroline Bos (UN Studio). In recent years, they have all completed projects at ICA. While all of this may seem simply to be life in six degrees of separation, it has informed my thinking and reading about architecture in a profound way.

"Fertlizers: Olin/Eisenman" came about while talking with Detlef Mertins, Chair, Department of Architecture at Penn, who brought to my attention the history of the twenty-five (or so) built and unbuilt collaborative projects of the two men. As a contemporary art museum, our way of working with architects is to commission them to create a new project. Instead of showing models and plans of past projects, we proposed that Olin and Eisenman represent the language they have developed over the past twenty-five years. To document and explore the history of their collaborative practice, ICA produced a book that extends the three-dimensional to two. In truly collaborative form neither this exhibition nor the book represents the work of either architect or landscape architect as separate, but is a hybrid of both—a third strand of being—which I am proud to see take shape at ICA.

As individuals, the two could not be more different in their practices or as people, and it is unusual for both landscape and building architects to have such a fruitful and generative relationship. Through their respective practices, Olin and Eisenman have developed a unique language and new terminologies for a thoroughly integrated approach to site development where neither building nor surrounding environment is given priority. What would the Wexner Center be without those extraordinary, disorientating plinths and the indigenous grass that grows wild next to the calculated (dis)order of the building.

For "Fertilizers" the architects have created a space that is disorienting and even physically dizzying. For instance, while ascending or descending the ramp one must hold the handrail or risk losing one's equilibrium. Nausea is not unusual. (Peter Eisenman himself refused to make the ascent for this very reason, but toddlers reveled in the experience). The "forest of trees" alters the usual flow of passage with its density of nearly identical "trees." The forced perspective of seemingly endless trees can be disorienting. This kind of play of perception, which includes body and mind, are at the heart of Eisenman and Olin's collaborative architectural projects. Their work brings to mind experiential and monumental works by sculptor Walter De Maria (*The Earth Room*, 1977 and *The Broken Kilometer*, 1979), and the light installations of James Turrell, where disorientation, perspective, foreground and background all become a singular extraordinary experience of moving, seeing and being.

I thank Peter and Laurie for generously creating this project at ICA. In the scope of their history together this is a small, but important, knot on the long rope of accomplishments and collaborations, one that demonstrates, among many things, how hard those in their profession work, how few realized projects come from that hard work, and how important those not realized become to the ones that follow. The main essayist for this publication is Julia Czerniak, Associate Professor, Syracuse Architecture, who has for many years thought about this unique history. We are pleased to be publishing her essay. At the Eisenman office, I am very thankful to Cynthia Davidson, a publisher and writer, who has taken on many aspects of this publication. At Olin Partnership I want to thank Frank Garnier, Associate, who assisted with the logistics of creating this installation, and Daneil Mazone, Director of Marketing, for her help with the book and coordinating images. At ICA I've worked closely with our Associate Curator Jenelle Porter whose deep interest and love of the design profession has helped me with this project and this publication. In charge of the installation at ICA was Exhibition Coordinator and Registrar Robert Chaney. Along with Shannon Bowser, our Head Preparator, they have been responsible for researching the feasibility of building this project within budget. Robert and Shannon are constantly given projects with many challenges, and in the end the projects are done so magnificently, so flawlessly, one would never know those challenges existed. I am also grateful to Senior Curator Ingrid Schaffner for her insightful guidance, and to the entire curatorial department for their help in every aspect: Curator of Education Johanna Plummer, Assistant Curator Elyse Gonzales, and Whitney Lauder Curatorial Fellow Naomi Beckwith. Jill Katz, Manager of Marketing and Communications, does a brilliant job getting the word out there. My assistant Chris Wieman was very helpful in pulling details together. On the funding side, I am endlessly indebted to our Director of Development, Marilyn Pollick, who worked very hard to raise additional funds for this project, and her staff: Barbara Allen, Denise Berry and Elysa Voshell. And finally, my thanks to our incredible business administrator Cassandra Green.

The main funding for this commission came from Philadelphia Exhibitions Initiative (PEI), a granting program of the Philadelphia Center for Arts and Heritage, funded by The Pew Charitable Trusts and administered by The University of the Arts, Philadelphia. At PEI I would like to thank our friend and colleague Paula Marincola for her deep understanding of the importance of the integration of design and architecture into the contemporary art dialogue. We are also grateful for funding from Elise Jaffe + Jeffrey Brown and the Goldberg Foundation, Inc. ICA acknowledges support from the architectural and design community: Amuneal Manufacturing Corp.; The Accent on Architecture Grants Program, supported by grants from the American Architectural Foundation, CNA Insurance Companies and Victor O. Schinnerer & Company, Inc.; Atkin Olshin Lawson-Bell Architects; Ballinger; KieranTimberlake Associates LLP; MGA Partners, Architects; and Minima Inc. For additional funding we thank The Horace W. Goldsmith Foundation, the Commonwealth of Pennsylvania Council on the Arts, The Dietrich Foundation, Inc., the Overseers Board for the Institute of Contemporary Art, friends and members of ICA, and the University of Pennsylvania, and for in-kind support, Loews Philadelphia Hotel.

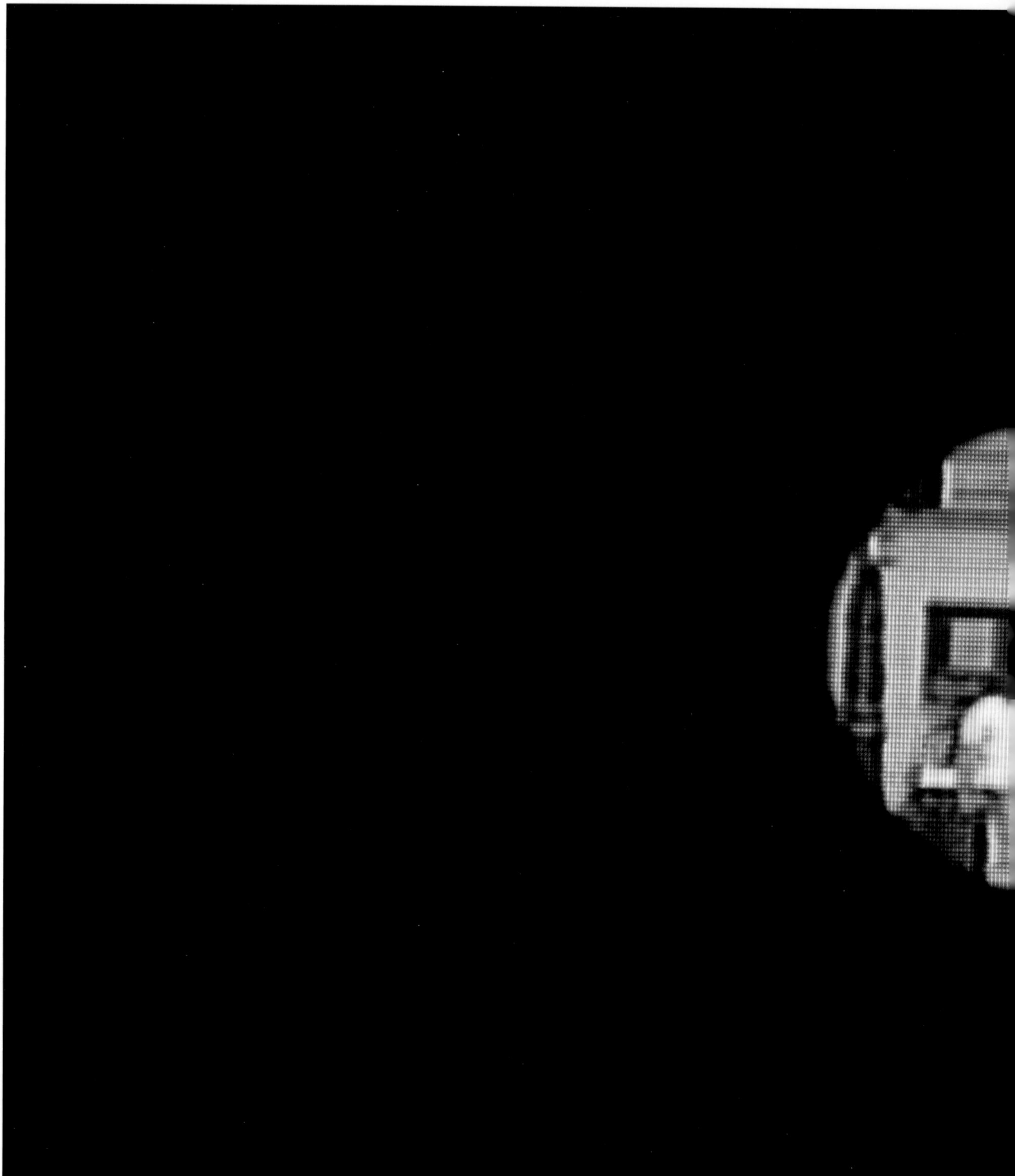

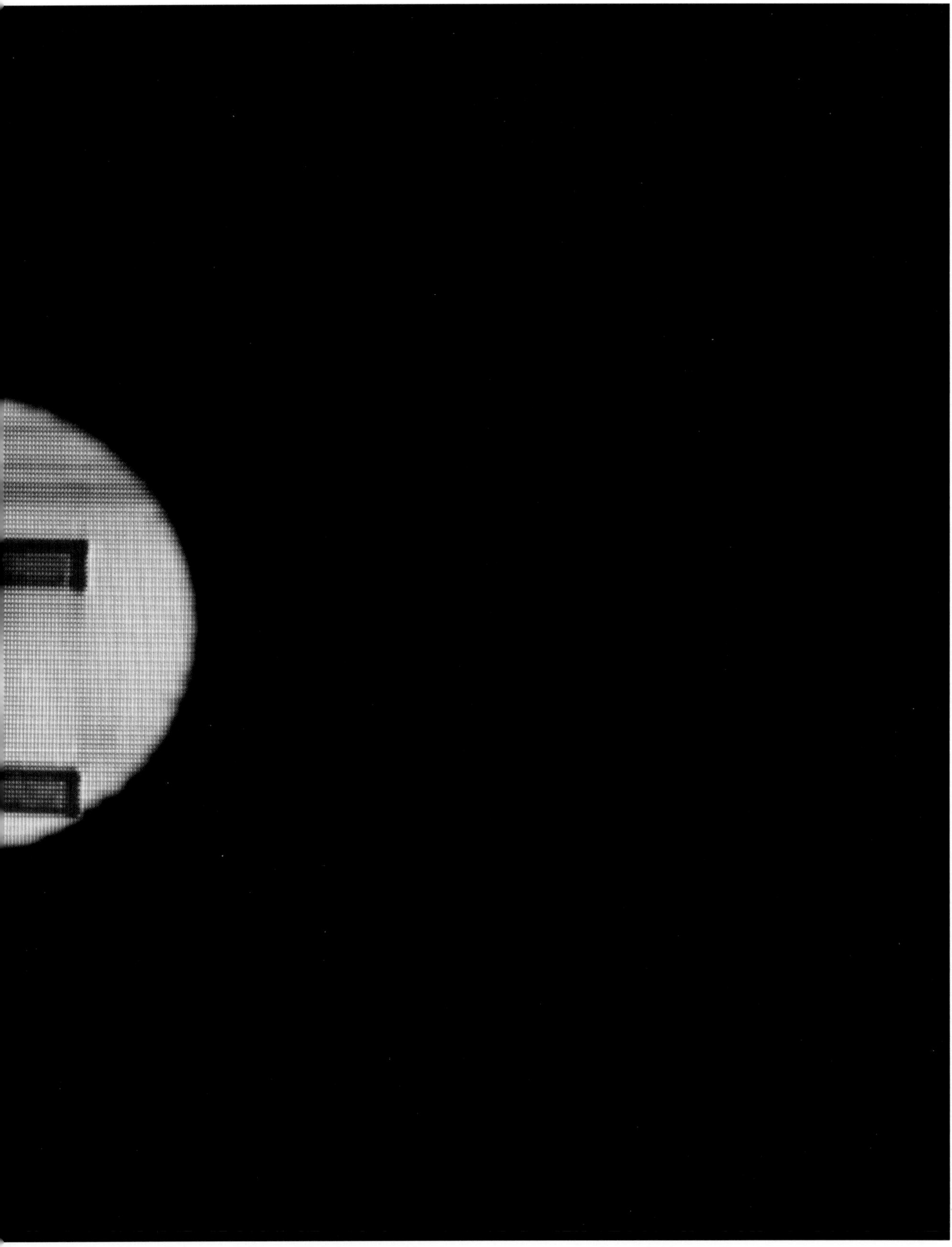

INSTALLATION VIEW, FERTILIZERS

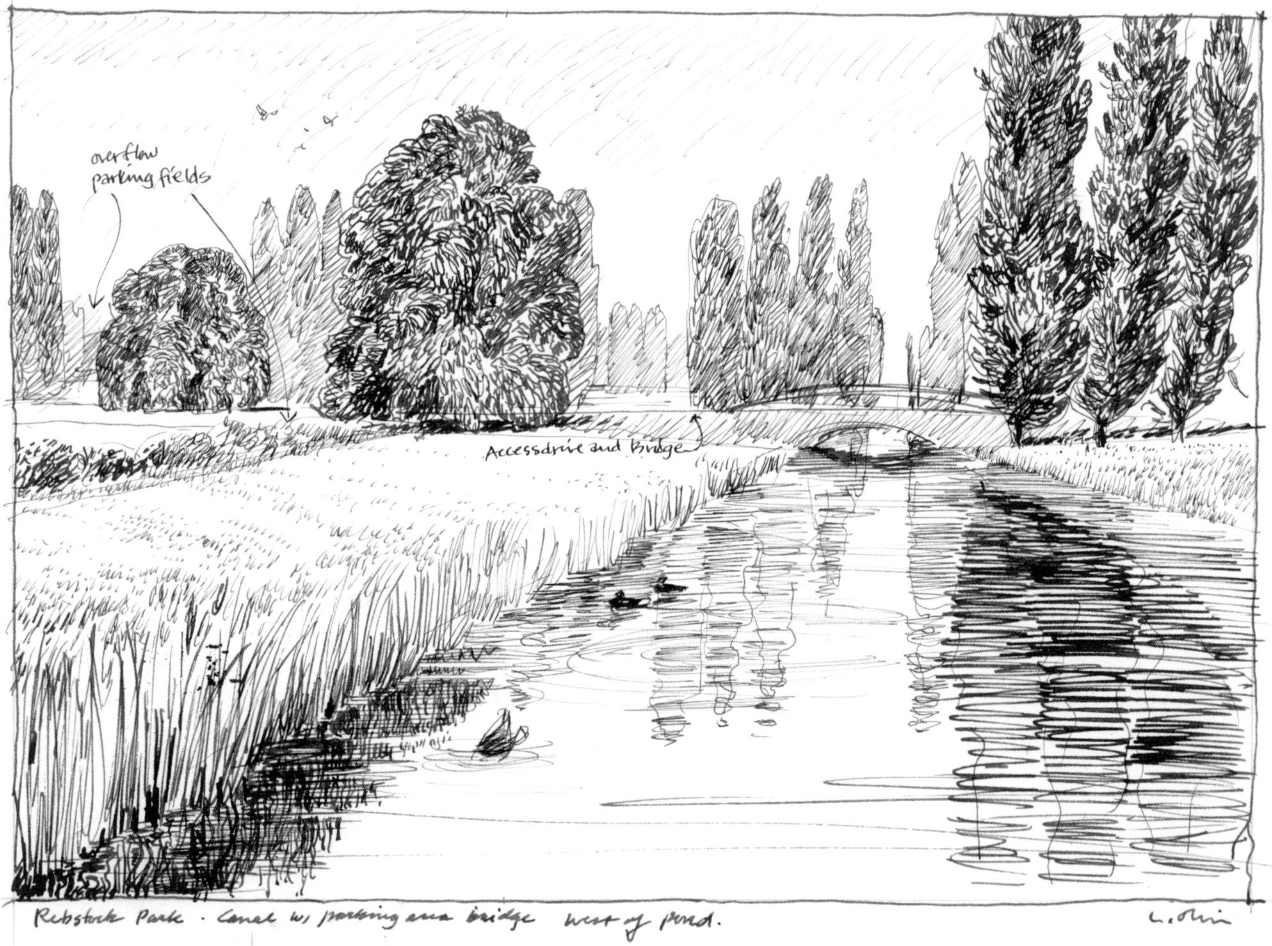

LAURIE OLIN, DRAWING FOR REBSTOCKPARK MASTER PLAN

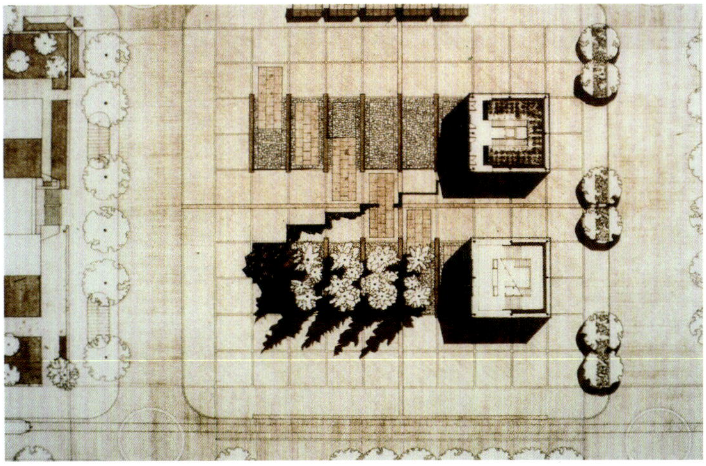

LANDSCAPE'S ARCHITECTURAL LOGICS: THE OLIN/EISENMAN PROJECTS

At Ohio State, I remember the point where Peter said, "It's great, we got it," and I said, "Peter, we only have these three lines." He said, "Yes, but they're the right lines." I said, "Well, I don't know if it's a building or a path." He said, "It doesn't matter; we'll figure it out." —LAURIE OLIN, ON THE DESIGN OF THE WEXNER CENTER

The longtime collaboration between architect and theorist Peter Eisenman and landscape architect Laurie Olin is as unique as it is unlikely, producing experimental work that has shaped our culture's expanding perception of what buildings and landscapes are, how they look, and what they do. Their approach to twenty-five projects over twenty-six years reflects the shifting relations between architecture and landscape during a time when the disciplines were playing a tactical game, continually swapping major and minor roles. The Olin/Eisenman projects coincide with a widespread attempt to retrieve the "art" of landscape by allowing design to assert the discipline's constructedness—as opposed to the presumed moral correctness of a "naturalism" that had dominated the field since the rise of the environmental movement and the publication of Ian McHarg's influential *Design with Nature* in 1969.

Design critic R.E. Somol has suggested that landscape's postwar move away from its conventional associations with composition and planting was enabled by appropriating architecture's modernist preoccupation with "space and structure"[1]—as exemplified in projects such as Dan Kiley's Miller Garden (1955). In turn, architecture's recent concern with "surface and contingent event"[2] and deployment of the language of "emergence," "ecology," and "field" draws unmistakably and successfully from landscape discourse and sensibility—so much so that architects frequently outnumber landscape architects as leads on influential design competitions such as Downsview Park in Toronto (1999).

Within this context of productive exchange, the Olin/Eisenman collaboration began in 1980 with the Portland Pioneer Square competition. This would be a fortuitous juncture: Eisenman's interests were shifting from object to ground, while Olin, after interacting with classical archeologists at the American Academy in Rome, discovered a renewed sense of the layered potential of a horizontal surface. This project's location in the Pacific northwest, near Olin's childhood landscape of Alaska, proved more consequential than their subsequent competition scheme, in that it revealed a shared interest in how natural systems (with their association with force and dynamism) can inform urbanism and produce forms in ways that challenge conventional processes.

Olin and Eisenman's subsequent concern with *ground* and *time* constitutes a major project that undergoes collaborative highs and lows, initiated by processes and outcomes that would be reiterated, reinvigorated, and reorganized over the next twenty-five years. Disciplinary preoccupations with "ground"—and its associations of lowness and limit, solidity and foundation, even basis and principle—hybridize with those of "land"—and its implications of a territory defined by people

DRAWING FOR PIONEER COURTHOUSE SQUARE COMPETITION

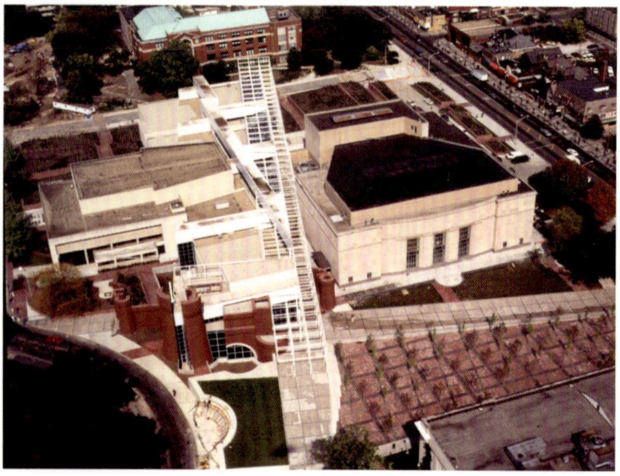

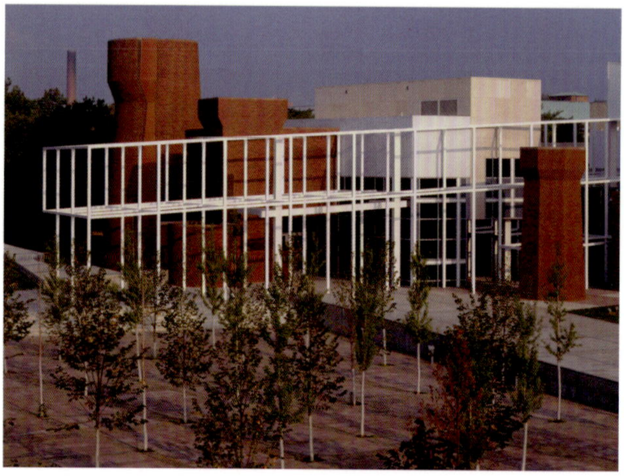

and their relationships to a living earth (through cultivation, establishment of boundaries, and claims of ownership). This ground-land hybrid is the site of the ongoing game of disciplinary exchange between Olin and Eisenman. Time in this exchange is favored over space, from the synchronic mapping of vastly different diachronic scales (geological, historical, seasonal, and diurnal), to movement and perception, to a preoccupation with the formative logics of the design process itself, and to the subtle ways landscape materials change on a site.

To discuss this work is to recognize that few of the proposals are built (only the Wexner Center for the Arts in Columbus, Ohio; the Holocaust Memorial in Berlin; and, currently under construction, the City of Culture of Galicia, Santiago de Compostela, Spain).[3] Thus representations, many of them produced in Eisenman's office and well publicized in lectures, books, journals, and exhibitions, form the basis of their critical reception and their contribution to the discourse of architecture and urbanism. Yet few of Olin's landscape drawings have had such visibility and scrutiny. Despite their shared concerns, Eisenman's representations (in which landscape is a blind spot) and Olin's drawings (where landscape is envisioned) suggest different concerns.

What follows is a survey of ground and time in a number of their collaborations, and an examination of the organizational strategies and diagrammatic structures of this work as viewed *through the lens of landscape*. The projects' derivations (how they begin and are developed), articulations (how they are activated in material ways), and effects (how they appear and perform) suggest that in various ways at numerous scales, the projects; 1) merge intellectual and ecological agendas that challenge landscape's "naturalized" appearance; 2) critique figure/ground contextualism in a way that challenges both grounds (as base conditions, origins, and essential figures) and, subsequently, landscape as the background for architecture; and 3) according to Olin, "refer to and represent ideas of change and process while positioning them into some sort of long-term frame."[4] The subject matter is emergence and mutability, yet the material manifestations are for the most part fixed. Olin is skeptical about what he calls the passing fashion of employing change as part of "the fact as well as the idea of design," a practice that will lead to "impermanence and designs that self-destruct." Nonetheless, the critique of the Olin/Eisenman projects in advanced design circles as "just representation" often overlooks the more nuanced ways and scales that time plays out.

The Wexner Center (1983+) is the beginning of a series of collaborations undertaken in the early to mid-1980s that reflect the designers' preoccupation with architecture's textual logics and the capacity of architecture and landscape to be read. These projects work with memory based in language and history, driven essentially through a study of site. At the Wexner Center, Eisenman and Olin initiated a process that they would repeat and refine: first, identify the intrinsic and extrinsic information that produces a project's organization (in this case, a collision of grids and the memory of the armory that once occupied the site), and then "figure out" how that memory can be articulated and developed. The massing concept of the Wexner Center is one instance of "figuring." What Eisenman termed an "archeological earthwork"—essentially landscape and scaffolding—was the first incarnation of a figured ground, a pursuit to which Olin and Eisenman would often return. Olin's use

WEXNER CENTER FOR THE ARTS

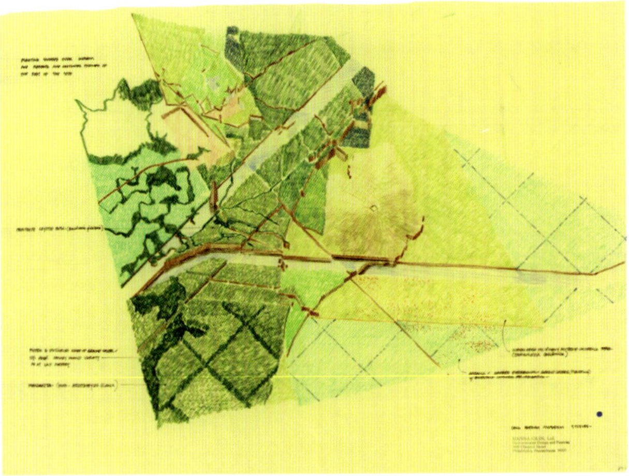

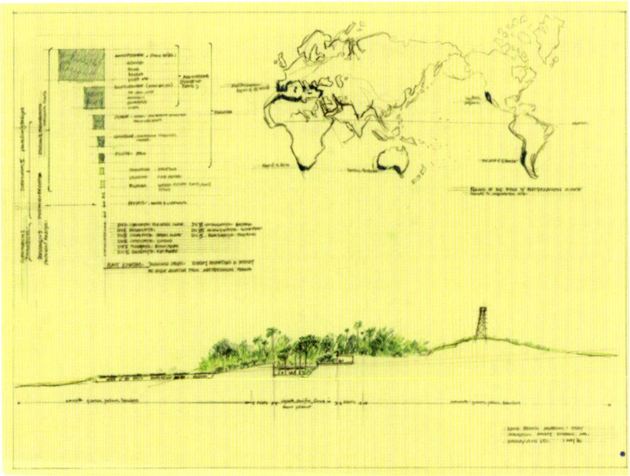

of a "wallpaper" of three ornamental grasses in the project, one tall and spiky, one fluffy and green, and one with seed heads, was meant to evoke the midwestern prairie, but it also had the more provocative intent to challenge landscape's subordinate, calm, and supine role and render ambiguous building/ground relations. The disrupted pattern simulated nature's accidents, and was, as he describes, "in your face, taller than you were, extremely dynamic and not what the Ohio people like or wanted." This reversal of landscape's normative role as a background to architecture (in the horizontal dimension as a ground on which an object sits; in the vertical, a framing scene) parallels the work of designers such as Peter Walker (Burnett Park, 1983) and is continued in contemporary work by Hargreaves Associates and Martha Schwartz.

The projects for the University of California, Long Beach (1986+) and the Carnegie Mellon Research Institute (1988+), produced when both Eisenman and Olin were teaching studios at Harvard, advance their interests in memory, history, and language. These early projects rely on their contents to refer to landscape, a tactic later replaced when computational techniques enable smooth and fluid form to do the job.

At Long Beach, perhaps the most articulated example of their shared sensibility, the building takes its form from a synchronic mapping of the histories of the site—of the ranch that once existed there, the campus, and the changing configurations of fault lines, a river, a channel, and the coastline—and is supplemented by iconic elements such as an oil-rig tower and a pier. By engaging multiple scales of time, the project neutralizes the value of each. This process reflects Eisenman's interest in "reading the building as an architectural artifact, a palimpsest of its own history,"[5] even one of its future. The thick mat of information that this mapping process produces is undeniably a landscape, a particular form of ground, in that its contents imply such things as measure (property ownership), economies (the ground as resource—oil), and patterns of domestication.

The programmatic conflation of a museum and an arboretum furthers the reading of the project as continuous ground, where almost the entire museum was to be below earth forms. The geometry of the arboretum, the surface of this ground exploration, overlays a loose field of plants onto a grid—a sort of "outdoor filing cabinet." These landscape materials play a large role in articulating the project's extruded plates. Olin's diagram of Southern California as a Mediterranean climate informs the planting palette, patterned through upland and riparian plants juxtaposed with Mediterranean and agricultural species.

The Long Beach project proposal has significant implications for landscape discourse. First, landscape is generative: its disciplinary logic (for instance, the gridded disposition of landscape program, superimposed with a pastoral composition) produces, not just articulates, the geometry of the organizational armature. The estuary and shifting coast that contribute to this effect are used dynamically: they "erode" a path through the site. This organization challenges the assumptions, in 1986, of how a designed landscape looks. Second, the project's layered and shifting ground offers new ways of seeing: it continually exposes different surfaces to viewers as they move through the ensemble. This organizational strategy encourages what Olin calls "the happy accident, where you set things in motion that produce convergences

LAURIE OLIN, DRAWINGS FOR UNIVERSITY ART MUSEUM, CALIFORNIA STATE UNIVERSITY, LONG BEACH

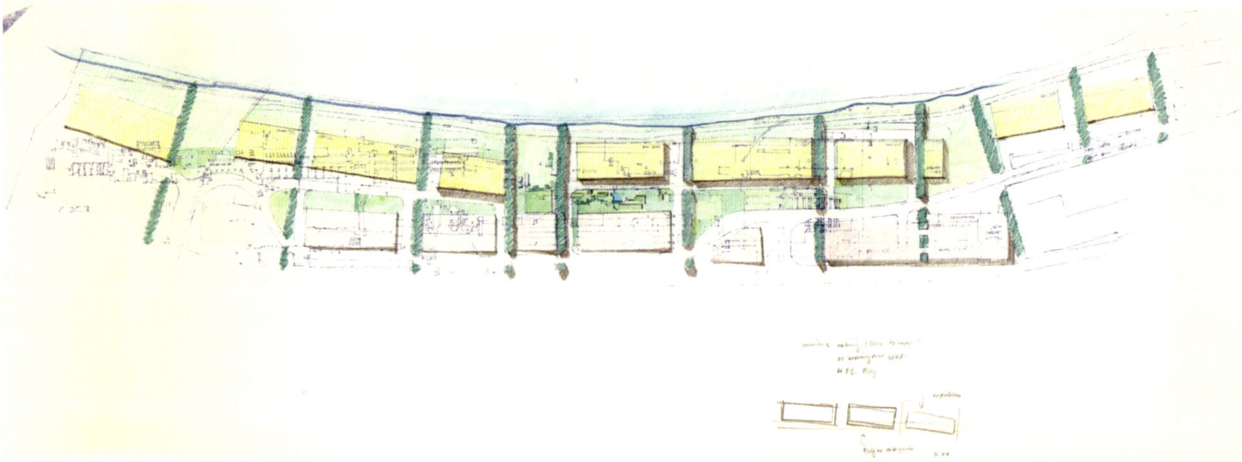

and coincidences that you couldn't invent." The interest in new ways of seeing has unintended disciplinary effects. This desire for simultaneity, with roots in collage and montage, challenge conventional ways of seeing landscape through a singular point of view or as a carefully orchestrated set of views. By calling the Wexner Center a "landscape," Olin intends precisely this: the need to move fully through and around the project to grasp its contents.

Finally, Eisenman's interest in fractal geometry and nonscalar mathematics—the ability to describe the same elements, from clouds to typhoons, across a range of scales—inspired for Olin a way to critique landscape practice as overly dependent on human scale. For example, his rescaled estuary within the arboretum (articulated through plants) changes the relationship of the body to the landscape by simulating a perception of the ground as if one were flying above it.

By the time the pair collaborated on the Carnegie Mellon Research Institute (CMRI)—a master plan for the Pittsburgh technology center and design for a new biotechnology institute—Eisenman's interest in the textual logics of sites seems supplanted by an engagement with the mathematical logics of Boolean geometry, a geometric model for computer processing. Olin's continued preoccupation with what he calls "place memory," or "the memory of the evolving nature of places themselves, the physical evolution of the land that is often hidden or absent except in traces left behind," spurred him to produce, at CMRI, his richest ground to date.

Carboniferous-era forests exposed by glacial run-off, a green river snaking through the site, hedgerows that mark the property lines of early riverfront settlers, the evocative foundation ruins of a steel mill, rusting steel parking garages, and a string of buildings on top of asphalt parking lots—these all constitute a template of past and future information from which to draw when designing. Moreover, the material development of the project aided the articulation of the site's embedded histories. For instance, Olin proposed using hard anthracite coal, with its striking high luster, for vertical shifts and berms that separated pedestrians from cars. For Olin, the innovation of this reiterated process and its subsequent material development is its inversion of a design method dear to the discipline: the typical McHargian process of mapping sites for analytic purposes now becomes generative. This technique (synchronic mapping) and its effects (site as open-ended text) foreshadow much landscape work to come.

Between their work on Long Beach and CMRI, Eisenman and Olin collaborated on the Biocentrum (1986+), a technical and educational institution and campus outside of Frankfurt. This project favored the operational over the figurative, and projected an infrastructure that provided a matrix for the future development of the university. Reinforcing strategies of extension implied by infrastructure, the site is further articulated through a series of horizontal bands formed by buildings (themselves resulting from the action of the three most basic processes by which DNA constructs protein: replication, transcription, translation) and landscape. This interest in infrastructure would recur in their work five years later in Germany: Rebstock Park in Frankfurt (1990+) and the Banhoff Friedrichstrasse Redevelopment in Berlin (1994), where it both resulted from and drove the development of the ground as a geologic, hydrologic, vegetative, and circulatory system—an ecological infrastructure that works.

DRAWING FOR CARNEGIE MELLON UNIVERSITY RESEARCH INSTITUTE

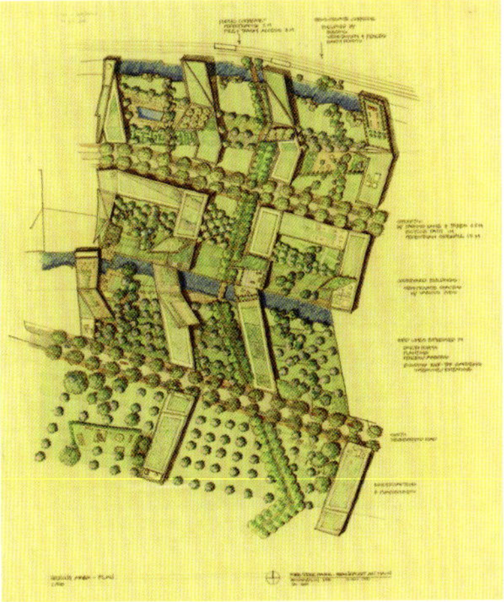

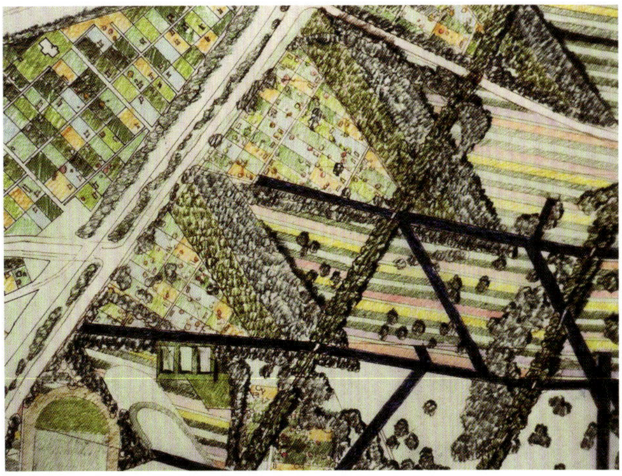

The Rebstockpark Master Plan in Frankfurt is an urban landscape of housing, offices, commercial space, and a large urban park proposed in 1991 as a critique of the "static urbanism" of figure/ground contextualism.[6] Much has been written, by Eisenman and others, on the analog of catastrophe theory, the strategy of folding and the design processes that forms the fictive structure and promised effects of Rebstockpark.[7] Evident and inferable information on the building lot are appropriated and reconfigured as a complex weave of elements that extend into the site's larger context, here the regional greenbelt. Additionally, urban aspects of the site's morphology (offices, shops, houses, recreation, and parking) are interspersed with elements drawn from the regional agricultural landscape (orchards, meadows, produce gardens, woodlands, irrigation ditches, hedgerows, and canals), thereby creating an artificial place in the city with both urban and rural characteristics. This reconfiguration is enabled by the structure of a regular grid overlaid by a distorted one that, when connected, create lines of motion through which the ground planes and buildings are folded.

The promises of the scheme—its alternative figure/ground and city/nature dialogues—are made manifest through both the architectural and landscape strategies. Eisenman refers to the site weave as promoting a "ground surface … which becomes a topologic event/structure," that inevitably dissolves—yet subsequently reframes—normative relationships of old/new, object/context, and figure/ground.[8] In Olin's terms, the potential of the project "may afford new and different relationships between people, their daily routines, and the environment," a proposition supported by the thoughtful and detailed development of the landscape plan.[9]

Formally, the landscape elements—walks and roads, vegetation, drainage swales, and landform—were used to articulate the folded grid, producing an infrastructure that gives both a new form and image to the park, all the while addressing its social and ecological programs. These programs, developed by Olin, provide respite from increased urbanization while focusing on air quality and movement as well as the hydrologic cycle—measures intended to help balance regional natural systems of vital importance to the ecology of the city.

To this end, the two principal devices integral to the landscape infrastructure are extensive tree rows and drainage swales. The tree rows were developed as various combinations of canopy, understory, and orchard tree species, such as apple, cherry, and peach. Monoculture plantings seen in traditional urban parks are here replaced with rural and agricultural landscape typologies such as the farmer's hedgerow. Organized in several orientations and layouts, the trees join patches of fields, shrubs, and grass in an effort to control microclimate. A strong formal element made of the drainage swales and canals forms an integrated site network, dramatizing the conservation of rainfall, the cleansing of waste effluents, and the redirecting of water flow back to the earth. This variety of landscape elements and their organization provide moments of interface, or ecotones, where one ecological environment meets another, producing favorable conditions for increased species diversity and wildlife habitat.[10]

Olin acknowledges that the strategy of folding provides an arbitrary geometric system that is an armature for the emergence of Rebstockpark, and certainly its structure can be seen to represent complex processes. Although much of nature can

LAURIE OLIN, DRAWINGS FOR REBSTOCKPARK MASTER PLAN

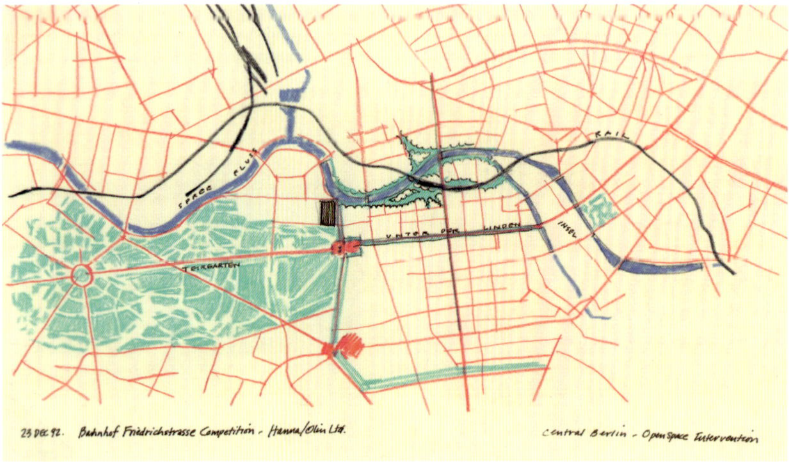

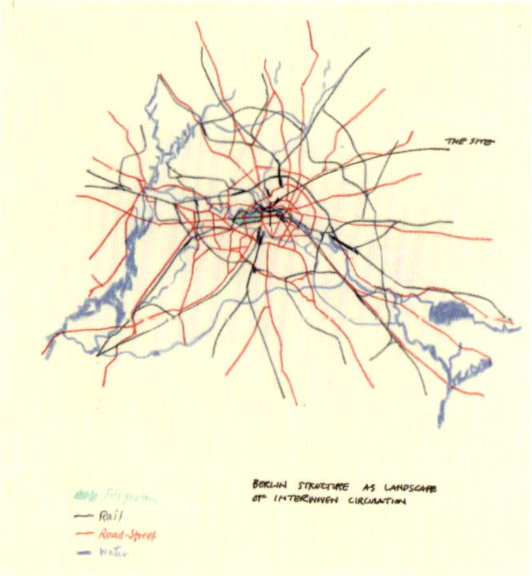

be explained through mathematical equations, for a landscape that actually works to be designed by using one is not only unusual but promising in its effects.

Whereas Rebstock's resulting ecological infrastructure was accidentally produced through an architectural process, the organizational armature for the Banhoff Friedrichstrasse competition was unmistakably driven by landscape. Much less developed than Rebstock, the innovation here is thinking of the city as a topographic, hydrologic, and vegetative network at diverse scales. At the largest scale, Olin's drawing of Berlin as a landscape shows an intertwined circulation system defined by rivers, canals, railroads, and roadways. The project site is a microcosm of these intertwined strands overlaid onto what was a poorly drained and marshy part of the city. Adjacent to this site, another scale of infrastructure is evidenced in the Tiergarten, a nineteenth-century large park used as an imperial pleasure ground. Its plan is comprised of layers of pathways, water, and vegetation that have both accumulated and been erased over time, such as the allées and rond-ponts, sinuous walks, and glades. This structure inspired a network of green pedestrian ways that mirror and analogously extend the systems in the Tiergarten onto the project site, bringing vegetation, light, ventilation, and a drainage system into a dense configuration of building—an ecological infrastructure that predates the term landscape urbanism.[11]

Eisenman and Olin continued their long-standing research focus on ground and time in two projects of the late 1990s: the competition for a new campus center at the Illinois Institute of Technology (IIT) in 1997 and the City of Culture of Galicia (1999+) where they were aided by new computational techniques and inspired by the contemporary possibilities of the diagram. The smooth surfaces and fluid forms of these projects—which could be called "earthworks"—look very different from the ground projects of the 1980s. For Eisenman, this shift relates to the morphogenetic ideas of matter (the notion that matter contains the internal processes to make form) and the possibility of exerting horizontal forces that have nothing to do with gravity, both of which locate themselves in the processes of the project's emergence.

Eisenman suggests that in their project for the IIT student center, "the material reality of site is used to critique the idealism of Mies's static objects."[12] Using an overlay of the grid of IIT (drawn from the building edges) and the ideal Miesian grid (24 x 24 x 12 feet) that spatializes the ground, they produce an underground city where "landscape objects" are suspended. Their polemic, using landscape as a warped and wrinkled field to reframe the plane of the IIT campus, disturbs the idealism of Mies's horizontal plane and replaces the abstract plain of Chicago with the textured undulations of the prairie.[13] This "expansive landscape gesture," Eisenman argues, assimilates the static idealism of Mies's grid in a new dimension of temporality.[14]

The temporality of the ground is advanced in Olin's nuanced development of this prairie. Olin's interest in the prairie (seen already at Wexner) is characterized by its formation by natural processes (such as the depositing of sediments, geologic uplifting, cycles of glaciation and erosion) as well as the harmonious texture of a variety of grasses and wildflowers.[15] Using these landscape elements along with earth forms and pavement,

LAURIE OLIN, DRAWINGS FOR BANHOFF FRIEDRICHSTRASSE COMPETITION

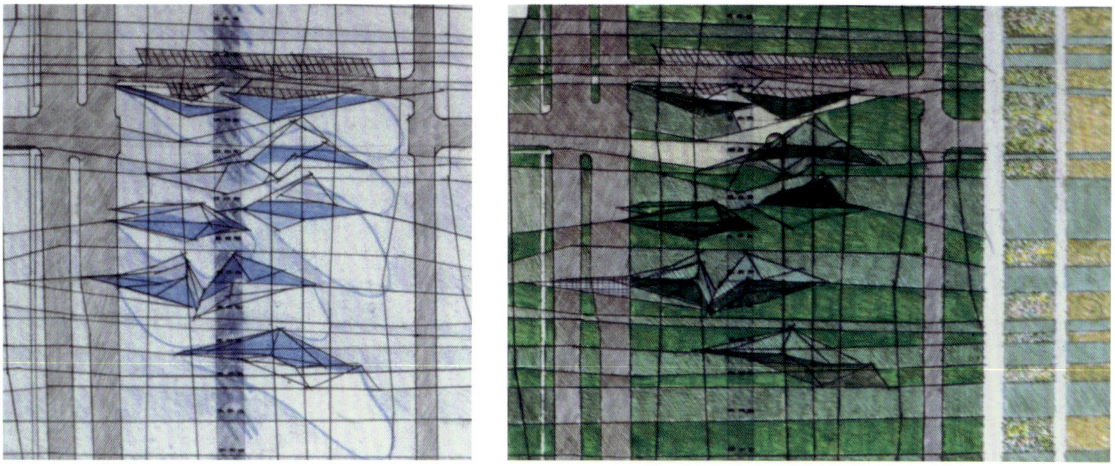

the landscape plan consists of large swaths planted with prairie grasses and wildflowers that change with the seasons, contrasted with another set of strips of contemporary lawn grasses. Olin's drawing of the field shows, sequentially, the fresh or light growth of spring, the flowering growth of summer, the golden growth of autumn, the snowdrift pattern of winter. It is a surface that is always changing, where materials shift over time according to local conditions of soil and moisture—revealing, for instance, shorter grasses on top of knolls and longer ones in swales.

Not only do Eisenman and Olin reconfigure the campus ground into a field of figures, but the strips of prairie grasses replace perennial grasses—the most common grass affiliated with campus greens—which alleviates the need for an array of chemical and mechanical maintenance practices. These prairie strips manage their own water intake, require no irrigation or mowing, and support habitat. The general field strategy of the scheme, with a highly permeable surface area, deals with much storm water on site. More important, it offers an image of an untended lawn (a surface produced by landscape's complex articulation) as an alternative to the campus green or quad (a space produced by building enclosure) so ingrained in the American psyche. This is different from other contemporaneous attempts at figuring campus ground. In Hargeaves Associates' campus green at the University of Cincinnati, the translation of one landscape (a braided river geometry) into another (the subsequent figural forms) produced figures *on* a ground. The ground of the campus green remains for the designers, in the loose signification of the site's history, authentic. In Eisenman and Olin's project, the improbability of the prairie as a campus landscape is suggested by the reading of the ground—with its suspended landscape field figures—as something thin, fragile, and synthetic.[16] Here landscape, in its translation to architecture, appears and performs differently. The thick "emergent landscape of field-figures" not only foregrounds landscape but positions architecture as a "proliferation of backgrounds."[17]

The derivation of the organizational logic for the City of Culture of Galicia repeats the processes of projects before it, beginning as a series of plans overlaid as a palimpsest: the medieval street pattern of Santiago, the abstract Cartesian grid, and the topological surface of the original hillside. Eisenman's shift from a preoccupation with the index (the recording of an indeterminate time) to that of a code (which rewrites time as a series of forces) is consequential. In simpler terms, this move enables a diagram of horizontal forces instead of vertical ones, moving away from designs that are plan extrusions. The resulting city of six building programs, which Eisenman refers to as a "three-dimensional matrix of forces," are spaces and surfaces as smooth and fluid as the surrounding topography.[18]

Unlike the project at IIT, very little of this new ground surface is articulated with "natural" landscape materials. Instead, Olin's preliminary site drawing delineates the geometries of the matrix as a series of "pavements"—exposed roof, stone, and walkway—through which run an irregular eucalyptus grove and lines of trees. Eisenman's ground figures are unapologetically geologic, eruptions of the lower strata of the earth through a green surface in what has been called a reversal of architecture's normal relationship between the stereotomic (the earth) and the tectonic (the frame).[19] The thin

LAURIE OLIN, DRAWINGS FOR IIT STUDENT CENTER COMPETITION

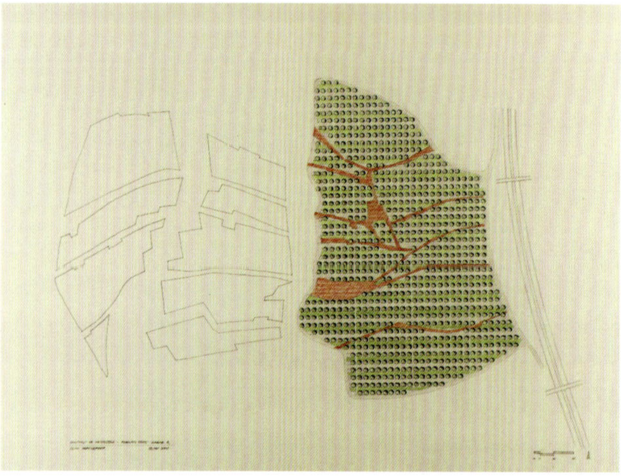

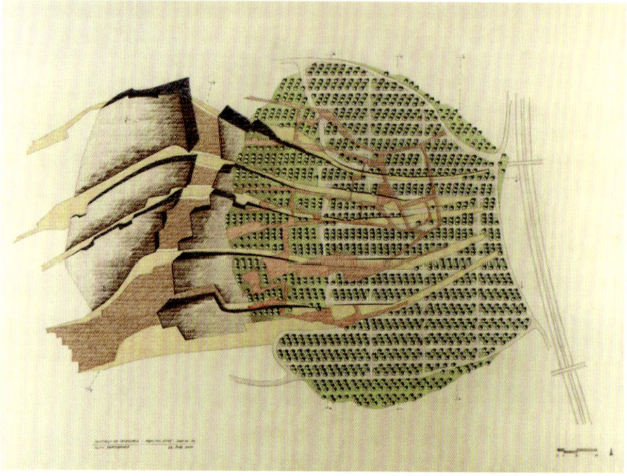

membrane and clear edge between landscape surface and building soffit at IIT has here been replaced with a malleable thickness, enabling a fluid and changing interior configuration. In an ironic twist, the most landscape-like ground the pair has produced is the most synthetic, engaging fully the games of building/ground, thick/thin, and full/empty explored in earlier work. Moreover, their sophisticated design techniques simulate the actions of natural processes. In the landscape, when a force (such as wind or water) acts on matter (such as soil), it produces an array of forms based on the internal logic of the material. "Streaming forces" on what can be called "matter-information" has here produced a complex ground that has the same smooth surfaces, spatial irregularities, and social occupations as a landscape.[20]

Whether these projects are buildings, landscapes, or grounds is insignificant. What is at stake is how these collaborative investigations reinvigorate the designer's respective disciplines. Eisenman and Olin do not need each other—for work, thoughts, or a career—but their collaborations generate something richer than each of them could produce alone. Their "right/right" approach to difference, that is, their validation of varied interests, is enabled by two thinkers who are united by what Olin describes as their "belief in meaning and representation."

It may be surprising to learn that Olin was never formally educated as a landscape architect. He studied architecture at the University of Washington and, after working in the office of Edward Larrabee Barnes from 1964 to 1967, became disenchanted with what he describes as the "fixation with objects to the detriment of broader situations and relationships, which are normally described as landscape." Although the use of the word "landscape" is ubiquitous these days, for Olin landscapes are a portion of the earth's surface that has been affected by human culture. For him, landscape does not privilege natural materials over synthetic ones. A landscape is a milieu, the physical or social setting in which something occurs or develops. Although Eisenman has not articulated his interest in landscape explicitly, many of his diagrammatic ideas are related to associated fields like science and natural systems, and the work evidences broader systems and serial extensions.

In the projects produced by the Olin/Eisenman collaboration, landscape's architectural logics stem from a sustained attempt to challenge the conventional practices of one discipline by adopting the logics of another. Sources for, meanings of, and the effects promised by the geometric infrastructure, the "regulating lines" of their project's organizations—by two architects—expand on received notions of landscape's temporality, spatiality, and materiality. And what of the equally provocative landscape logics of architecture (of surface, emergence, temporality, and ecology)? That story, already, is everywhere. The story of landscape's architectural logics, however, is just beginning to appear, and the Olin/Eisenman collaborations are a fertile example.

OLIN PARTNERSHIP, DRAWINGS FOR CITY OF CULTURE OF GALICIA

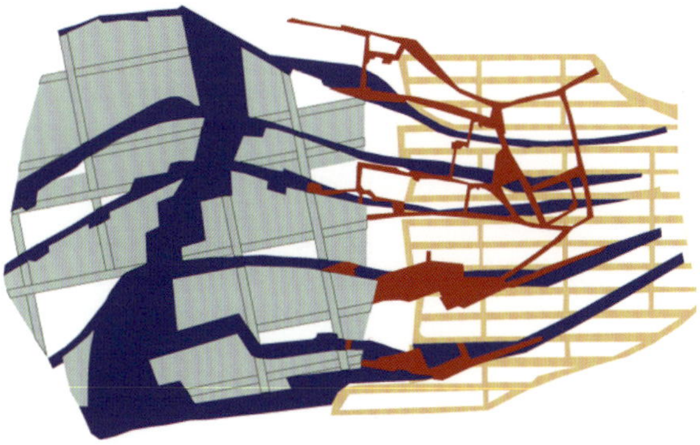

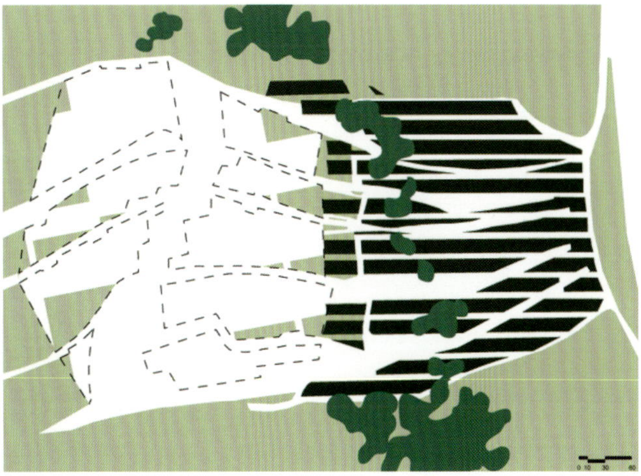

NOTES

I wish to thank Mark Linder and Melissa Vaughn for advice and criticism.

1. R.E. Somol, "All Systems GO!: The Terminal Nature of Contemporary Urbanism," in Julia Czerniak, ed., *Downsview Park Toronto* (Munich and Cambridge, MA: Prestel and the Harvard University Graduate School of Design, 2001), 128.
2. Ibid.
3. Parc de la Draga, Banyoles (1988) and Rebstock Park, Frankfurt (1991) are partially constructed.
4. This statement by Laurie Olin, and all quotations by him (except where noted), were taken from a series of discussions we had between January and July 2000. I thank him for his extraordinary generosity of time and for giving me access to his archives and sketchbooks.
5. Peter Eisenman, "The Museum Rediscovered," in *Cities of Artificial Excavation: The Work of Peter Eisenman, 1978–1988* (Montreal: Canadian Centre for Architecture and Rizzoli International Publications, 1994), 131–132.
6. See Eisenman's discussion of "grounds" in "Folding in Time: The Singularity of Rebstock," in *Folding in Architecture*, ed. Greg Lynn (London: Academy Editions), 23–26.
7. See Eisenman's discussion of the "agency of the fold" and the influence of catastrophe theory on the development of Rebstockpark in "Unfolding Events: Frankfurt Rebstock and the Possibility of a New Urbanism," in *Unfolding Frankfurt*, ed. John Rachman (Berlin: Ernst & Sohn, 1991), 8–17, and "Folding in Time," 23–26.
8. Eisenman, "Unfolding Events," 9.
9. Laurie Olin, "The Landscape Design of Rebstockpark," September 1992. This essay is published in German in *Frankfurt Rebstock, Folding in Time* (Munich: Prestel, 1992), 5. I thank the author for its translation.
10. For a more complete discussion on the landscape of Rebstockpark, see Julia Czerniak, "Looking Back at Landscape Urbanism: Speculations on Site," in Charles Waldheim, ed., *The Landscape Urbanism Reader* (New York: Princeton Architectural Press, 2006), 105–123.
11. The source of these landscape intentions is a short paper, "Berlin, Banhoff Friedrichstrasse Competition: Landscape Concepts," given to me by Laurie Olin.
12. Eisenman, *Eisenman Architects: IIT Student Center Competition*, February 1998. (Competition text in a booklet that accompanied the proposal).
13. Ibid.
14. Ibid.
15. Laurie Olin, "Mies-En-Scene," in *Eisenman Architects: IIT Student Center Competition*, February 1998.
16. Eisenman refers to Richard Serra "smashing a cube of black steel into the plinth of Mies's New National Gallery in Berlin as an analog for this project. It makes what appears to be an ideal and transcendental podium into something thin and brittle." (Competition text).
17. For more on this backgrounding, albeit not in the context of landscape, see Somol, "Five Easy Mieses," *ANY 24: Design after Mies*, 20–27.
18. The source for much of my understanding of Santiago is through "What Is a Diagram?" the Seligman Lecture given by Peter Eisenman at the Syracuse University School of Architecture (October 2004).
19. Luis Fernández-Galiano, "Code X in Three Movements," in *Code X: The City of Culture of Galicia* (New York: Monacelli Press, 2005), 15.
20. I thank Aaron Sprecher for the turn of phrase, "matter information."

Julia Czerniak is an Associate Professor of Architecture at Syracuse University and a Principal of CLEAR.

OLIN PARTNERSHIP, DRAWINGS FOR CITY OF CULTURE OF GALICIA

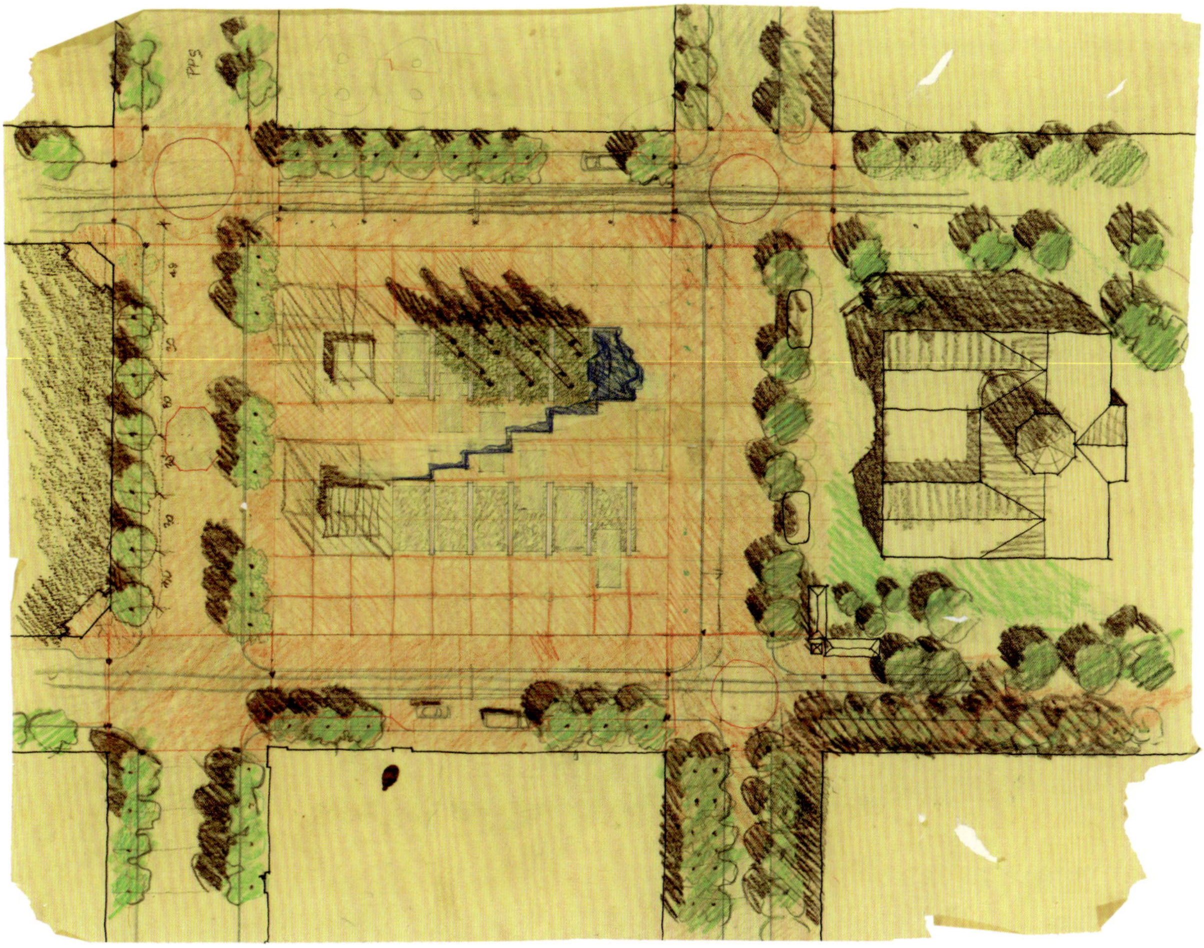

PIONEER COURTHOUSE SQUARE COMPETITION

Peter Eisenman, his then partner Jaquelin T. Robertson, and Laurie Olin first worked collaboratively on a proposal for a new city park occupying a full block in downtown Portland. The site of a parking garage, the block was to be cleared to make way for public space opposite the federal Pioneer Courthouse. In their competition proposal, Eisenman and Olin played off the strong, symmetrical form of the courthouse with a similar "form" made evident in the arrangement of paving stones in the new park and the introduction of two hipped-roof, glazed pavilions to stand at one end. That symmetry was then fractured by the introduction of a garden of regional vegetation (coastal conifers), a water feature, and stepped sections of pavement—all features that added a new layer of abstract references to the local ecology and history.

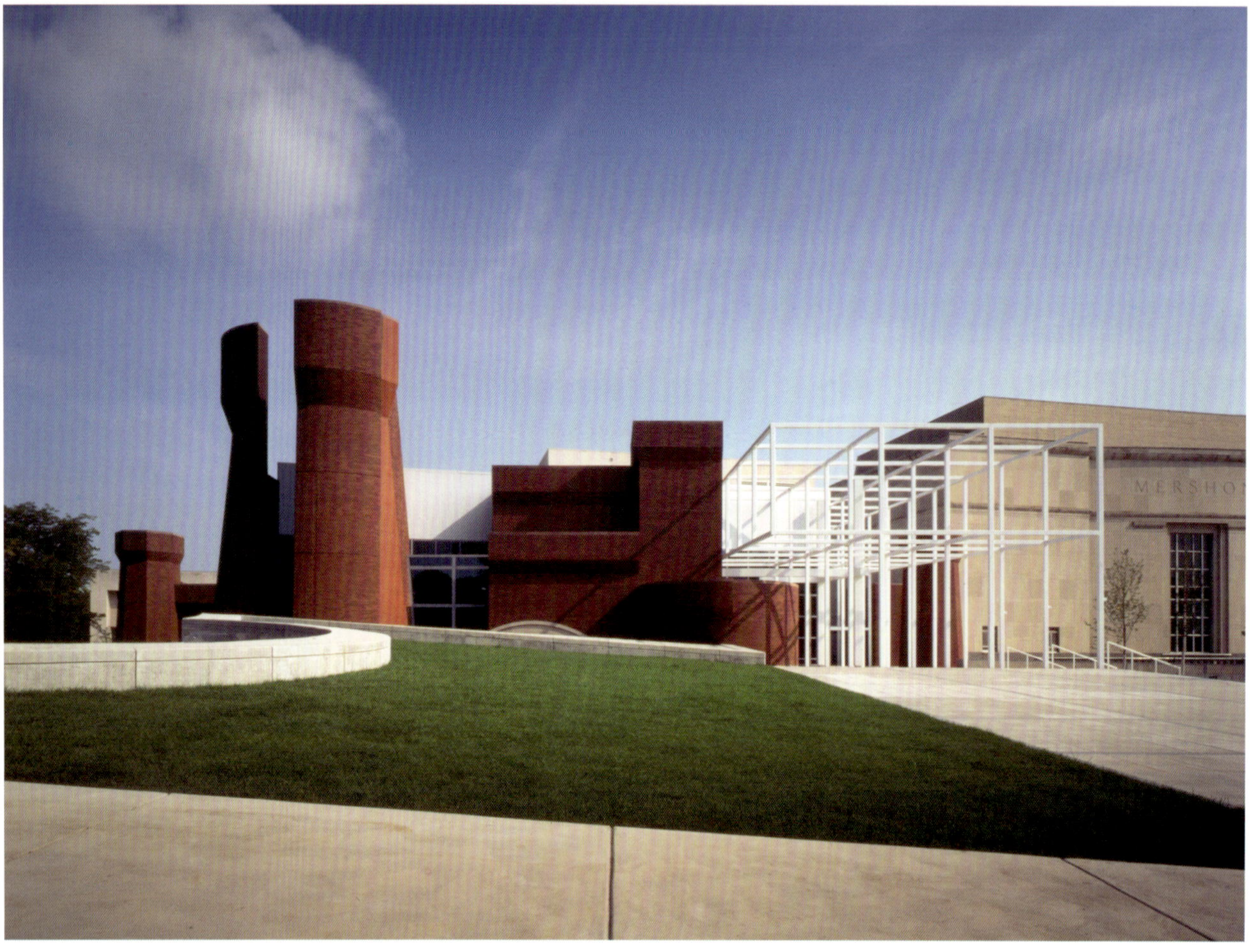

WEXNER CENTER FOR THE ARTS

As The Ohio State University campus grew in the nineteenth century it established a grid for the campus that was shifted off the Columbus city grid by twelve-and-one-quarter degrees. As the campus grew, it rationalized and extended this internal grid from the central campus Oval, reinforcing the university's separation from its urban context. But as the university continued to expand, many campus buildings became disconnected from the campus plan because they conformed to the Columbus grid.

The Wexner project sought to integrate the geometries of the city and campus grids within a new Center for the Arts that projects the image of belonging both to the campus and to Ohio. The city grid generates the new pedestrian path into the campus. The trajectory initiated by this path serves as a route of entry to the arts center, extends along the ragged northern edge of the Oval reinforcing its form, through to the main tower of University Hall, all the way to the flat end of the horseshoe of Ohio Stadium where the city grid picks up once again. Thus the confrontation between the city street pattern and the geometry of the Oval is given much greater dramatic impact.

The primary circulation spine of the Wexner was placed perpendicular to this new east-west axis. This glass-enclosed double north-south passageway cuts a new path between two older buildings by means of minimal interventions in them. With this precise cut the urban grid is not only referred to once again, but continues the curve of the Oval as a tangential vector, thereby giving the Center a second natural route of entry, and embedding it even more intimately in the double geometry of the site.

The new crossing, created as the intersection of these two "found" axes, is not simply a route but an event. It is appropriate for an on-campus arts center to be an architectural event in itself, a dynamic sequence of spaces rather than a monumental "palace." Conceived in this way, the site itself becomes the new architecture. The massing concept of the building is that of an archaeological earthwork whose essential elements are scaffolding and landscaping. It is as if the surface of the site were chiseled away and excavated to reveal the inlays of its own history and geography. The "scaffolding" of the intersecting grids inscribed on the plan provides a matrix connecting all the arts buildings and structures—a series of links to the various entries into the center's public and private functions.

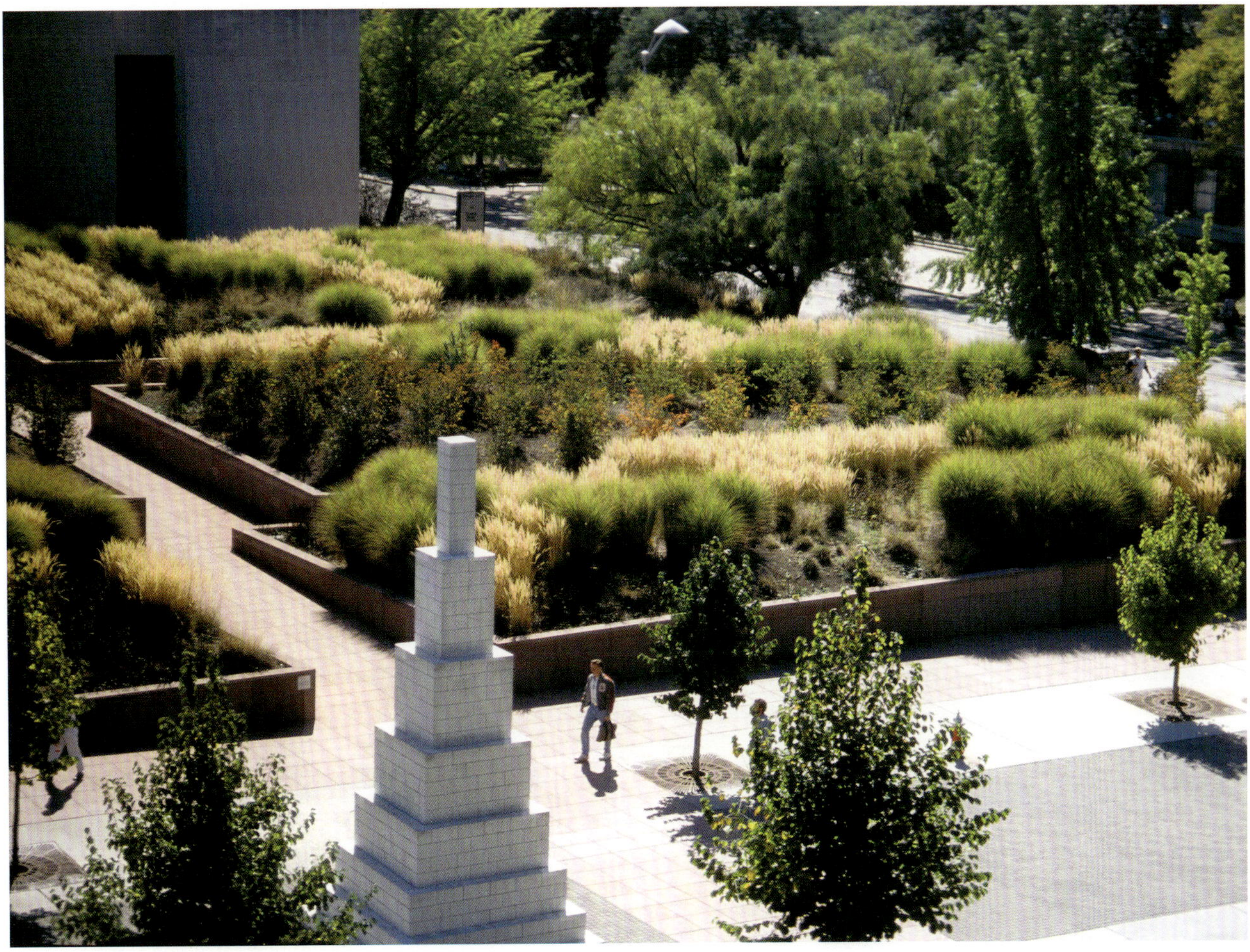

At a symbolic level, the matrix of paths creates a new "ground" for the existing buildings, a context for seeing relationships between them not previously possible.

Within this matrix is a series of landscaped sculpture terraces comprising the roof planes of below-grade performance, gallery, library, and service spaces. These landscaped volumes, calibrated to the height of surrounding buildings, are figured into the changing vistas along the routes of entry and passage. The principal vistas in all directions, and from a wide arc of approaches, are carefully considered in order to draw together isolated landmarks, local emblems, and elements of campus history into a coherent image.

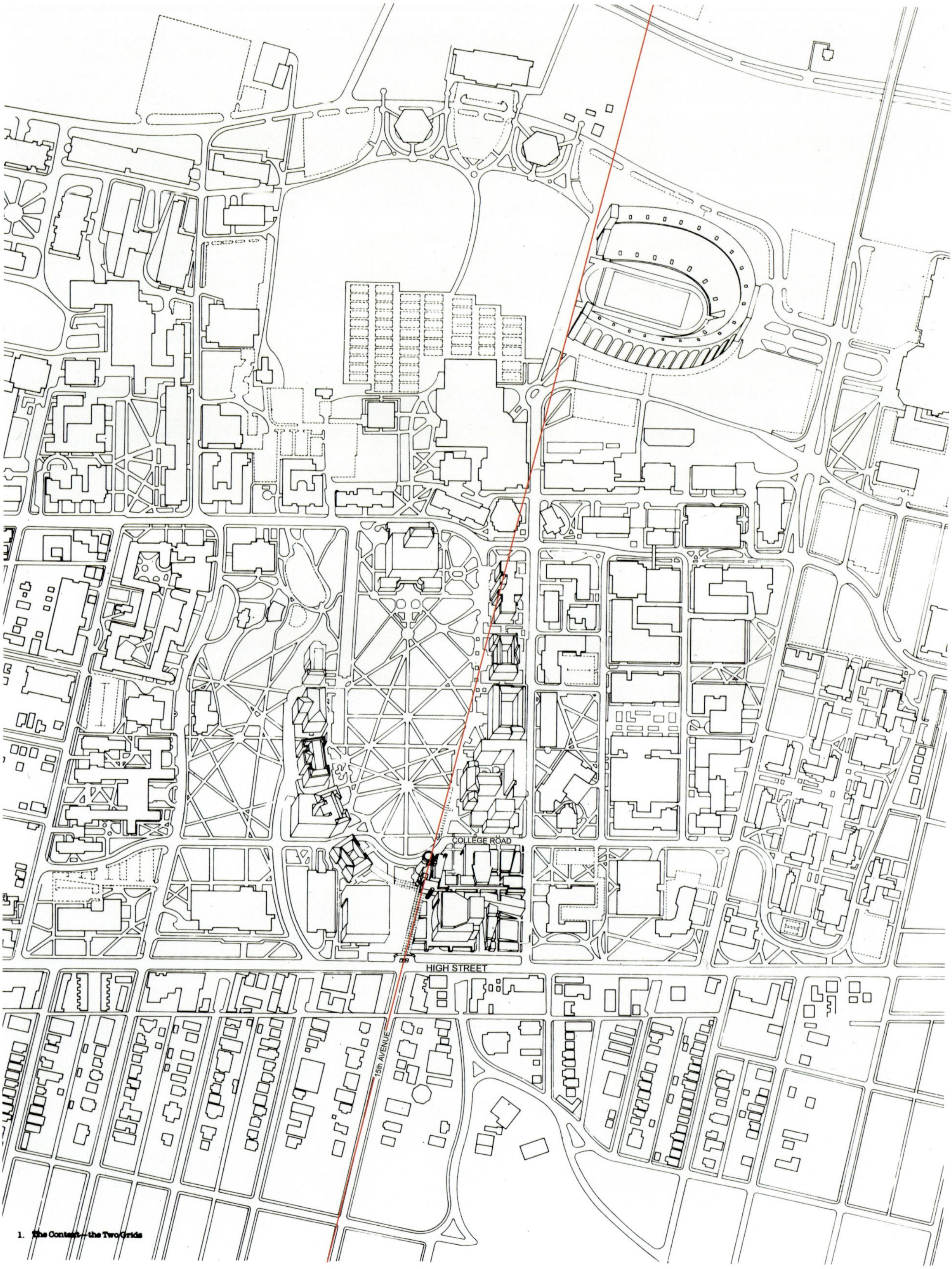

1. The Context—the Two Grids

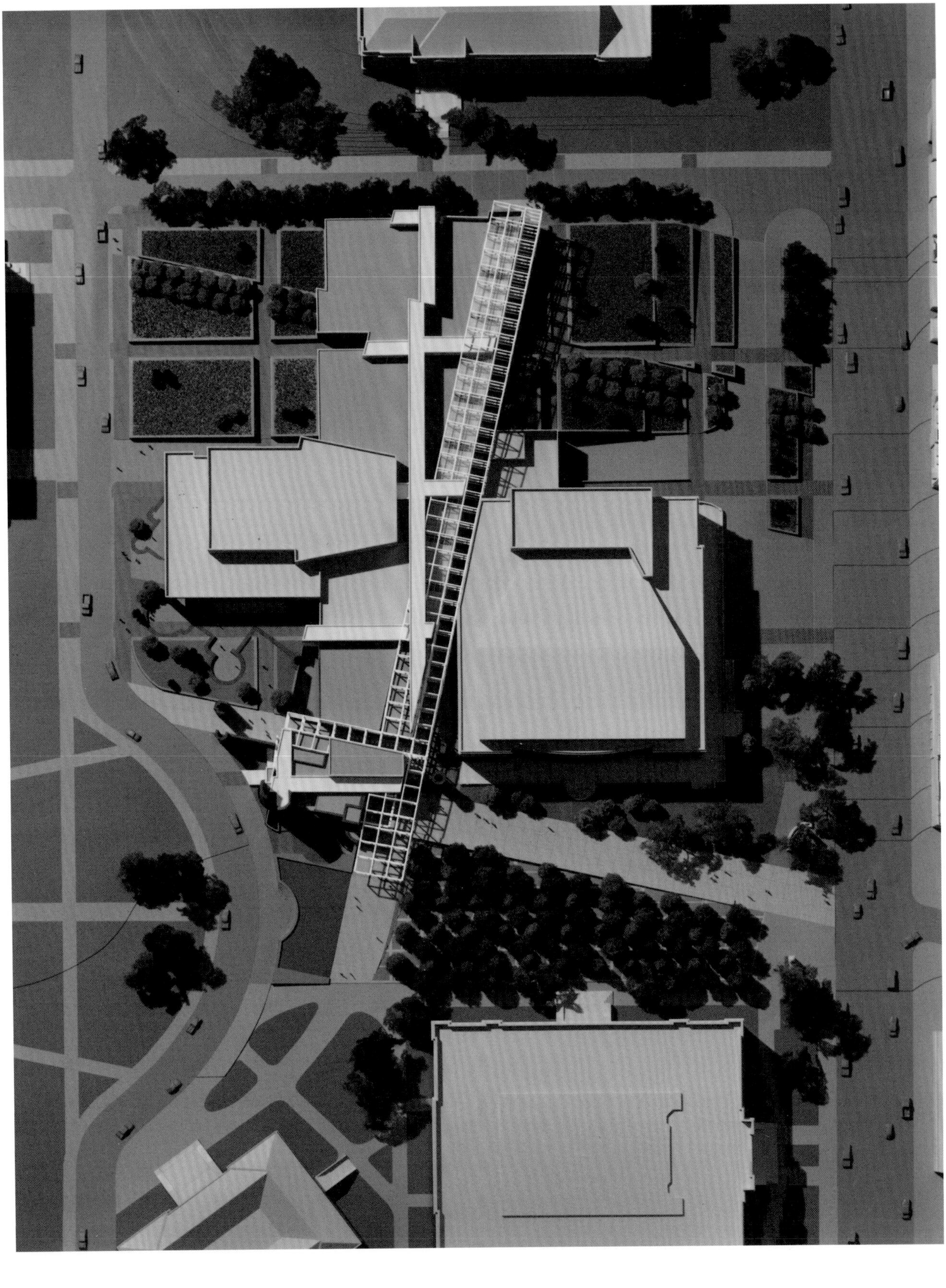

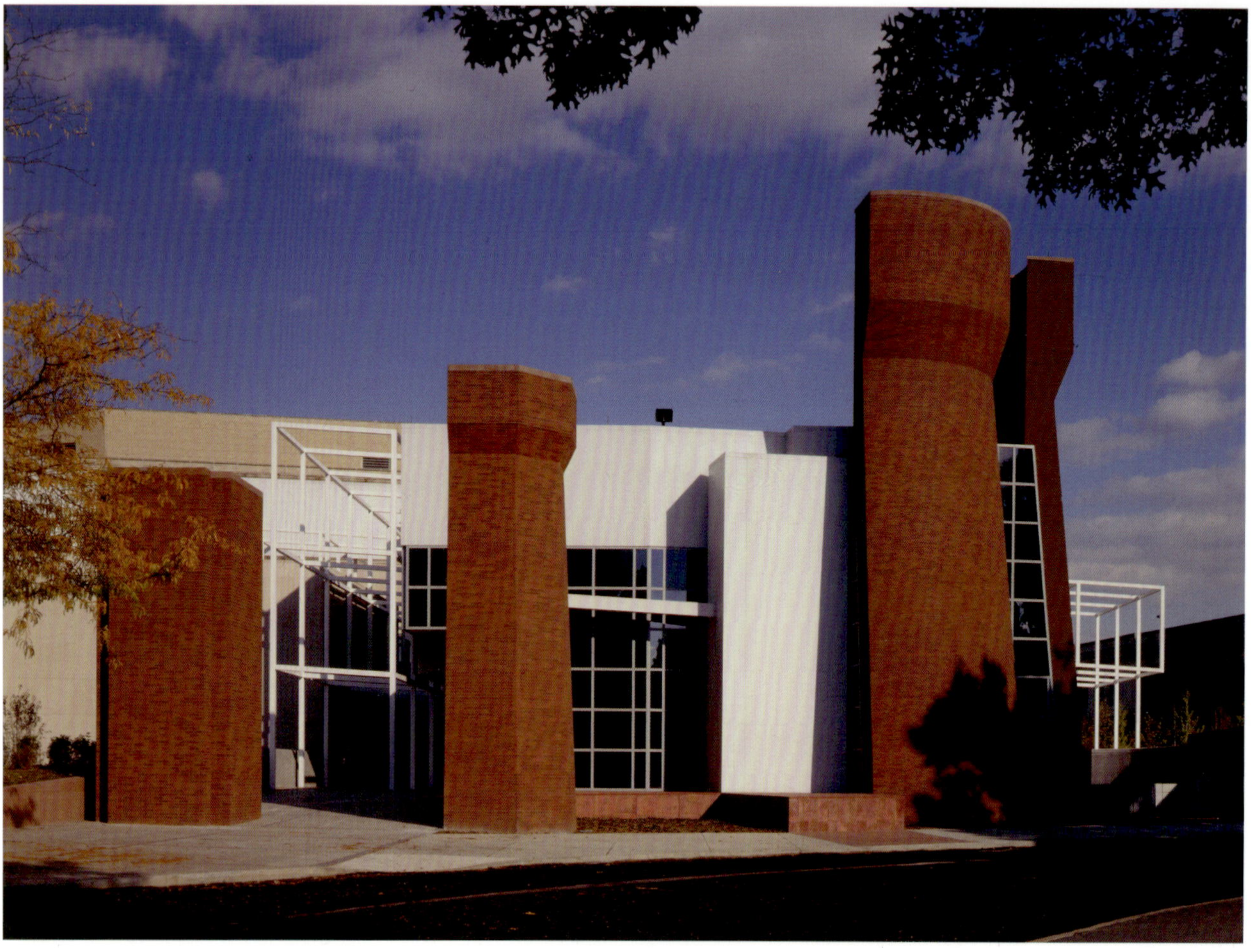

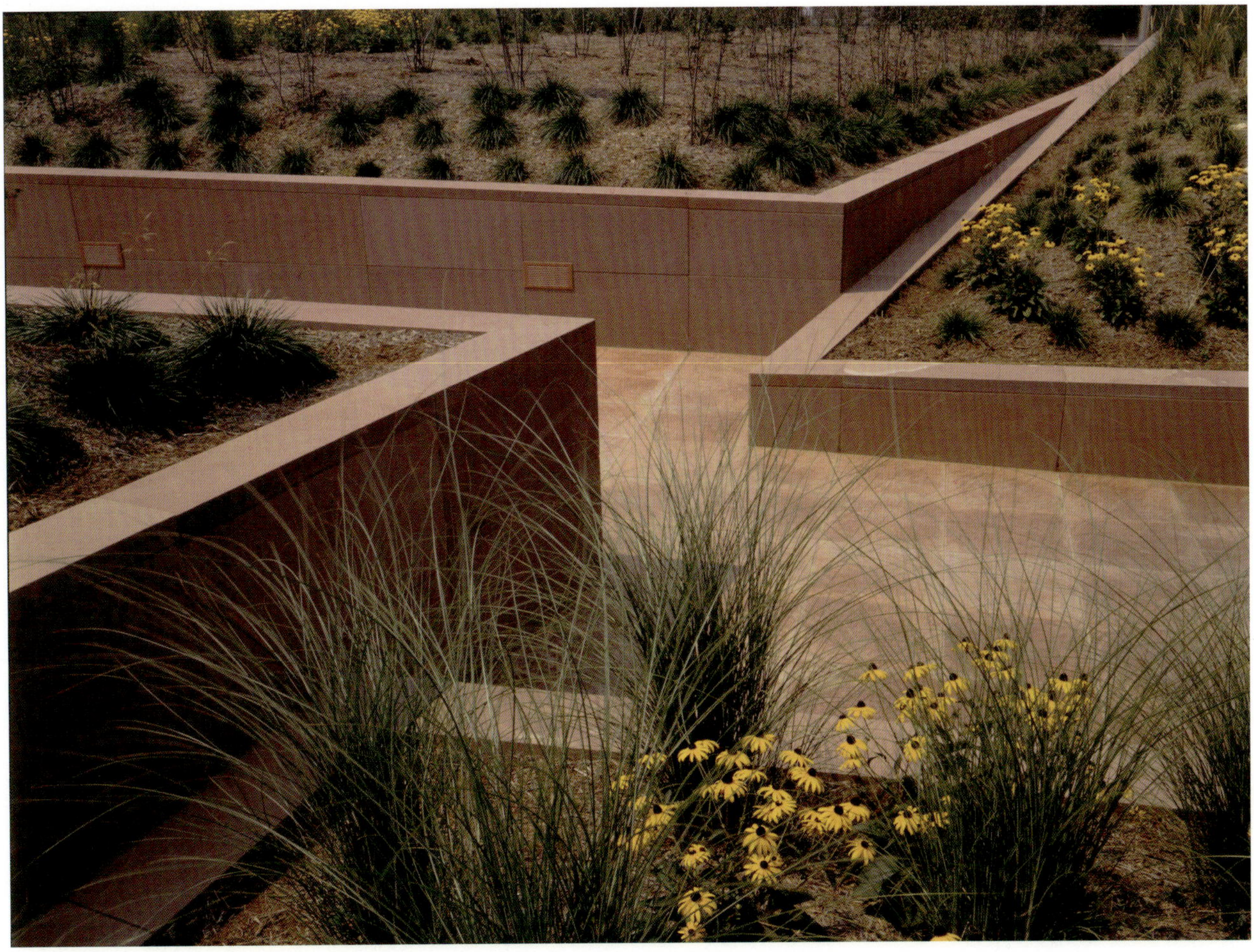

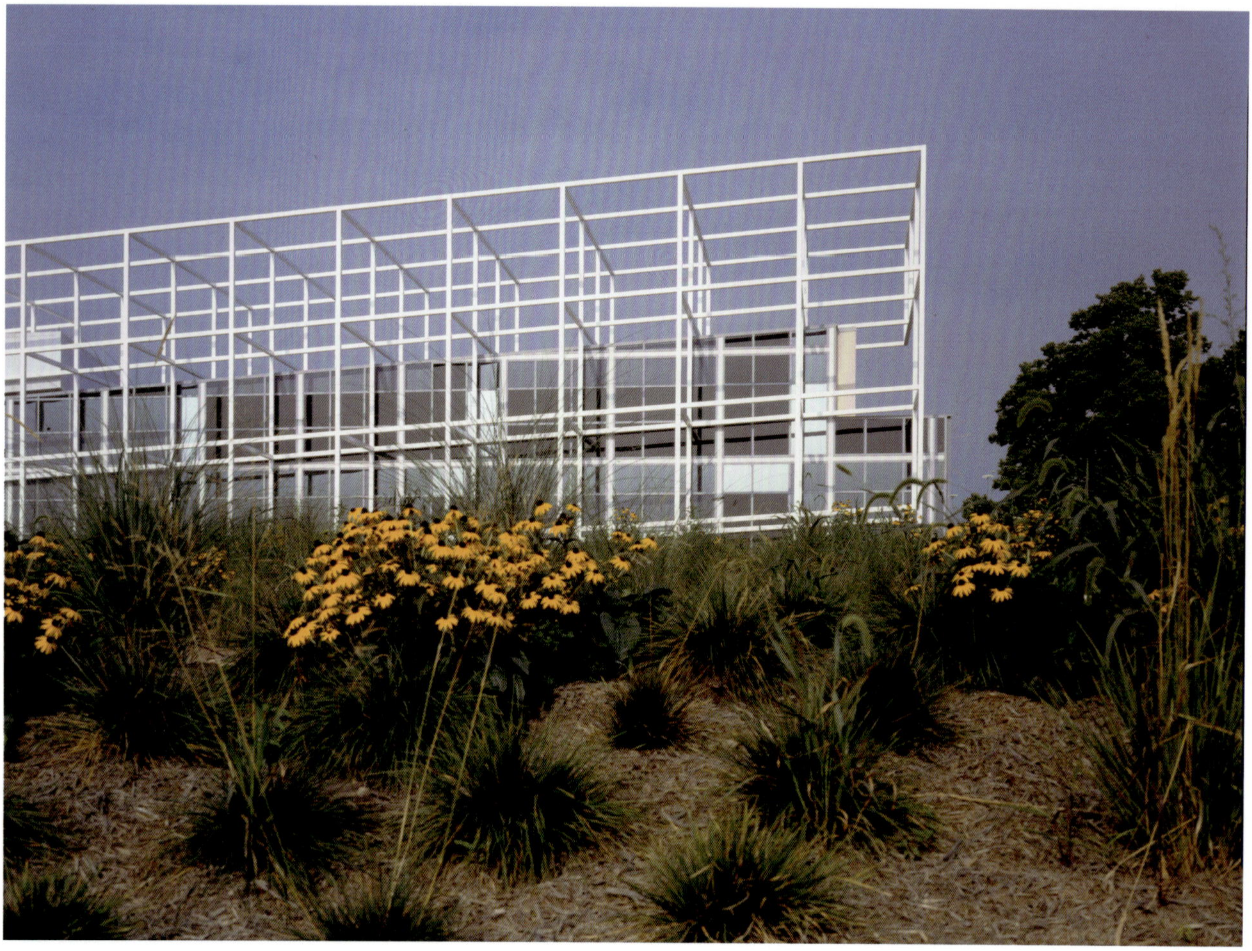

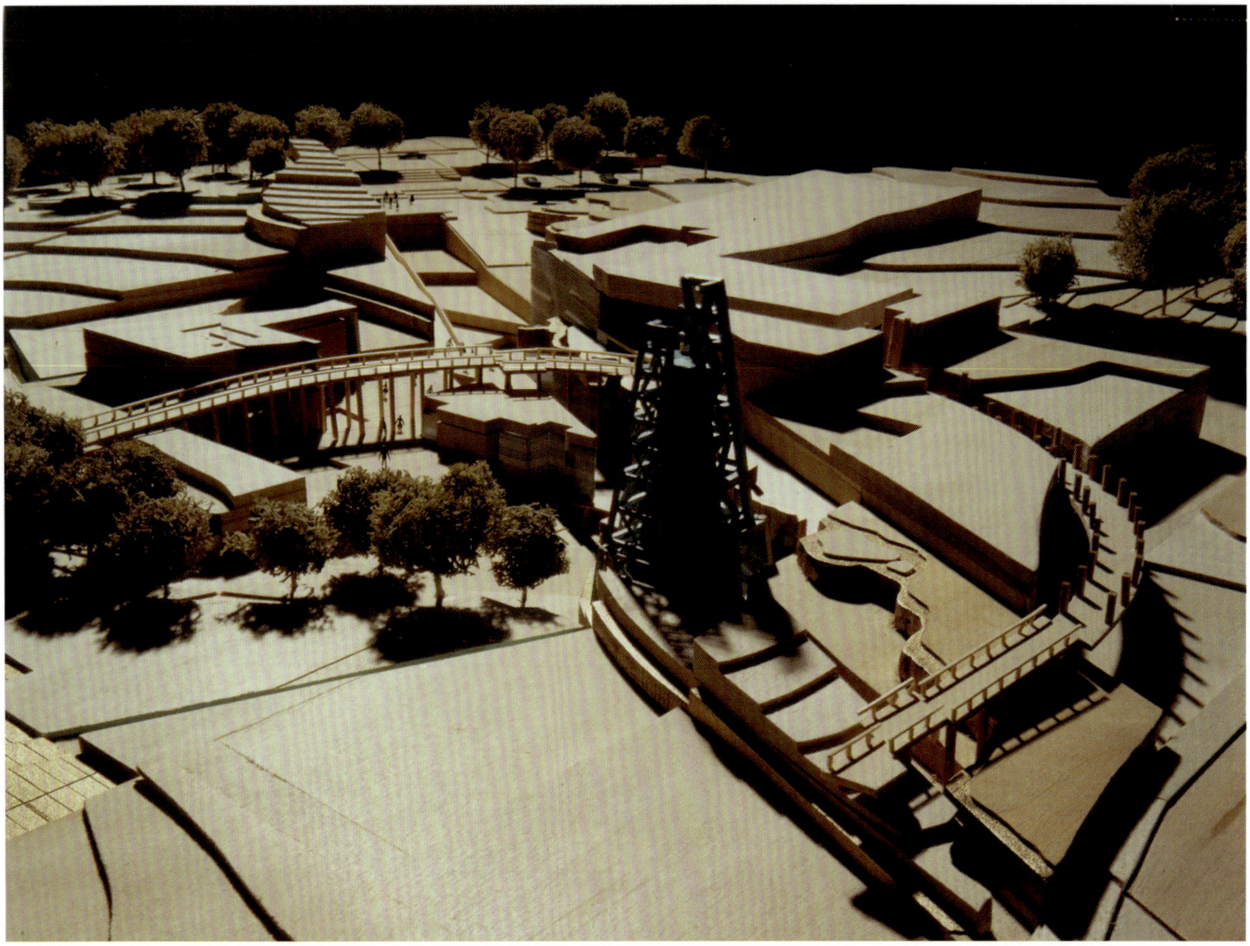

UNIVERSITY ART MUSEUM, CALIFORNIA STATE UNIVERSITY, LONG BEACH

On a twenty-three-acre site adjacent to the main campus entrance of California State University at Long Beach, Eisenman and Olin developed the architectural and site design for a museum of contemporary experimentation. Located in an arboretum, the design allowed the museum to be discovered and perceived as if it were an archaeological artifact.

The project is the outcome of a history "given to" the building. This "history" was compiled from a series of significant dates, beginning with the settlement of California in 1849, the creation of the campus in 1949, and the projected "rediscovery" of the museum in the year 2049. The idea was to imagine the site 100 years after the founding of the university, and 200 years after the California Gold Rush. The building takes its form from the overlapping registration of several local maps: of the ranch that once occupied the site, of the campus, and of the ever-changing configurations of fault lines, a river, a channel, and the nearby coastline. The "superposition" of these maps revealed analogical relationships that were obscured when some notations, such as social delineations, were accorded more importance. For example, the relationship of the channel to the museum site is similar to the relationship of the river to the entire campus site. Thus the building, largely submerged in the landscape, can be seen as an artifact, relating past and present conditions in a way that alludes to past, present, and possible future conditions. In addition, an elevated walkway, symbolic of the famous Southern California sea coast pier developments of the 1920s, provides a link between the north and south areas of the arboretum, traversing above and through the museum precinct.

Olin used Eisenman's predilection for grids to create a site matrix for displaying plants that was reminiscent of filing cabinets, or Renaissance-era curiosity cabinets, which were to contain the kinds of tropical and Mediterranean plants typically imported at the Long Beach port. These were sorted and distributed in a tumbling manner across the site, with an eye to access, types of trees, water, and how best to embed the museum within the whole. In addition to exhibition and performance spaces, the 67,500-square-foot building featured a series of terraced sculpture courtyards.

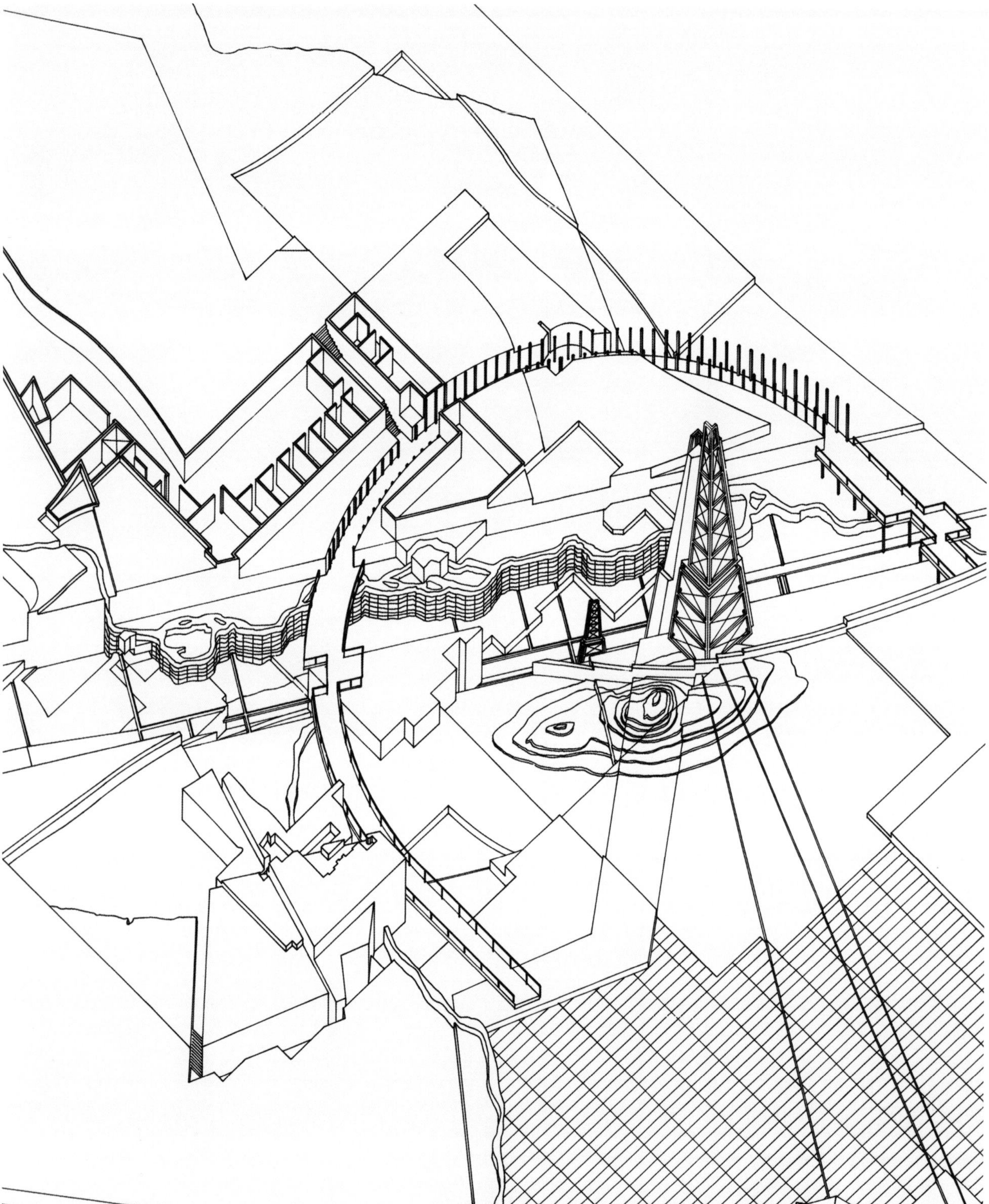

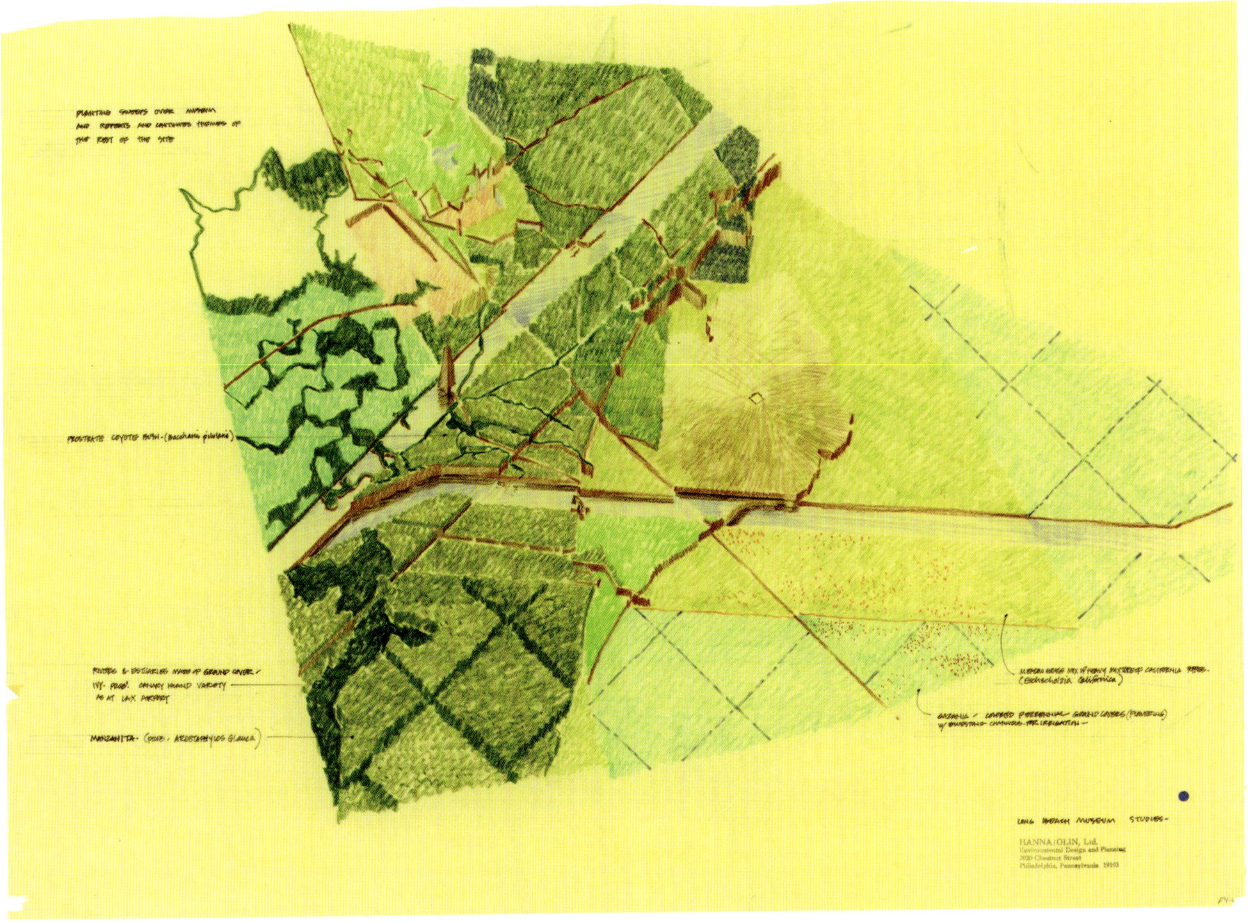
LONG BEACH MUSEUM STUDIES-
HANNA/OLIN, Ltd.
Environmental Design and Planning
2020 Chestnut Street
Philadelphia, Pennsylvania 19103

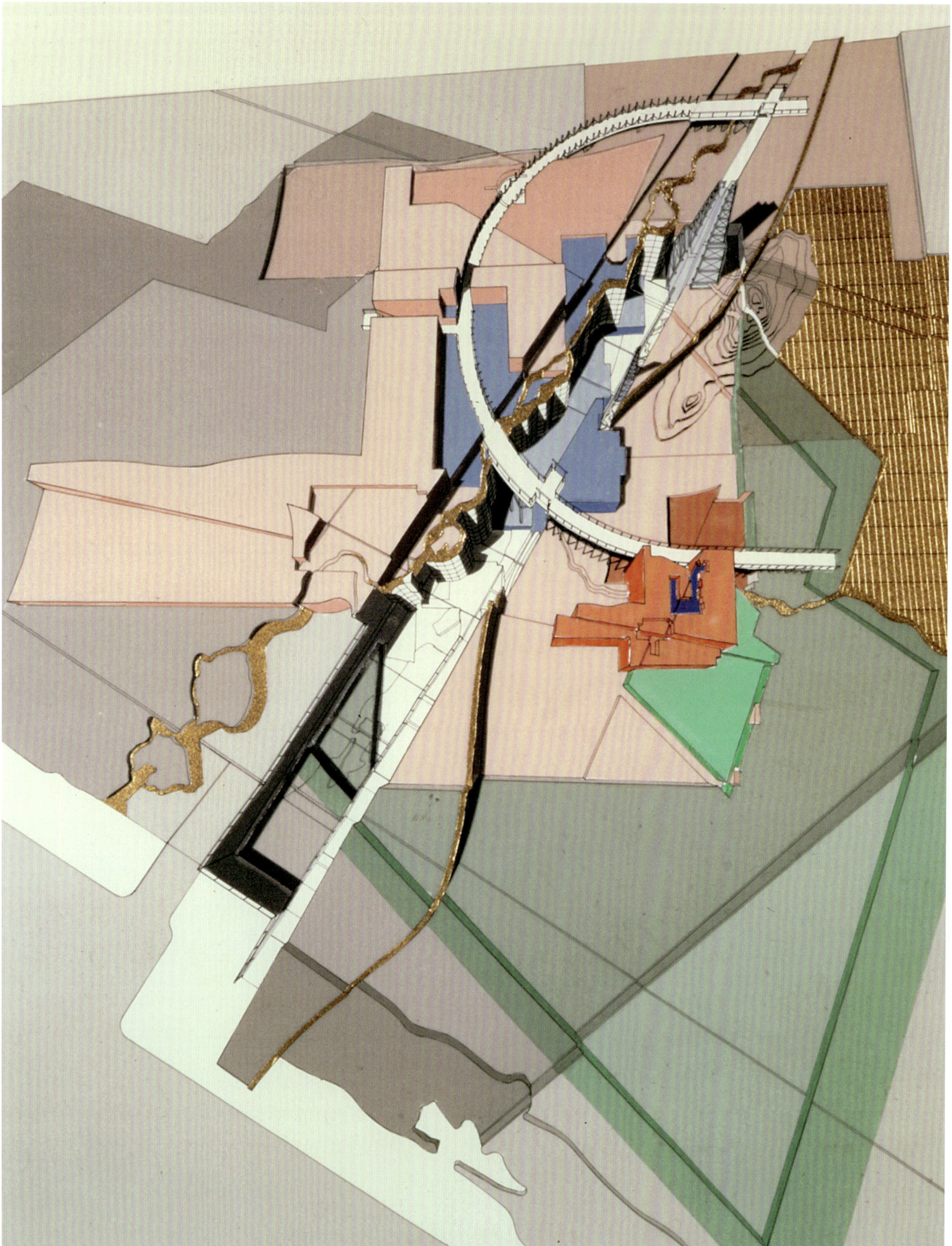

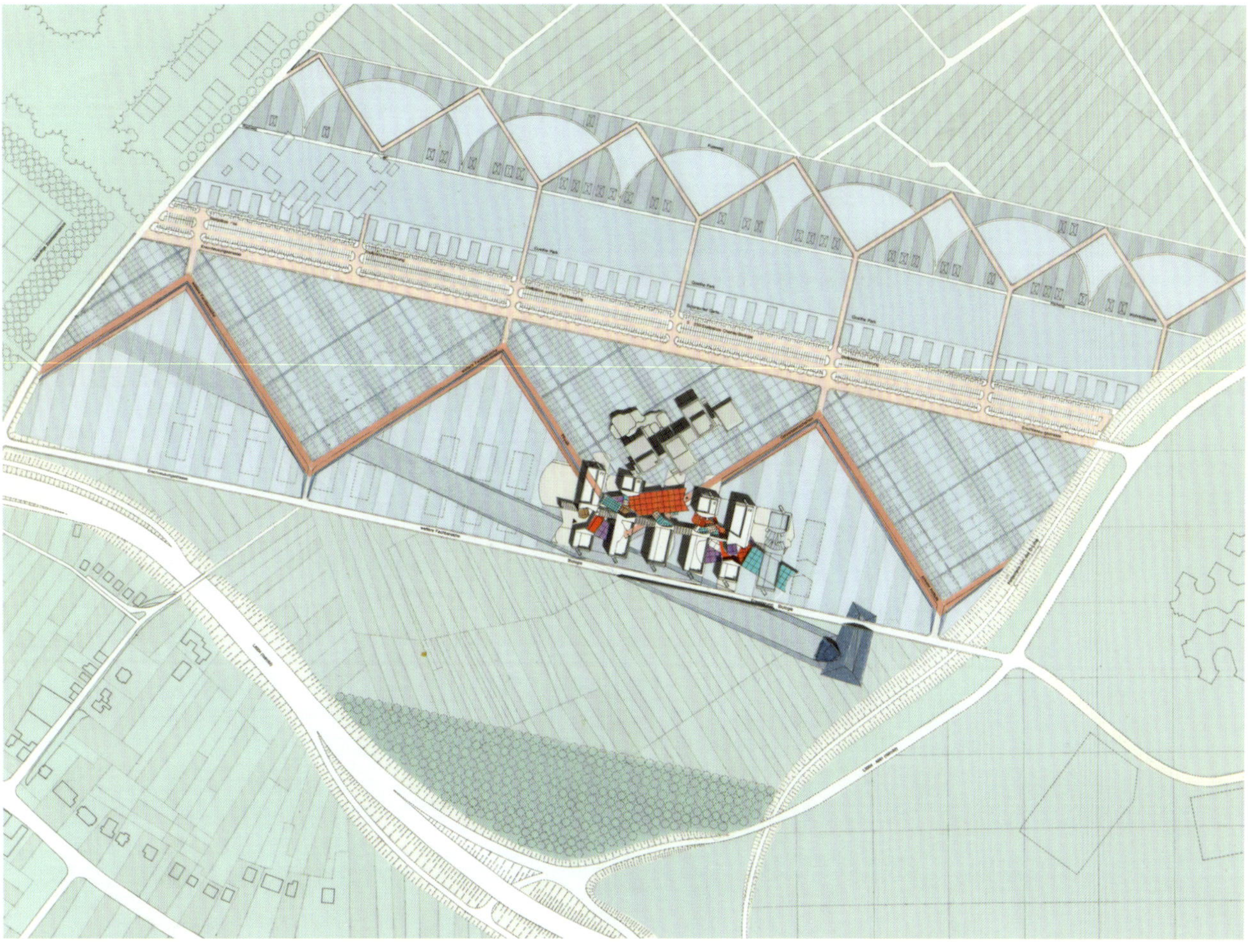

BIOCENTER / J.W. GOETHE UNIVERSITY

For the Biocenter at Goethe University, Eisenman began considering DNA and genetic research as it was unfolding at the time, exploring its ability to describe, record, and code biological, and possibly architectural, processes, while Olin began thinking about Goethe and his studies of color, optics, and plant biology, as well as his interest in landscape gardening and the morphology and development of plants.

The site was organized in a series of bands, each with a purpose and character: a forest with staff housing; a landscaped park that also served as a wildlife habitat and supported storm water management; test plots and experimental beds; parking and circulation for access and service as the Biocenter was built out; research facilities; and agriculture for locally produced organic crops. In the facilities band, Eisenman overlaid the biologists' figures of DNA chains on the site, following the precise sequence of the DNA chain for the protein collagen, which produces the necessary tensile strength of structure (as in bone). But rather than simply representing the physical configuration of DNA, the project articulates the three most basic processes by which it produces proteins: replication, transcription, and translation. By architecturally subjecting the biologists' figures to the very processes they describe, the interdisciplinary boundaries between architecture and biology are blurred. The final project was neither simply architectural nor biological, but rather an addition to a science complex that could be naturally expanded, like the DNA helix model, as future use demanded.

A proposed collaboration with site sculptor Michael Heizer, who was not interested in DNA or Goethe, resulted in the artist simply placing a giant boulder at the end of a track that he would scratch across all the bands of proposed development, rather like an enormous glacial erratic in its path.

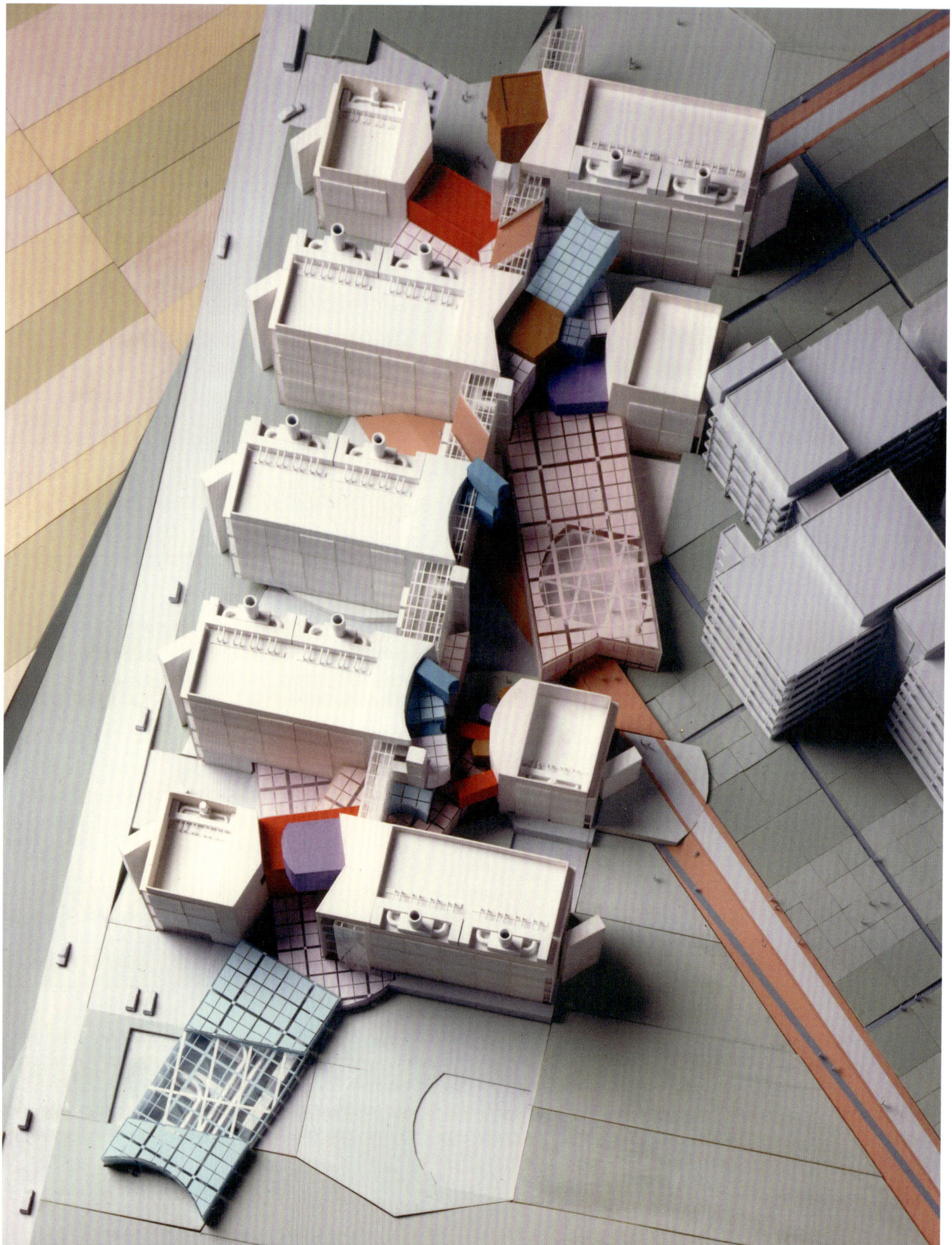

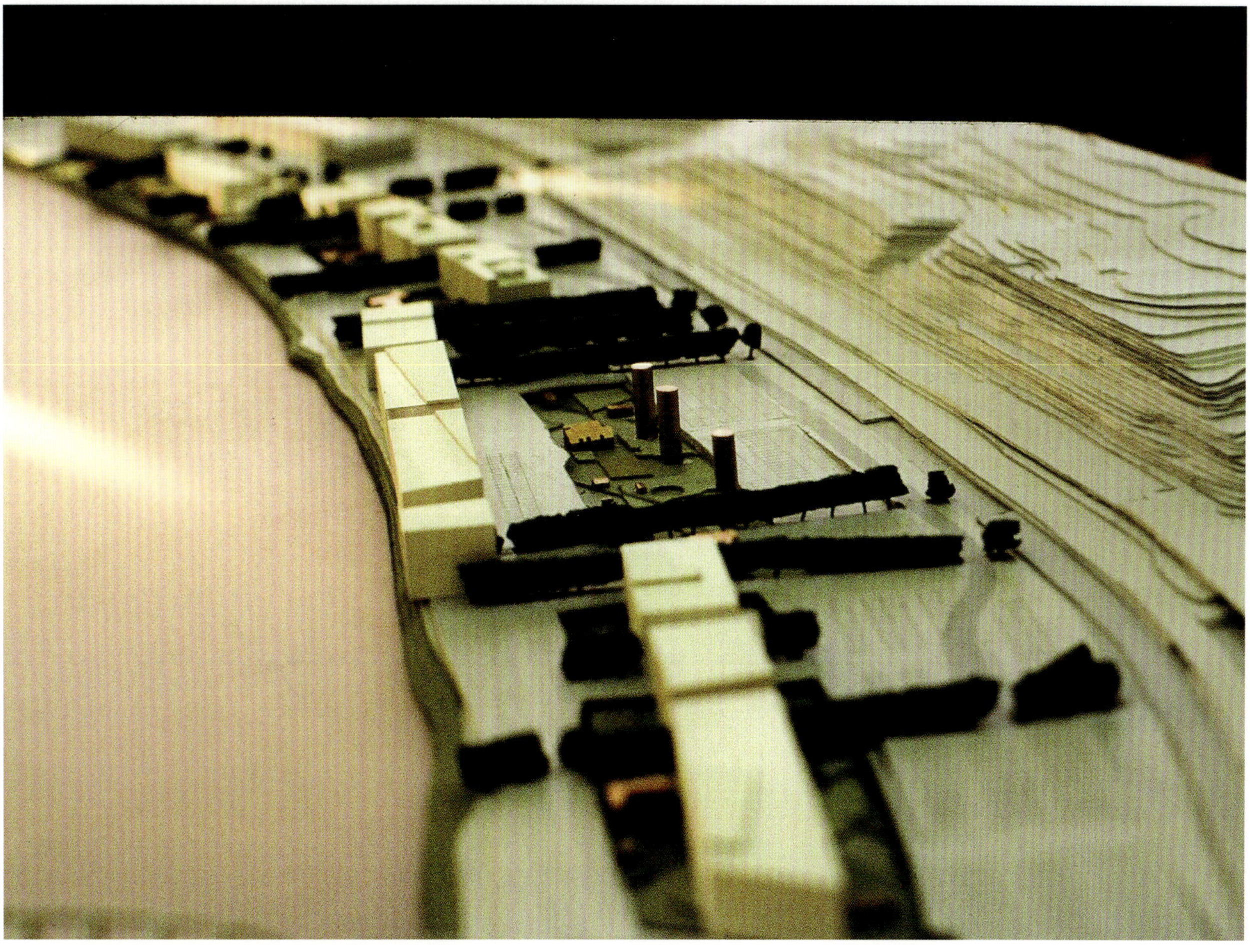

CARNEGIE MELLON RESEARCH INSTITUTE

In January 1988, Eisenman Architects was asked to develop a master plan for the Pittsburgh Technology Center and to design a new facility for the Carnegie Mellon Research Institute that addressed the "knowledge revolution" and represented Pittsburgh's revitalization as the first post-industrial city. Eisenman asked Olin to join the project, which was located on the site of a demolished Johns & Laughlin Steel Mill along the north bank of the Monongahela/Allegheny River.

Together, they overlaid the shifting historic property lines from colonial times to the present, as well as the footprint of the steel mill, on the site. Olin suggested developing contemporary needs such as parking as a sedimentary layer over the entire site and then eroding it to create social spaces—a "green river" that would form a continuous park or garden while exposing fragments of the steel mill's foundations, industrial archeaology, and imposing the parking and biotech research buildings. Concurrently, Eisenman worked with structural engineer Guy Nordenson to develop a set of structures based on aspects of Boolean geometry to produce multiple pairs of cubes—solid and framed—for the science facilities. In keeping with earlier projects, these structures were both within and above the ground, the surface of which appeared at various elevations, inside and outside, above and below the program spaces.

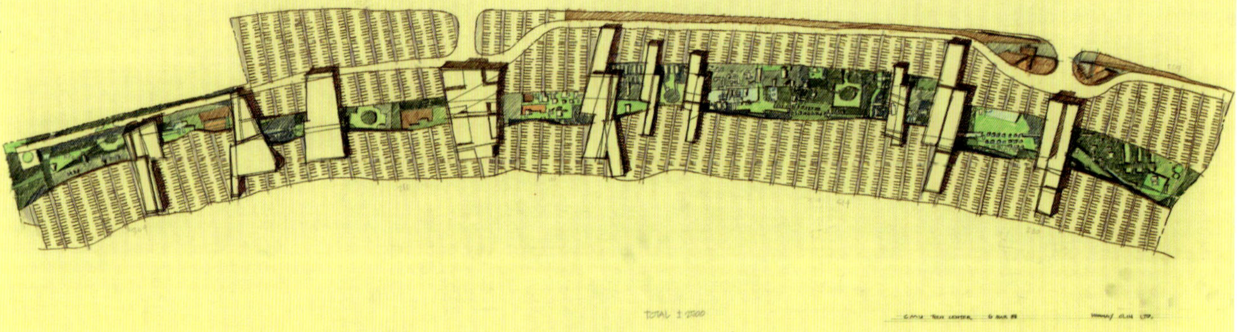

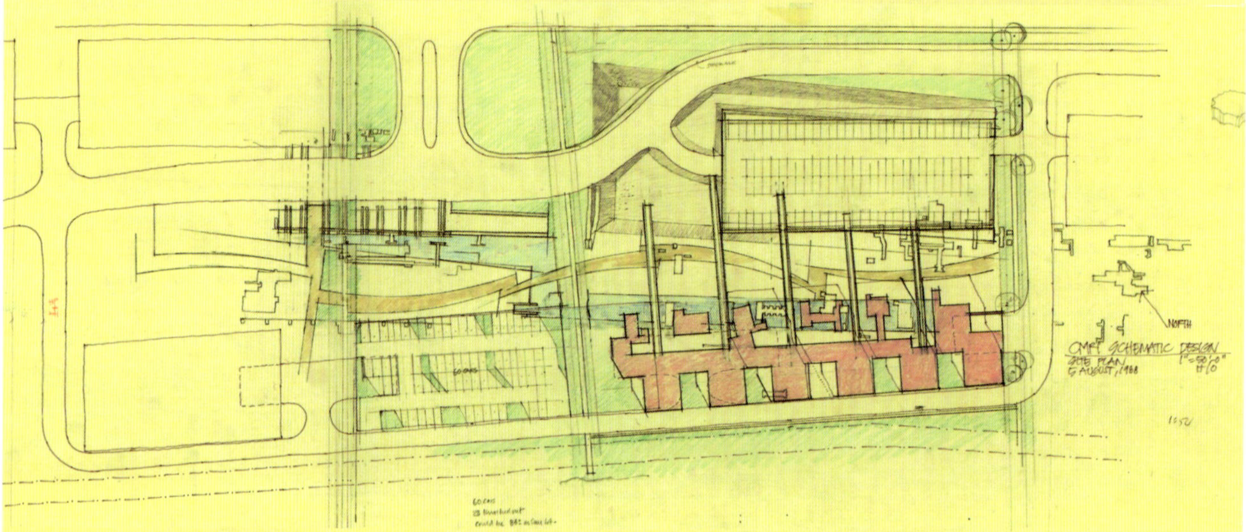
NORTH
CMRI SCHEMATIC DESIGN
SITE PLAN
5 AUGUST, 1988
1"=50'-0"
#10

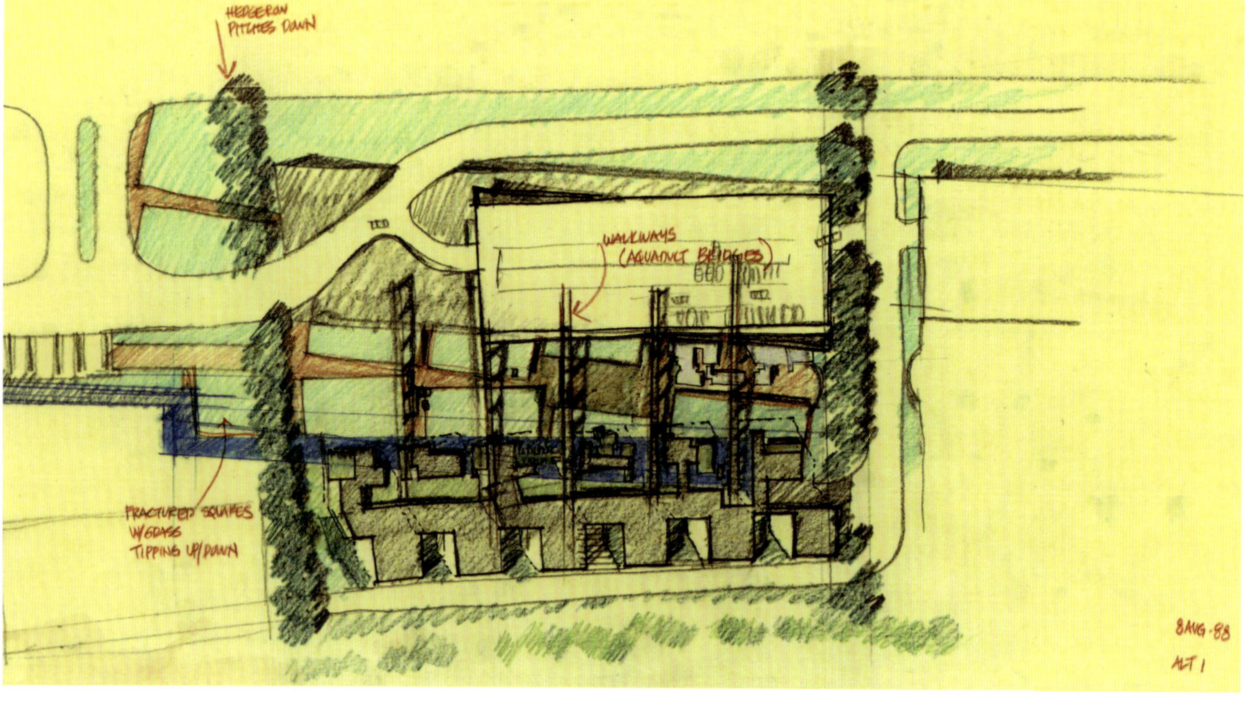
HEDGEROW PITCHES DOWN
WALKWAYS (AQUADUCT BRIDGES)
FRACTURED SQUARES W/GRASS TIPPING UP/DOWN
8 AUG-88
ALT 1

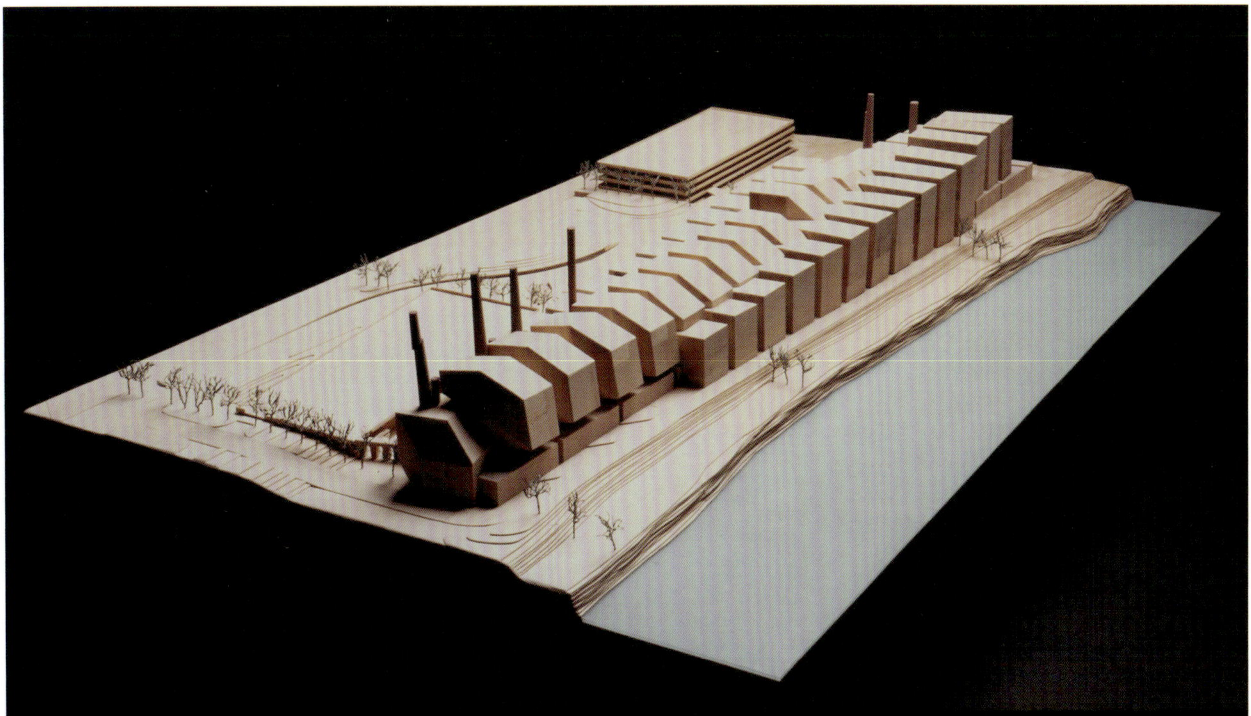

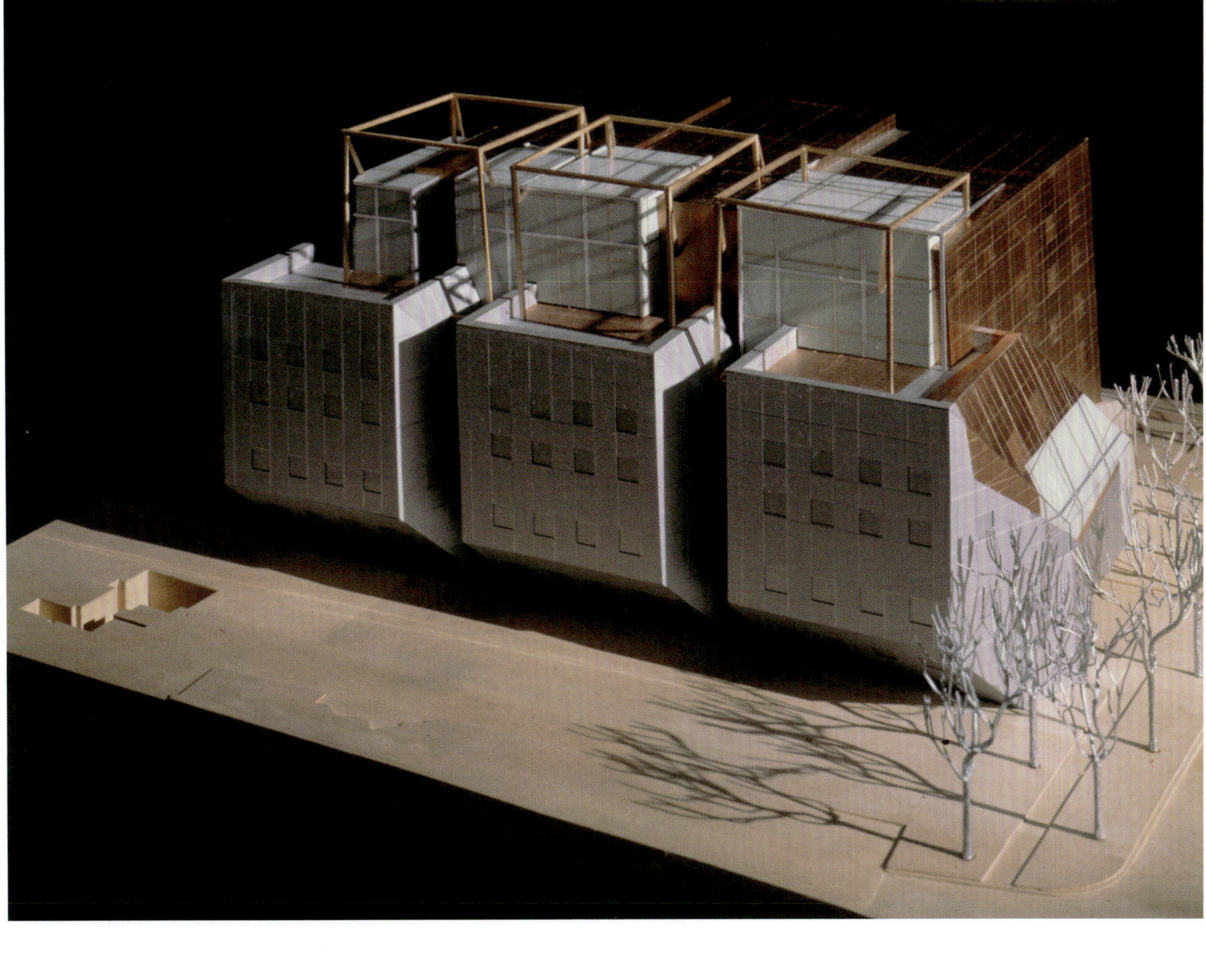

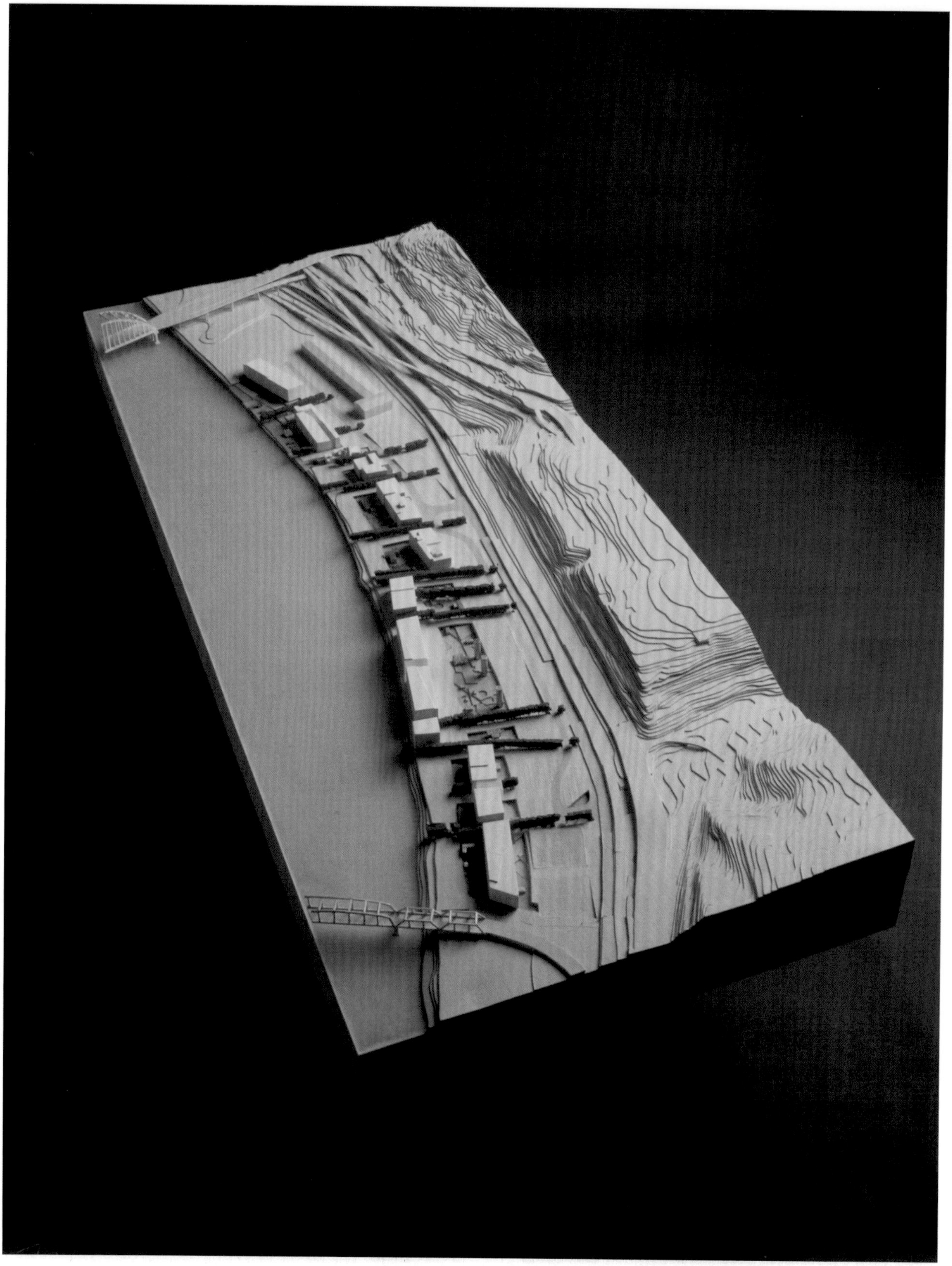

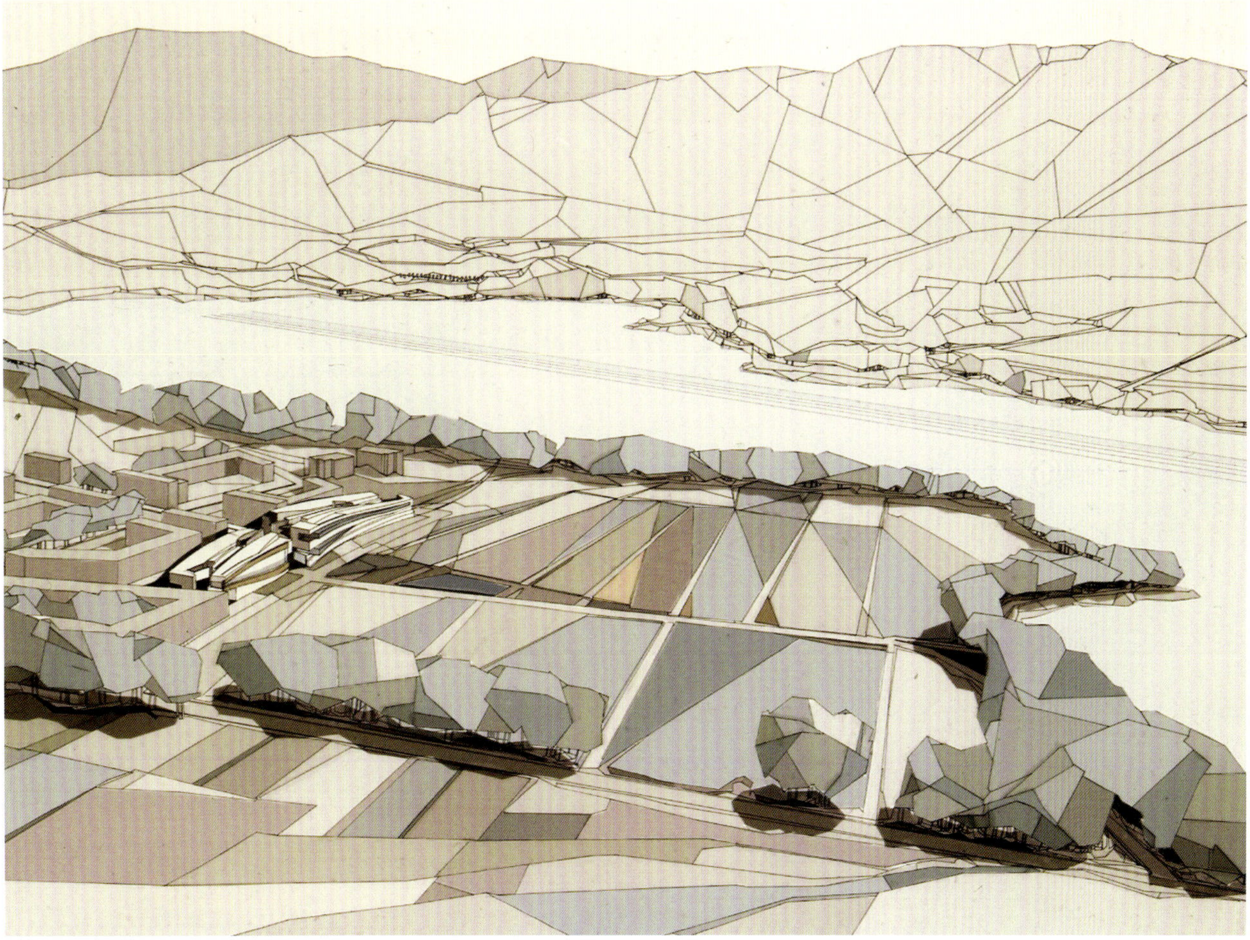

BANYOLES OLYMPIC HOTEL AND GARDEN

The project for a hotel at the site of the 1992 Barcelona Olympics rowing events is not a building in the traditional sense; rather it is part of the landscape, which in turn becomes part of the building. Located on a lake north of Barcelona, this Olympics rowing facility was to become a tourist hotel and lakeside community park and gardens after the games. Eisenman and Olin developed an overall strategy of a series of alternating elongated trapezoidal or triangular terraces that would climb from the lake shore up a peninsula, gradually becoming intertwining volumes that formed a building. The whole composition was bisected by an axis that was transformed from the hotel entry to a passageway into the park and then a walk down to the water, giving access to various elements of the hotel, its terraces and gardens, and finally to a park with agriculture, hedgerows, and fields.

Three different trace conditions of time inform the project: time past as represented in the form of the agricultural divisions on the site at the turn of the century; time present in the extension of the building forms into the landscape; and the trace of the two motions made in the arcing sweeps of an eight-oared rowing shell.

Banyoles is one of the clearest examples of Eisenman and Olin's interest in conceiving architecture and landscape as a continuum in which each is an extension of the other, and can be conceived in the same terms. It is all landscape, it is all architecture. When Barcelona and Catalonia found themselves financially overextended in Olympics facility construction, the somewhat remote Banyoles facility was cancelled. The site development, however, had already begun, so the park was built in a manner recalling early schematic documents.

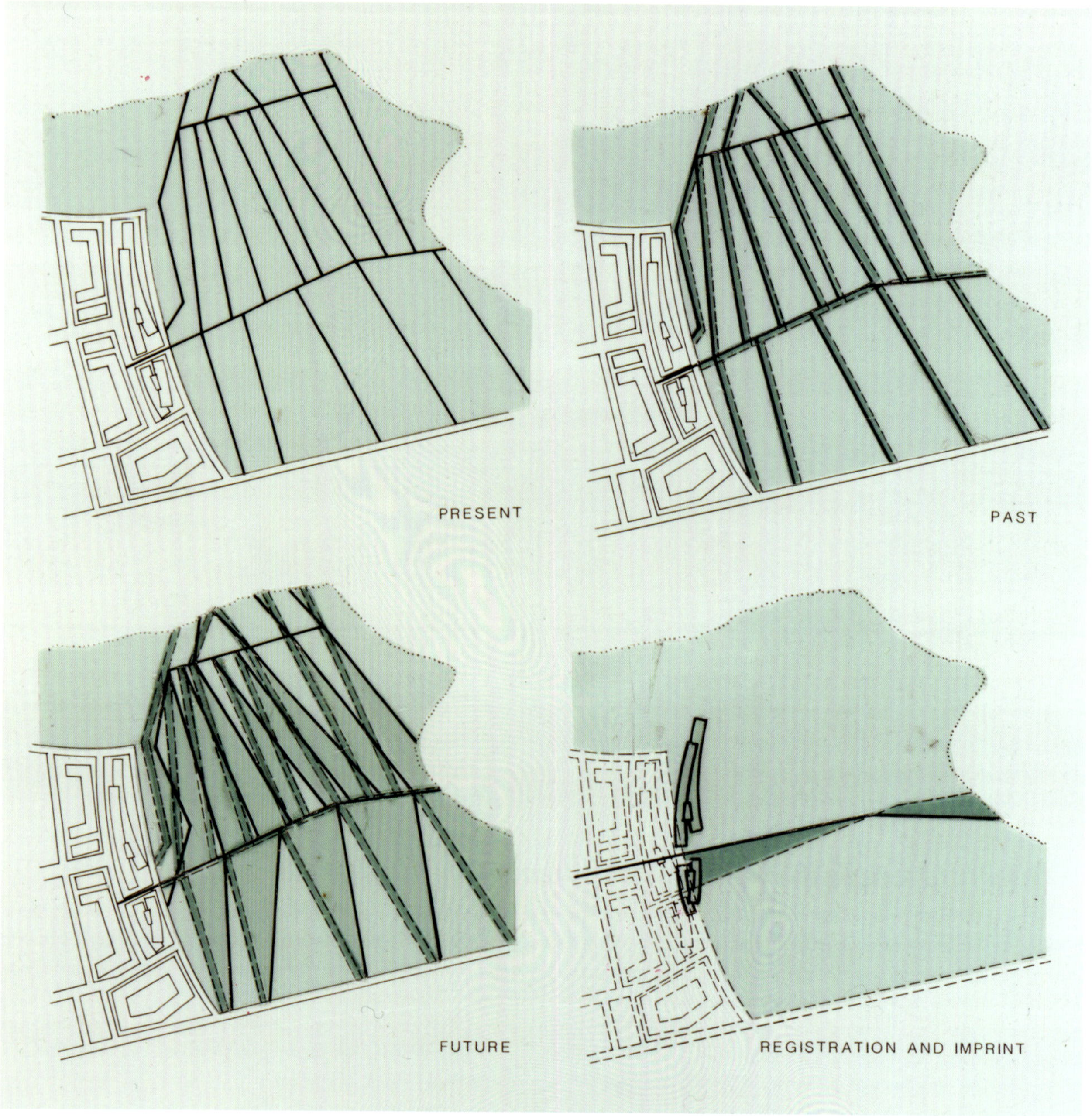
PRESENT
PAST
FUTURE
REGISTRATION AND IMPRINT

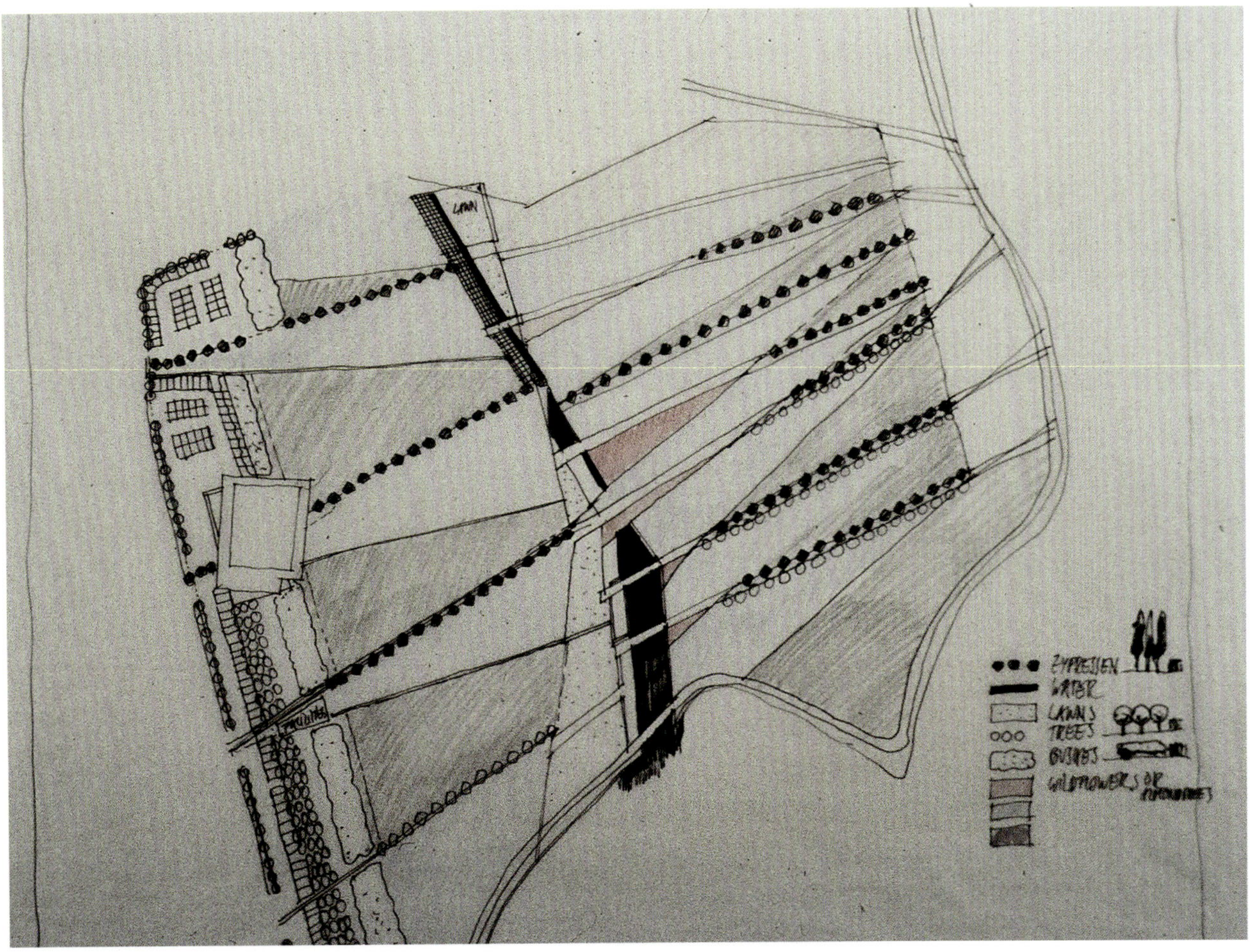
LAWN
ZYPRESSEN
WATER
LAWNS
TREES
BUSHES
WILDFLOWERS OR

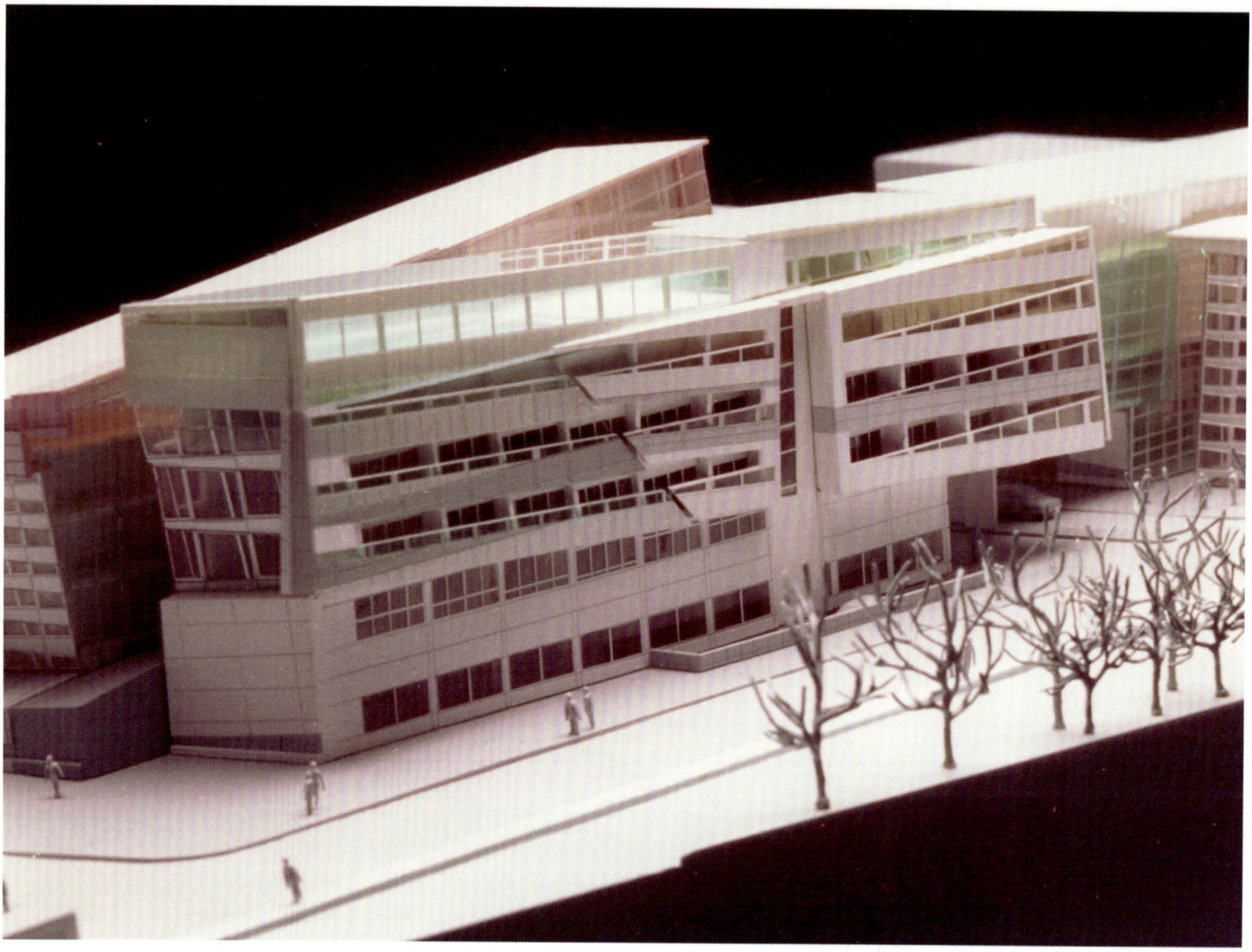

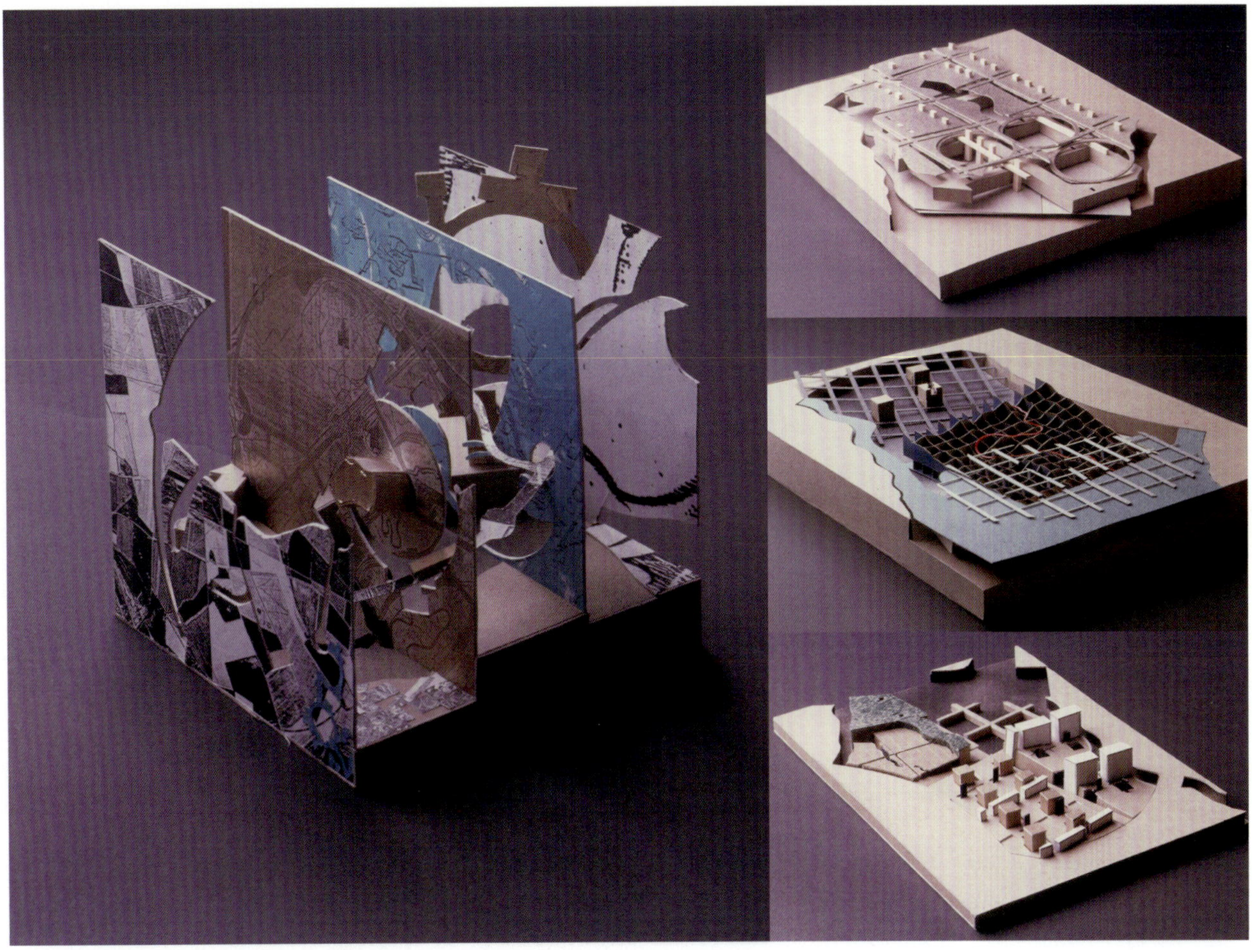

EURO DISNEY HOTEL

Unlike many of their projects wherein the surface and the subject matter are one and the same, here the expression of surface as a screen, or as one of many layers, is explicit. While somewhat skeptical about the Disney Corporation project in Europe, Olin and Eisenman saw the hotel project as an opportunity to produce a serious piece of work. A hotel and its requirements presented not only an opportunity to reflect upon the Disney oeuvre and Disney's portrayal of the American landscape, but also a chance to play with the Disney model in a way that could appeal to Europeans. Eisenman and Olin also noted the subterranean machinery of Disneyland and Disney World, the services and apparatus skillfully hidden from the stage set façades and superstructures that visitors see.

The proposed scheme was composed of a ground layer of small bungalows—a cross between Monopoly houses and Mickey's and Minnie's abodes—that were placed around half of a freeway cloverleaf that resembled Mickey's ears. Beneath this was a labyrinthine series of spaces that housed most of the hotel functions—ballrooms, restaurants, cafes, spas, services, et cetera—many of which opened to light from above (holes in the bucolic grid of houses, streets, and freeways). It was workable, funny, and critical. The "suits" at Disney hated it.

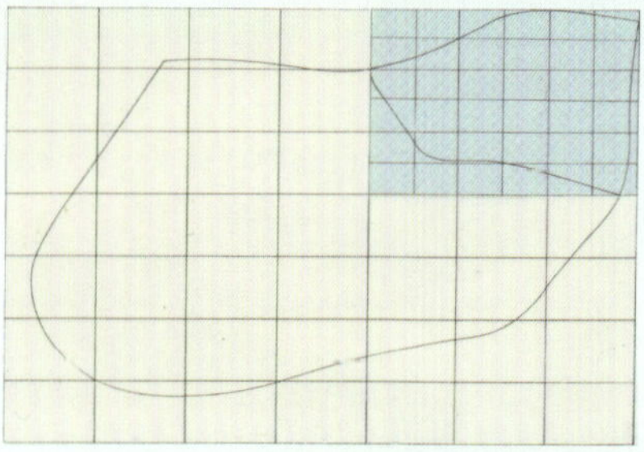

SUPERPOSITION OF NET

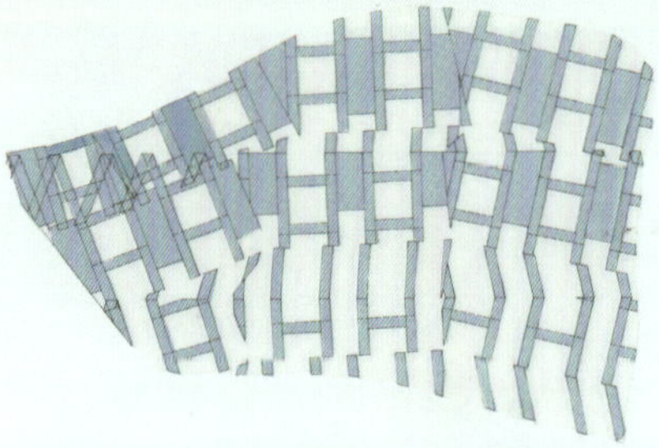

TYPOLOGICAL FABRIC

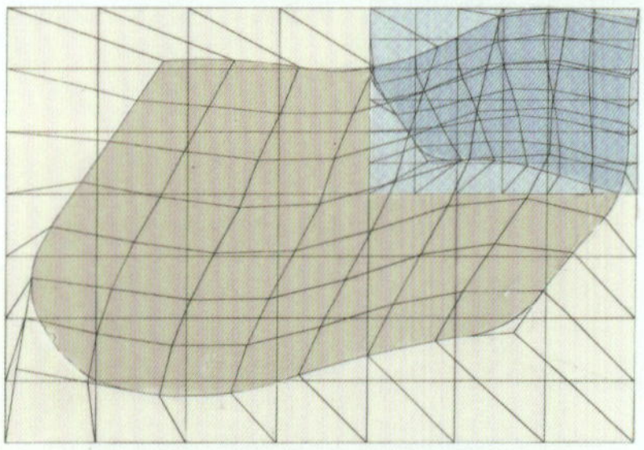

TRANSFORMATION OF NET

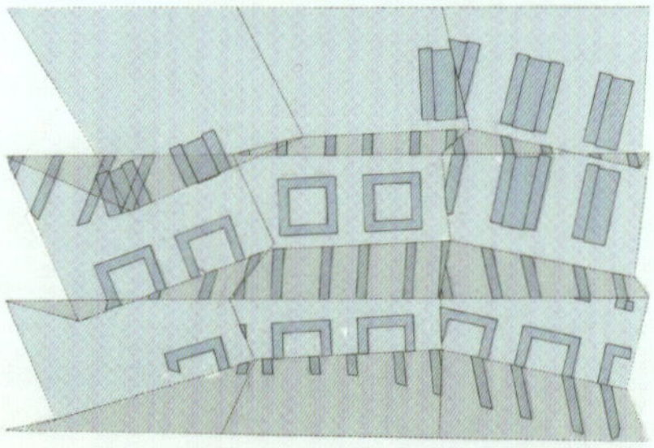

BUILDING TYPOLOGY

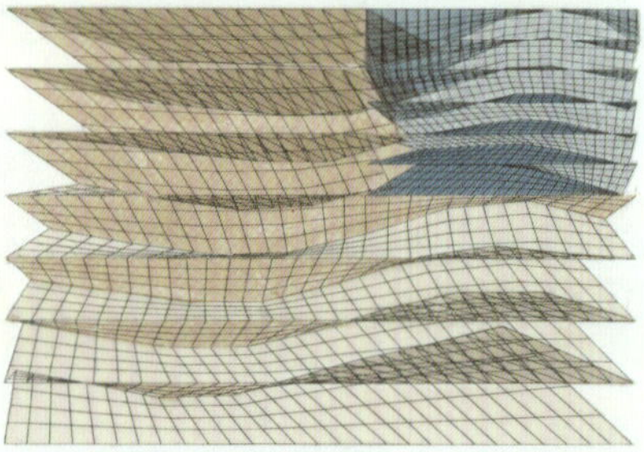

FOLDED NET

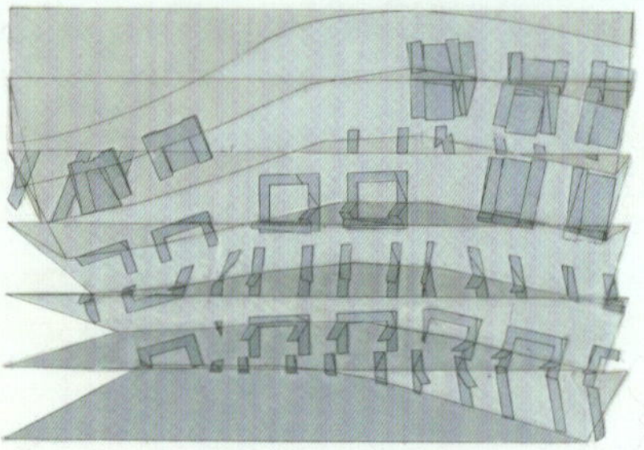

FOLDED TYPOLOGY

REBSTOCKPARK MASTER PLAN

The competition-winning Restockpark master plan was developed for a large site west of the historic center of Frankfurt, near the Messe (fairgrounds) and adjacent to a historic Seidlung designed by Ernst May prior to World War II. The site had once been the home of a suburban Schloss with its farm and grape vines (Rebstock). The Nazis turned it into an airfield, which in turn was heavily bombed by the Allies, only to become a gravel pit for postwar reconstruction.

The Rebstockpark project endeavored to reassess the entire idea of a static urbanism, one which only deals with objects rather than events, by taking into account the evolving reality of a media age where objects are no longer as meaningful as events. The "leftover" space of the Siedlung, in which object buildings seemed detached from their ground, was already antithetical to the blurring of the traditional figure/ground relationships that Eisenman and Olin had been working on for some years. Using the concept of folding—Gilles Deleuze's idea of *le pli*—Eisenman and Olin compressed two grids, large and small, on the site to generate contingent readings that can be seen as folding and unfolding site figures. The perceived dimension of the fold, versus the edge of the line, both mediates and reframes the condition of figure and ground.

Development of the scheme resulted in a zoning plan (*Bebauungsplan*) adopted by the city and subsequently used as the basis for implementing development of the site. Orchards and other green features were interlaced with the residential areas. Elements included: social housing, schools and day care, neighborhood shops, office and commercial buildings, an extensive recreation program, an enormous grape vine-covered parking garage, vast fields to provide overflow parking for the numerous fairs (and that become parks or flower farms at other times), sports grounds, expanded community gardens. Also, some reforestation was planned with a series of linear water features and storm water facilities to provide habitat and aquifer recharge, and cooling and cleansing of urban air and water.

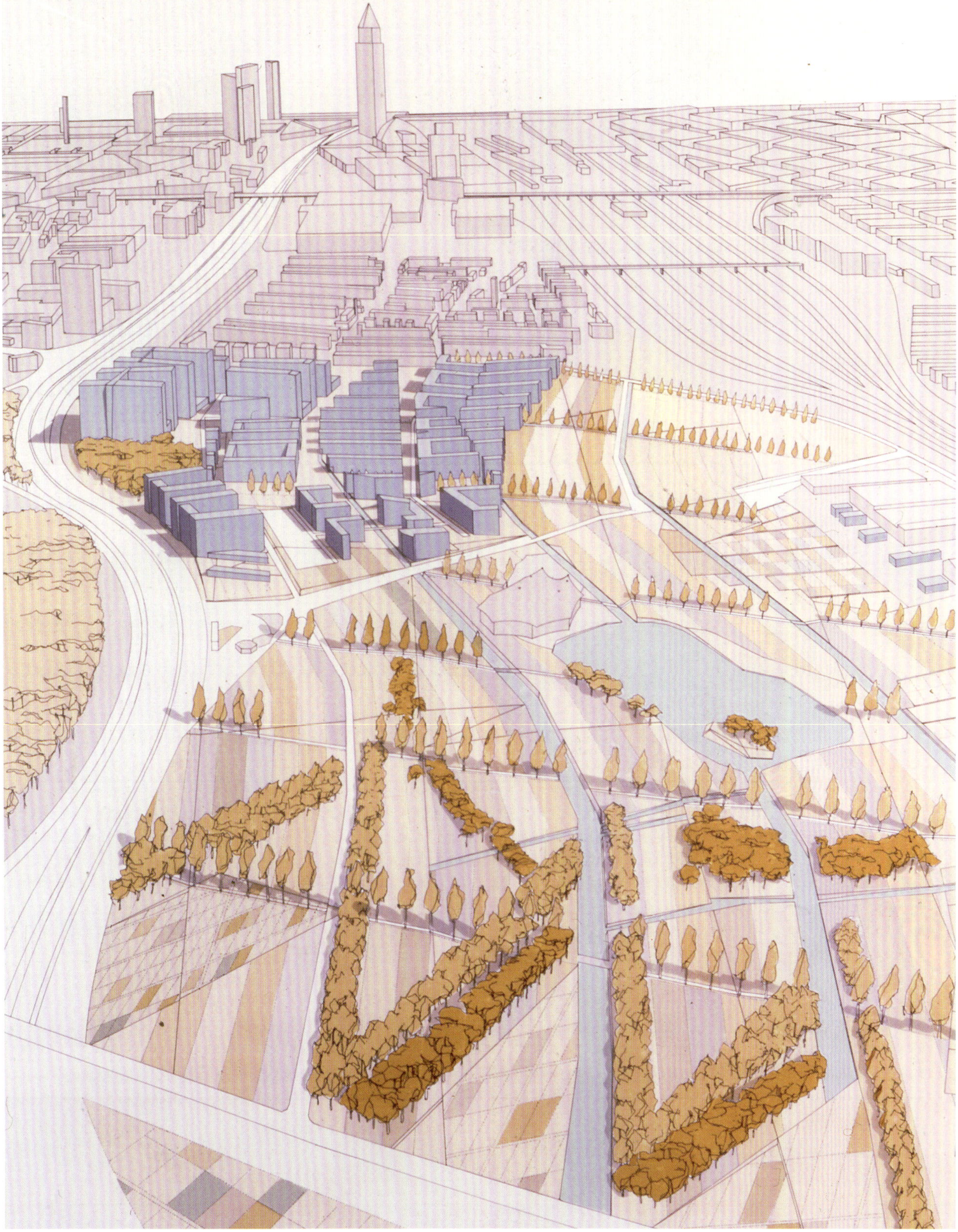

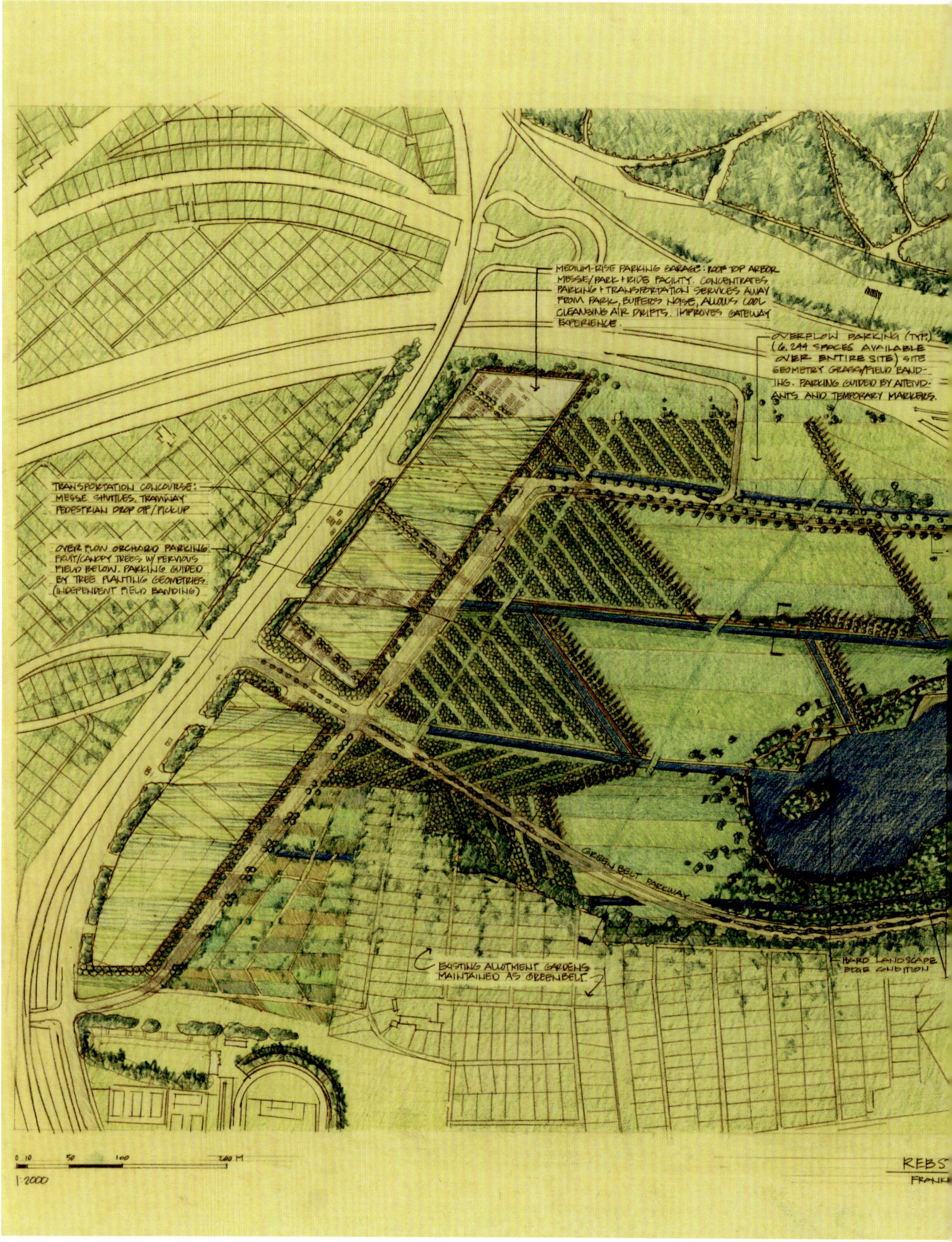
MEDIUM-RISE PARKING GARAGE: ROOF TOP ARBOR MESSE/PARK + RIDE FACILITY. CONCENTRATES PARKING + TRANSPORTATION SERVICES AWAY FROM PARK, BUFFERS NOISE, ALLOWS COOL CLEANSING AIR DRIFTS. IMPROVES GATEWAY EXPERIENCE.
OVERFLOW PARKING (TYP.) (6,244 SPACES AVAILABLE OVER ENTIRE SITE) SITE GEOMETRY GRASS/FIELD BANDING. PARKING GUIDED BY ATTENDANTS AND TEMPORARY MARKERS.
TRANSPORTATION CONCOURSE: MESSE SHUTTLES, TRAMWAY PEDESTRIAN DROP OFF/PICKUP
OVERFLOW ORCHARD PARKING: FRUIT/CANOPY TREES W/ PERVIOUS FIELD BELOW. PARKING GUIDED BY TREE PLANTING GEOMETRIES. (INDEPENDENT FIELD BANDING)
GREEN BELT PARKWAY
EXISTING ALLOTMENT GARDENS MAINTAINED AS GREENBELT.
HARD LANDSCAPE EDGE CONDITION
0 10 50 100 200 M
1:2000
REBS
FRANK

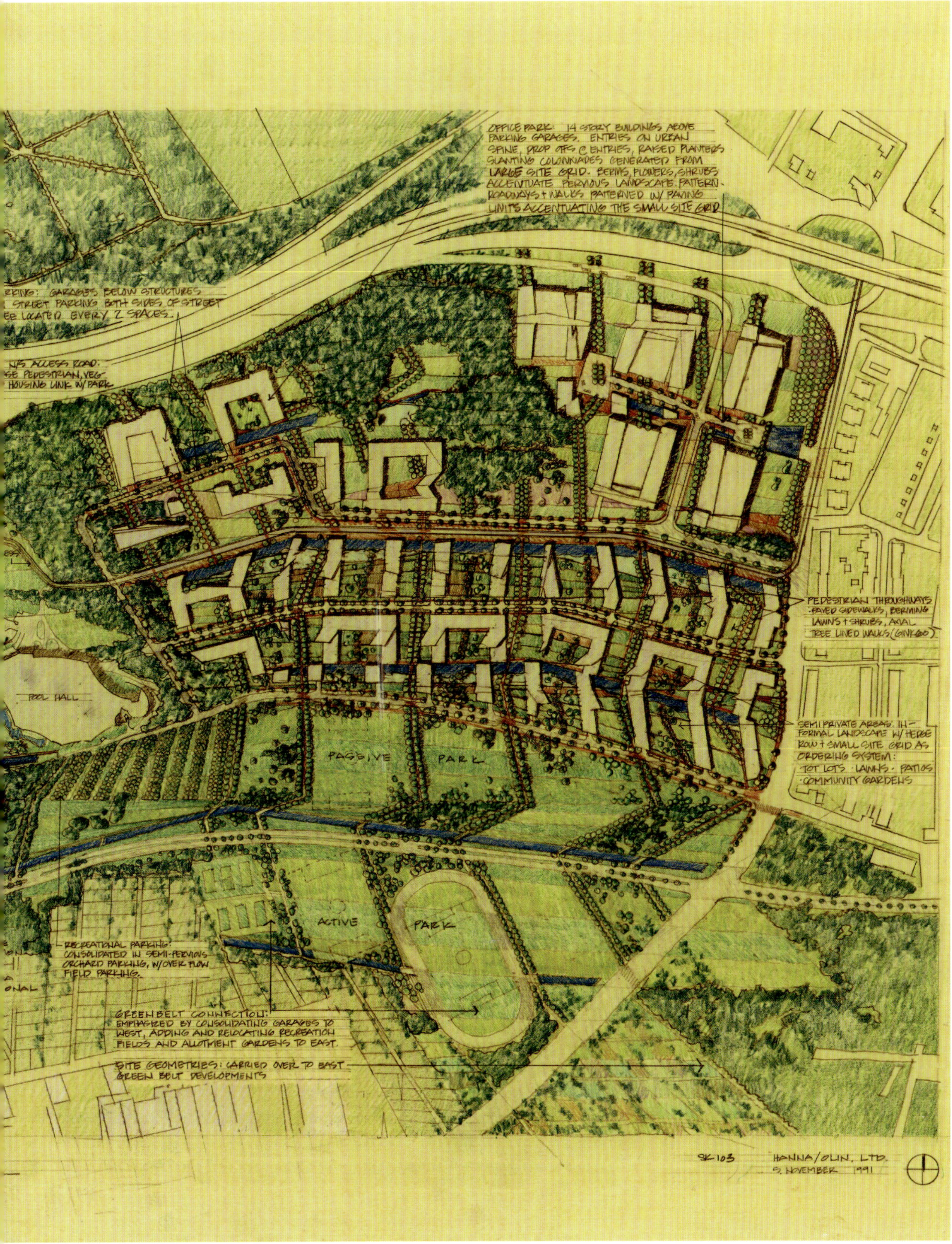
OFFICE PARK: 14 STORY BUILDINGS ABOVE PARKING GARAGES. ENTRIES ON URBAN SPINE, PROP OFFS @ ENTRIES, RAISED PLANTERS SLANTING COLONNADES GENERATED FROM LARGE SITE GRID. BERMS, FLOWERS, SHRUBS ACCENTUATE PERVIOUS LANDSCAPE PATTERN. ROADWAYS + WALKS PATTERNED W/ PAVING UNITS ACCENTUATING THE SMALL SITE GRID
RKING: GARAGES BELOW STRUCTURES
STREET PARKING BOTH SIDES OF STREET
EE LOCATED EVERY 2 SPACES.
N/S ACCESS ROAD:
SE PEDESTRIAN, VEG
HOUSING LINK W/ PARK
POOL HALL
PASSIVE PARK
ACTIVE PARK
PEDESTRIAN THROUGHWAYS: PAVED SIDEWALKS, BERMING LAWNS + SHRUBS, AXIAL TREE LINED WALKS (GINKGO)
SEMI PRIVATE AREAS: INFORMAL LANDSCAPE W/ HEDGE ROW + SMALL SITE GRID AS ORDERING SYSTEM:
· TOT LOTS · LAWNS · PATIOS
· COMMUNITY GARDENS
RECREATIONAL PARKING: CONSOLIDATED IN SEMI-PERVIOUS ORCHARD PARKING, W/ OVER FLOW FIELD PARKING.
GREENBELT CONNECTION: EMPHASIZED BY CONSOLIDATING GARAGES TO WEST, ADDING AND RELOCATING RECREATION FIELDS AND ALLOTMENT GARDENS TO EAST.
SITE GEOMETRIES: CARRIED OVER TO EAST GREEN BELT DEVELOPMENTS
SK103
HANNA/OLIN, LTD.
5 NOVEMBER 1991

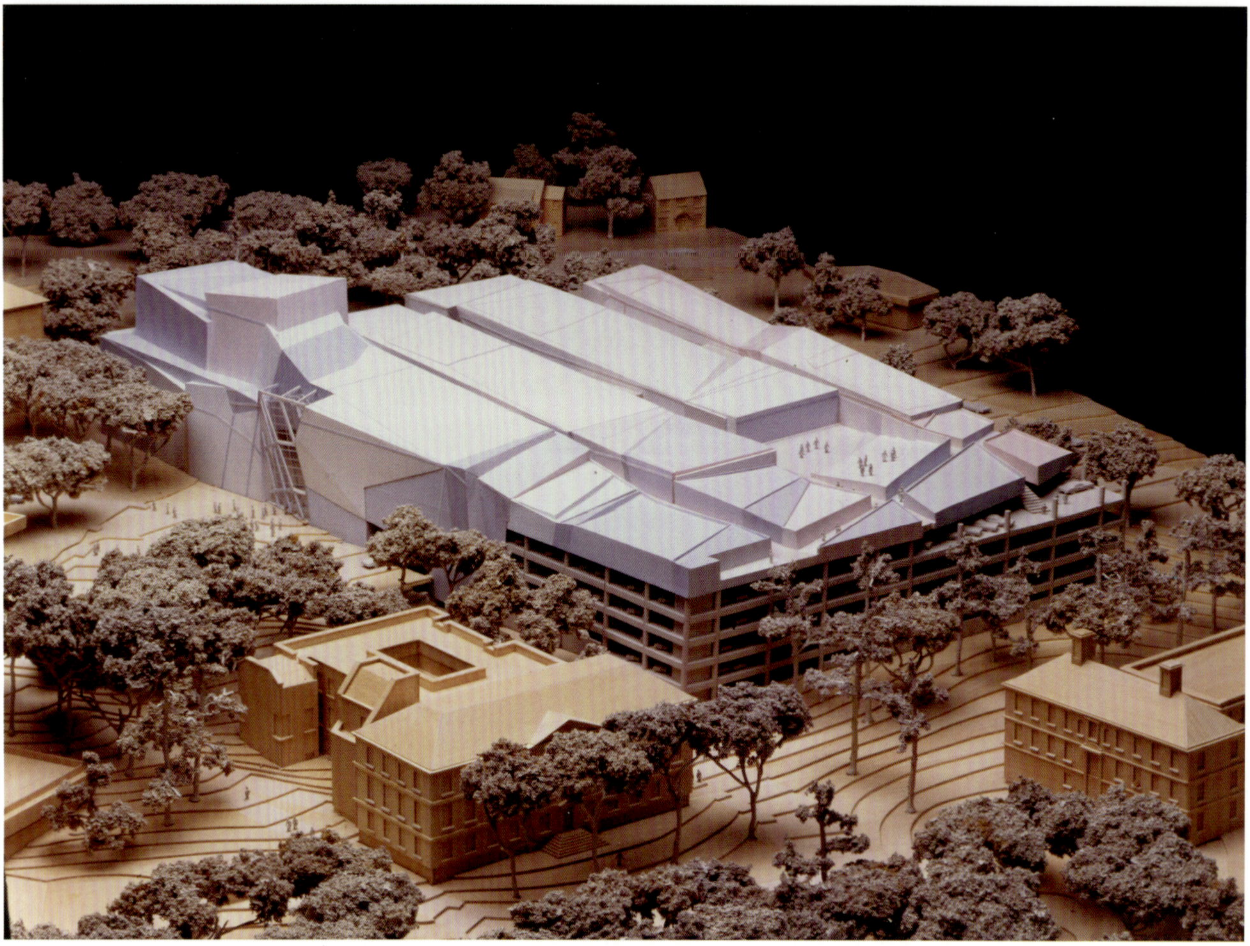

CENTER FOR THE ARTS, EMORY UNIVERSITY

The location near the edge of the Emory campus positioned the Center for the Arts to serve as a link between the community and the University, both through community-oriented performances and by physically providing a natural point of entry to the campus. The university had selected a highly visible site at an intersection on an edge of the campus. Noting a lovely stand of mature trees that was the last relic of the forest that once covered the campuses and region, Olin suggested shifting the site toward the recently built parking garage downhill from the trees.

The Center envelops an existing multiple-level garage structure on one side, and projects its main spaces onto a natural knoll. A promenade crosses the knoll and passes through the building lobby to arrive at an open amphitheater and sculpture garden. These in turn pass over one of the campus's many ravines, leading to the University art museum on the historical campus quadrangle designed by Henry Hornbostle.

The quadrangle is based on a grid system which, when extended to the center's site, is "deformed" by the topography of the ravine. This initial deformation approximates the five lines of a fundamental sine wave in musical harmonics; the wave is similar in amplitude and frequency to the ravine topography. These harmonic waves compress and extend the continuous surfaces of the Center's four main building bars, folding them in a multiplicity of configurations. Later, in the landscape plan, Olin created clusters of trees based upon several choruses from a late 1930s Duke Ellington tune.

The four performance halls are linked by an expansive, multi-level lobby traversing the length of the building and functioning as a link between the campus boundary and a new open-air amphitheater. Academic spaces for the Department of Theater and Film Studies and the Department of Music are located to the east of the lobby over the parking garage, and rehearsal and support space is provided adjacent to the performance halls.

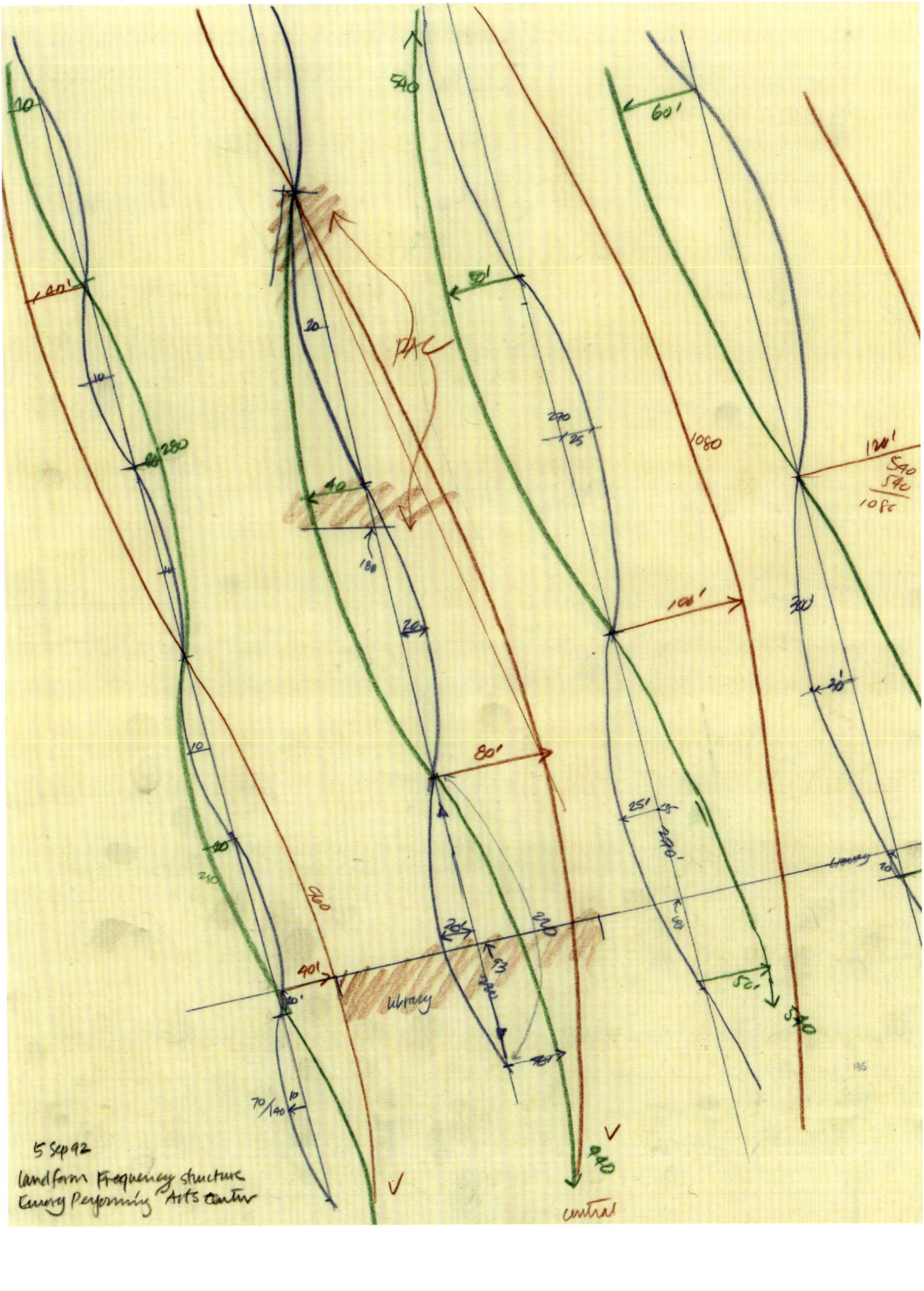
5 Sep 92
Landform Frequency structure
Emory Performing Arts Center
PAC
Library
central
540
1080
60'
50'
80'
100'
120'

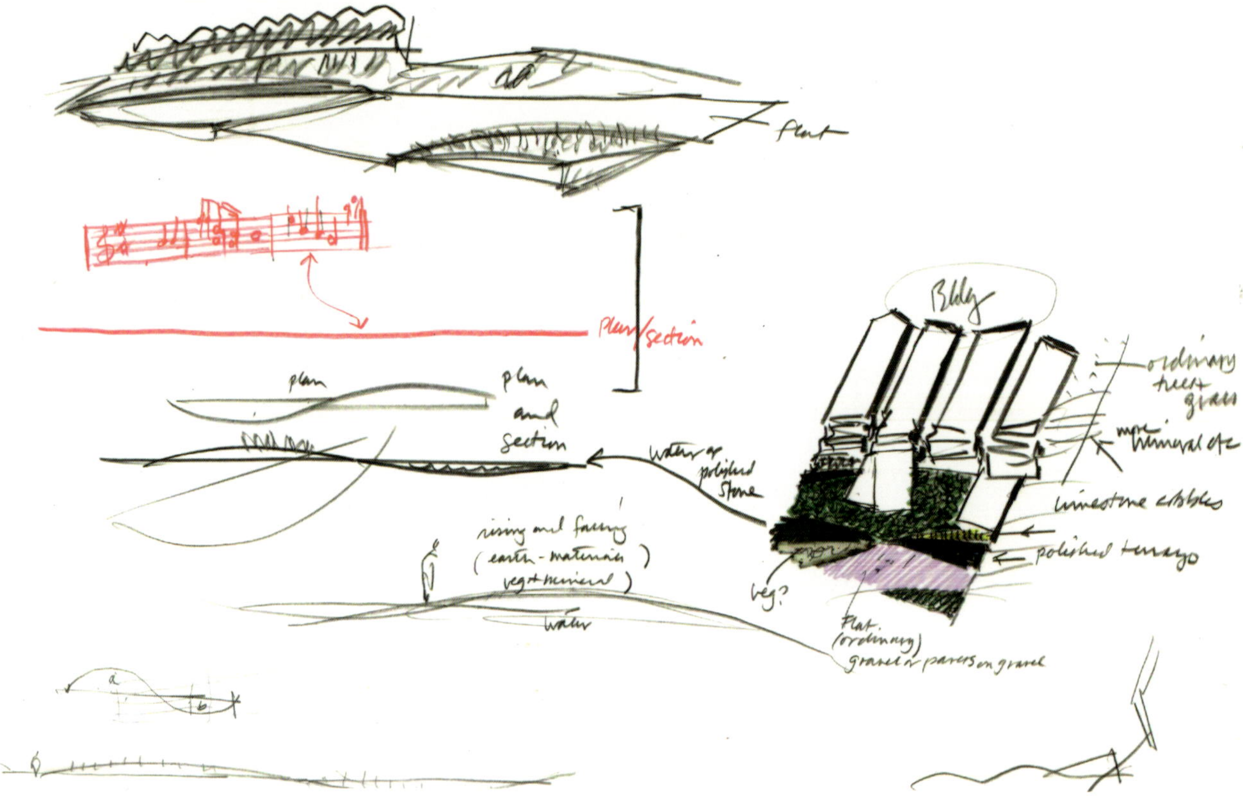
Flat
Plan/section
plan
plan and section
water or polished stone
Bldg
ordinary trees + grass
more mineral etc
limestone cobbles
polished terrazo
rising and falling (earth-materials) veg+mineral
water
veg?
Flat (ordinary) gravel or pavers on gravel

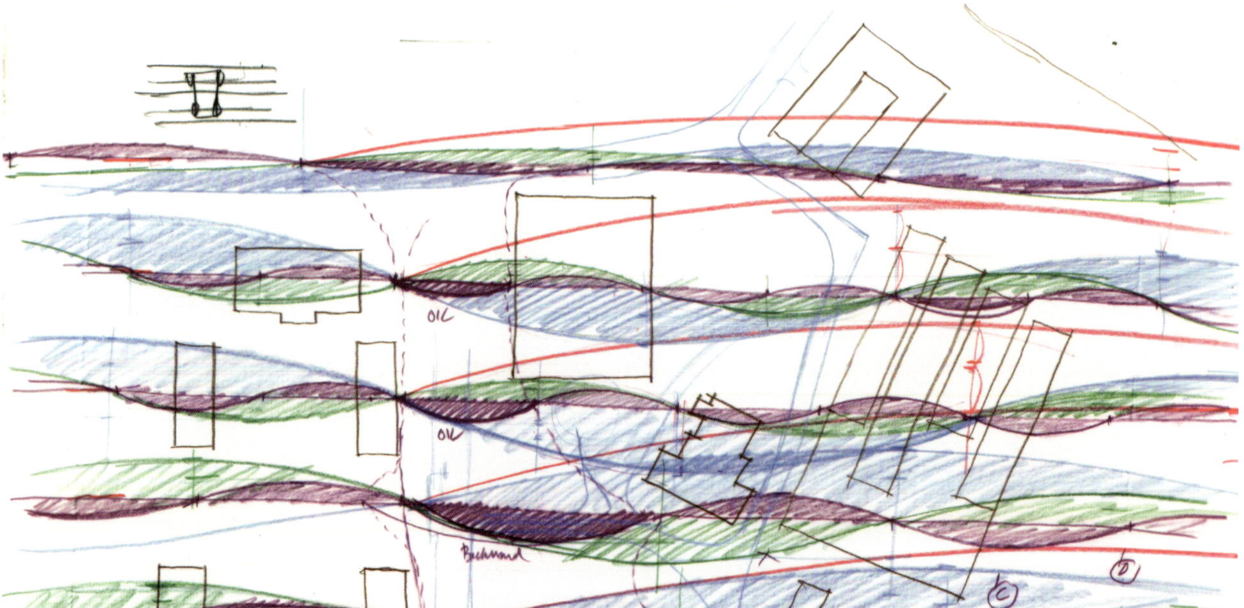
OK
OK
Backward
A primary arc/chord (note)
B
C
D

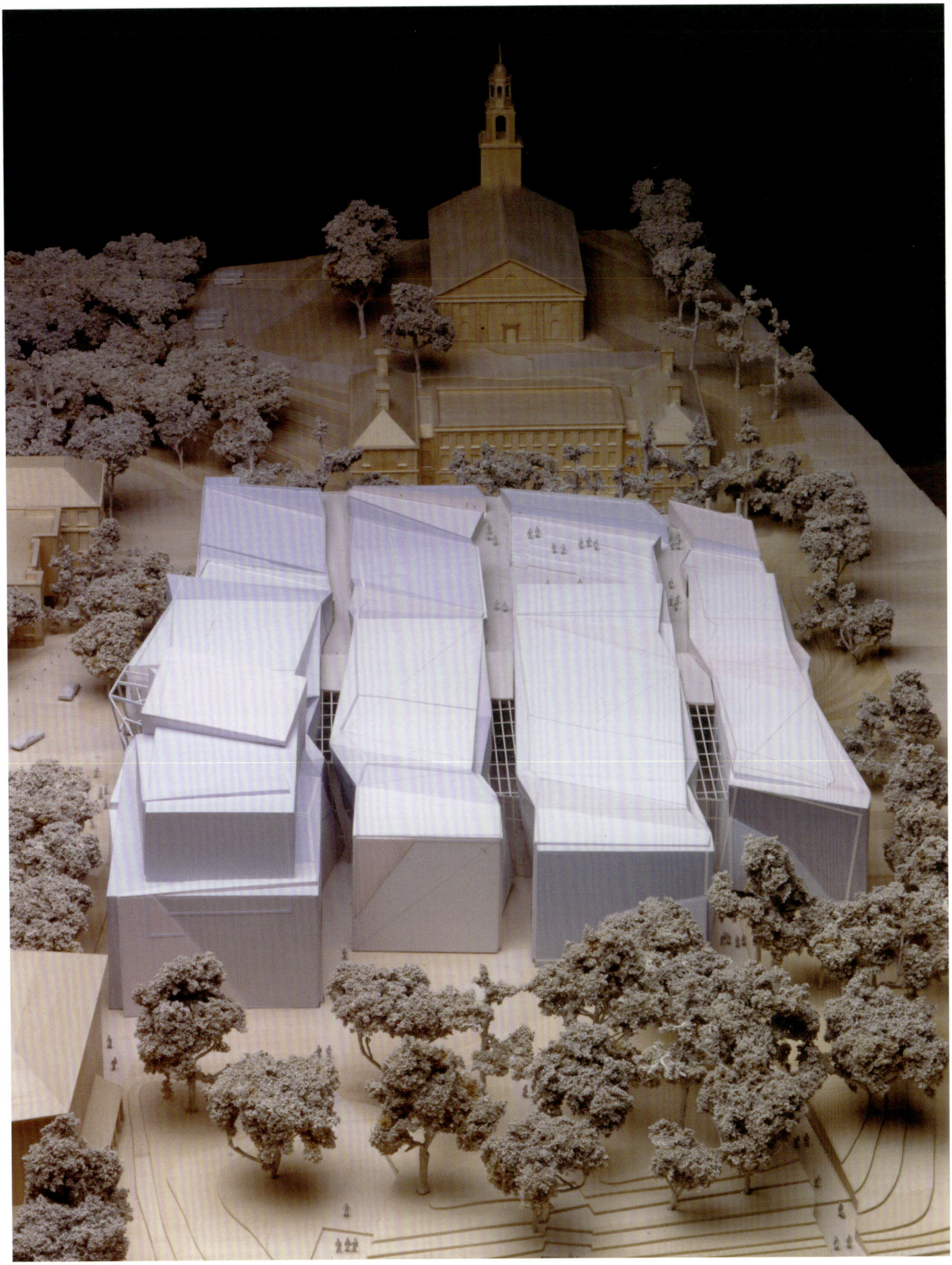

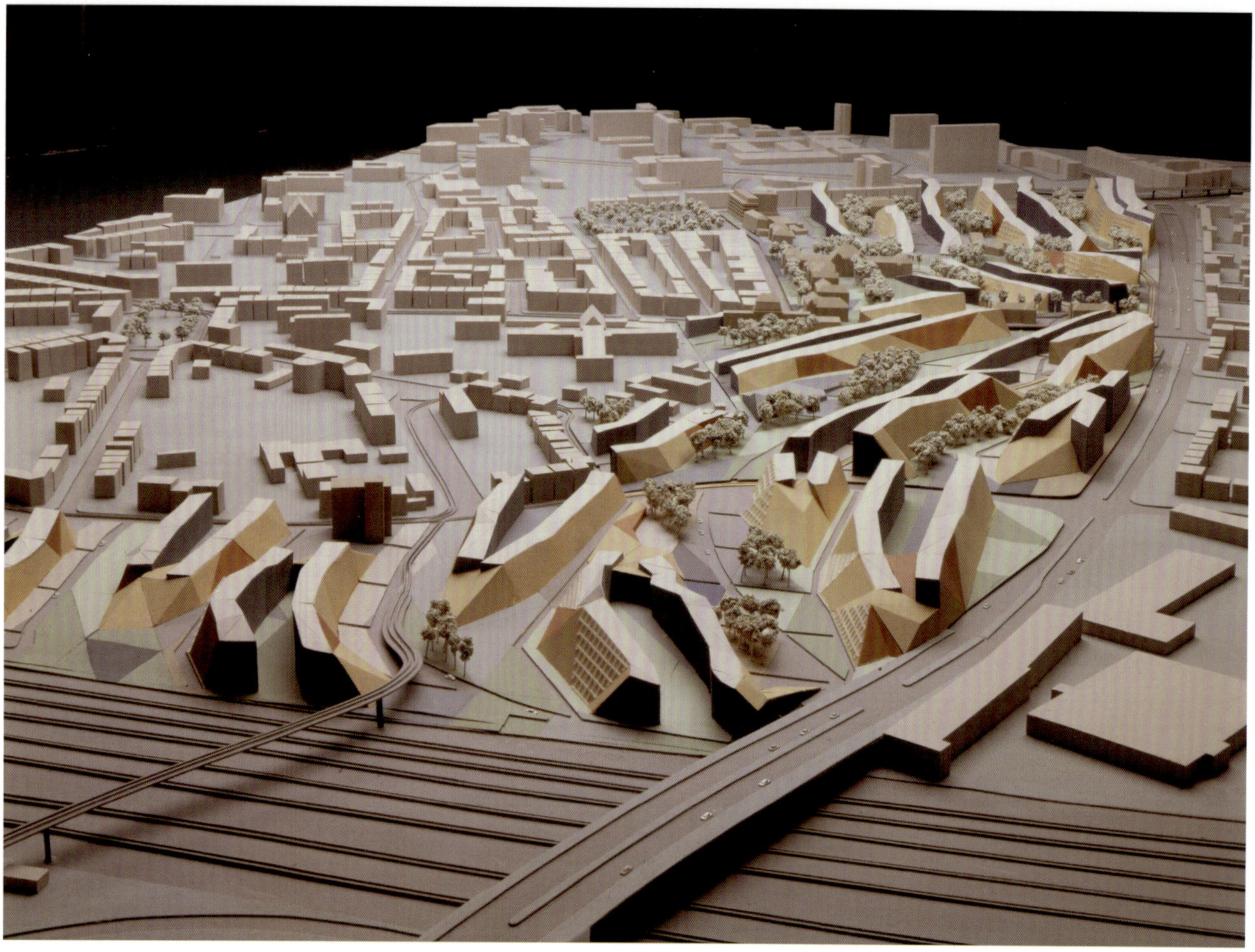

NORDLICHES DERENDORF MASTER PLAN COMPETITION

This invited competition was for a site to the north of the historic center of Dusseldorf, adjacent to two older residential neighborhoods restored after the war, and bounded on the east by rail yards and a perimeter bypass highway on the north. Sensing an opportunity to revisit issues of urban form and its character, Eisenman began exploring devices to produce an overall organization, a framework. Olin continued to look for an opportunity to use urban fabric as a "landscape," and to introduce natural processes at a larger scale into the city.

One of the specific but intangible limits on the site was the system of radar and radio that, because of the site's proximity to the flight path of the airport, causing a certain height restriction to be mapped on this project. This mapping derives from the intersection of the radar pattern with the radio pattern, which produces an interference, or moiré, pattern, which subtly changes over the dimension of the site and provides an idea of limit for physical design. This new mapping is then overlaid on the site, as a topological structure. Instead of the grid, there is a matrix produced by the stretching of the interference pattern in section over the site.

The matrix led to the formation of five-story apartment dwellings, which created a landscape of ridges and valleys that were adjusted to take advantage of solar aspect and air movement. Straight vertical facades formed normal streets and addresses, while sloping backsides with terraces formed "valleys" with linear parks and gardens. A series of north-south access paths was introduced providing vehicle-free pedestrian ways to schools, daycare, recreation and community facilities. The scale of the blocks and streets was remarkably like that of the traditional normative perimeter blocks of the adjacent neighborhoods.

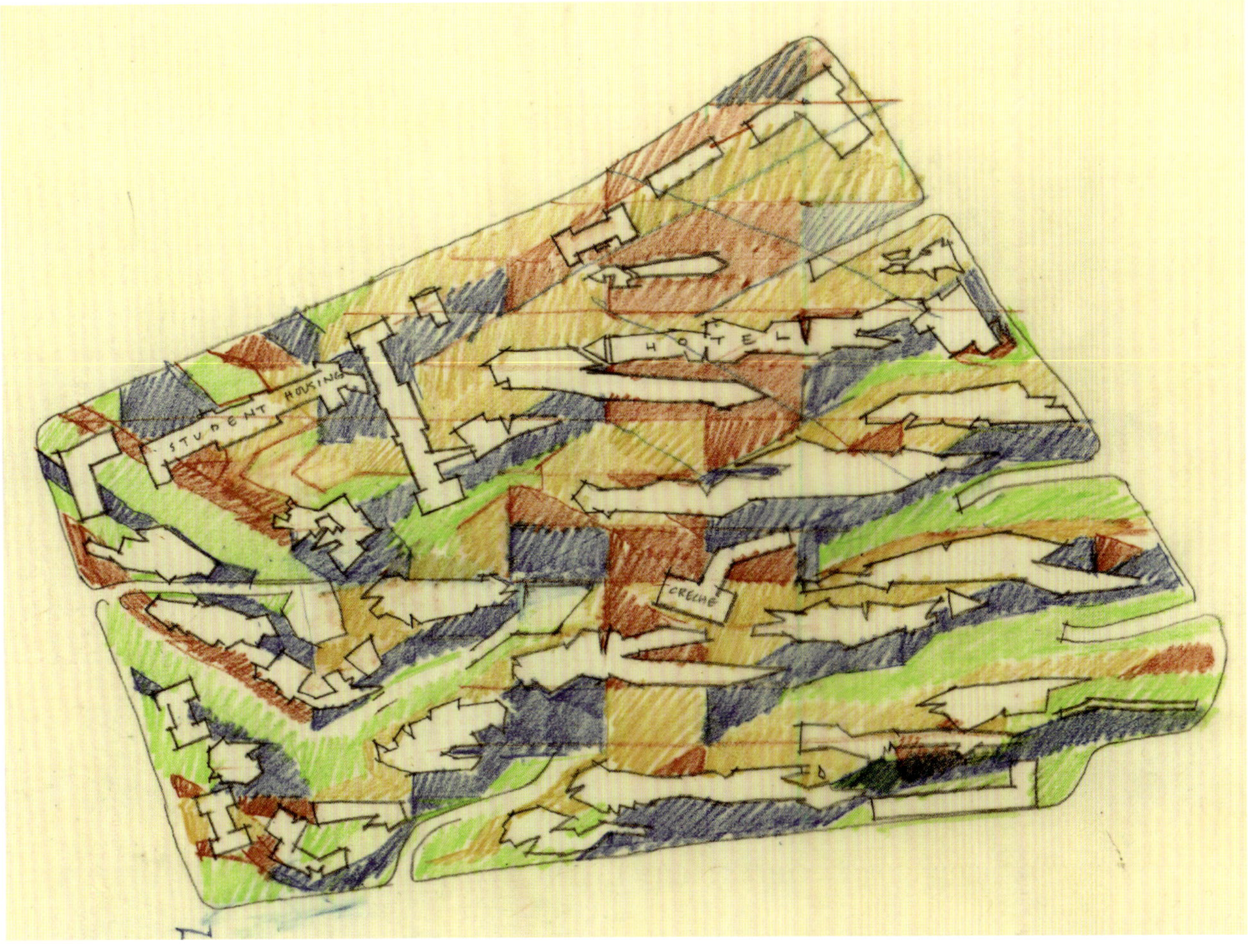
STUDENT HOUSING
HOTEL
CRECHE

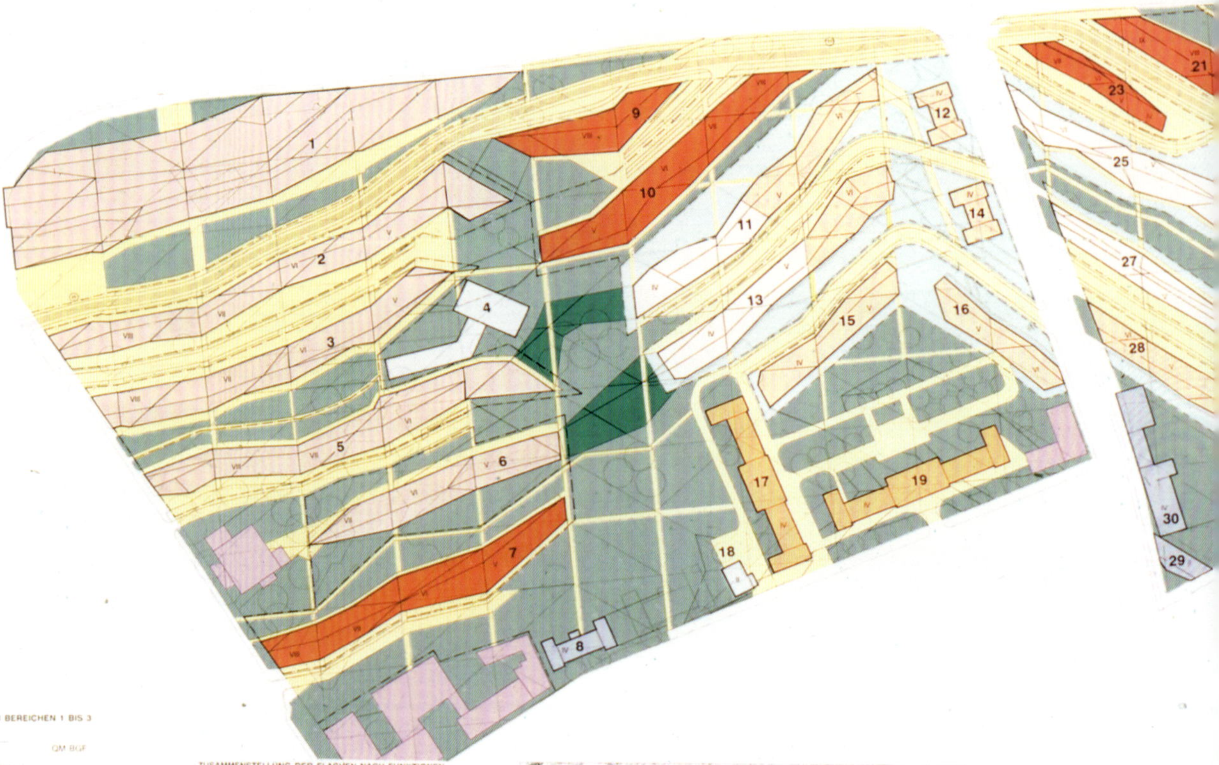

LUNG IN DEN BEREICHEN 1 BIS 3	
	QM BGF
ca. 170.000 QM	
	3.000
	2.200
ungsraume	4.400
	22.400
	2.800
	6.300
	24.900
	4.000
	21.200
	1.600
	4.900
	19.000
	3.100
	15.700
	25.600
	2.400
	13.000
	19.300
	14.100
	1.000
	13.800
	1.000
	6.100
	6.900
	6.500
	500
	6.500
	252.200
etall ca. 101.000 QM	
	20.600
	12.700
	20.000
	7.600
	16.000
	10.000
ermarkt	5.900
	14.000
	10.700
	1.000
	5.400
	5.600
	5.000
	134.500
tall und Schlachthof	
	17.300
	22.500
	4.500
	4.200
	18.000
	15.500
	13.500
	15.200
	13.600
	12.000
	4.000
	12.900
	22.800
	29.000
	205.500
	591.700

ZUSAMMENSTELLUNG DER FLACHEN NACH FUNKTIONEN

Funktion	BGF QM
Stadthalle	3.000
Buro-/Dienstleistungsflachen	366.200
Wohnbauflachen	142.700
Gewerbeflachen	55.000
Versorgungsflachen	18.400
Jugendzentrum	6.400
Kindergarten	2.400
GEPLANTE BGF INSGESAMT	**591.700**

ZUSAMMENSTELLUNG DER FLACHEN NACH BEREICHEN

Bereich 1 Landesgrundstuck

Funktionsbereich		BGF QM
Stadthalle		3.000
Buro-/Dienstleistungsflache, Hotel		184.800
Versorgungsflache		8.500
Wohnungsbauflachen		55.900
Sozialer WB	14.000	
Frei Finanzierter WB	28.900	
Studentenwohnen	13.000	
Kindergarten		2.400

Bereich 2 Grundstuck Rheinmetall

Funktionsbereich		BGF QM
Buro-/Dienstleistungsflachen		60.900
Wohnflache gesamt		61.300
Sozialer WB	20.000	
Frei Finanzierter WB	41.300	
Versorgungsflachen		5.900
Jugendzentrum		6.400

Bereich 3 Grundstuck Rheinmetall und Schlachthof

Funktionsbereich		BGF QM
Buro-/Dienstleistungsflache		120.500
Versorgungsflache		4.000
Gewerbeflache		55.000
Wohnflache gesamt		25.500
Sozialer WB	8.500	
Frei Finanzierter WB	17.000	

BESCHREIBUNG DER BAUABSCHNITTE

Eine mogliche Gestaltung der Bauphasen ist wie folgt:

Bauabschnitt 1	Erstellung der Stadthalle bis an die Wohnbebauung an der Johannstrasse
Bauabschnitt 2	Erstellung der Wohnbebauung und Teil der Burobebauung auf dem Teil des Landesgrundstuck, der sofort verfugbar ist, und auf Rheinmetall-West.
Bauabschnitt 3	Erganzung der Stadthalle und des Convention Centers mit Hotel und der dazu gehorenden Burobebauung. Bebauung Rheinmetall-Ost ohne stadtisches Grundstuck und ohne Schlachthof.
Bauabschnitt 4	Bebauung des Grundstucks Rechenzentrum und des stadtischen Grundstucks Ratherstrasse
Bauabschnitt 5	Bebauung des Grundstucks des heutigen Schlachthofs
Strassenbahn:	Die Strassenbahn kann in jedem der Bauabschnitte erstellt werden. Der Zeitpunkt ist abhangig vom Bedarf.

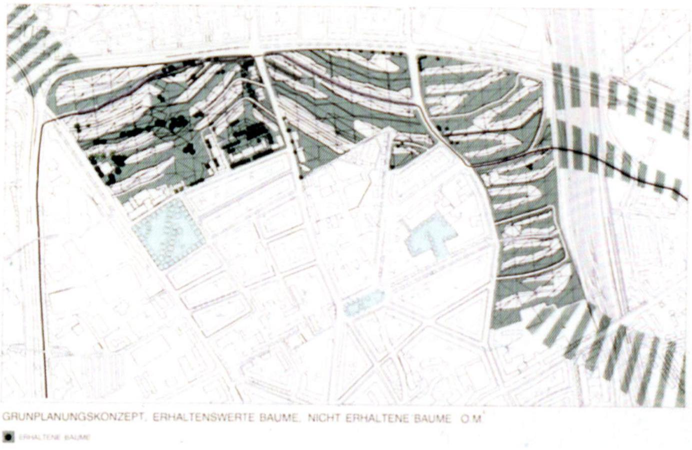

GRUNPLANUNGSKONZEPT, ERHALTENSWERTE BAUME, NICHT ERHALTENE BAUME O.M.

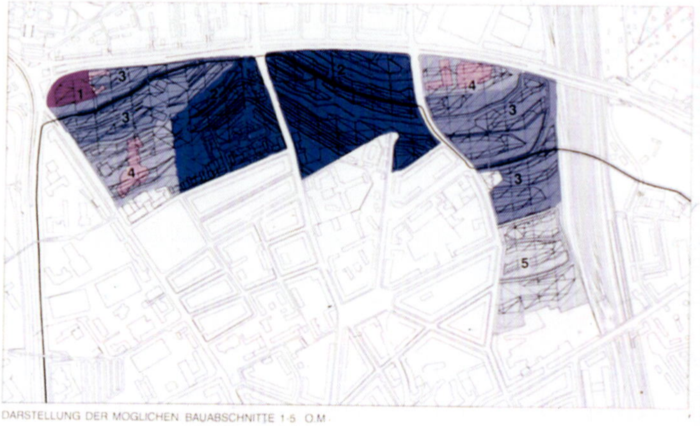

DARSTELLUNG DER MOGLICHEN BAUABSCHNITTE 1-5 O.M.

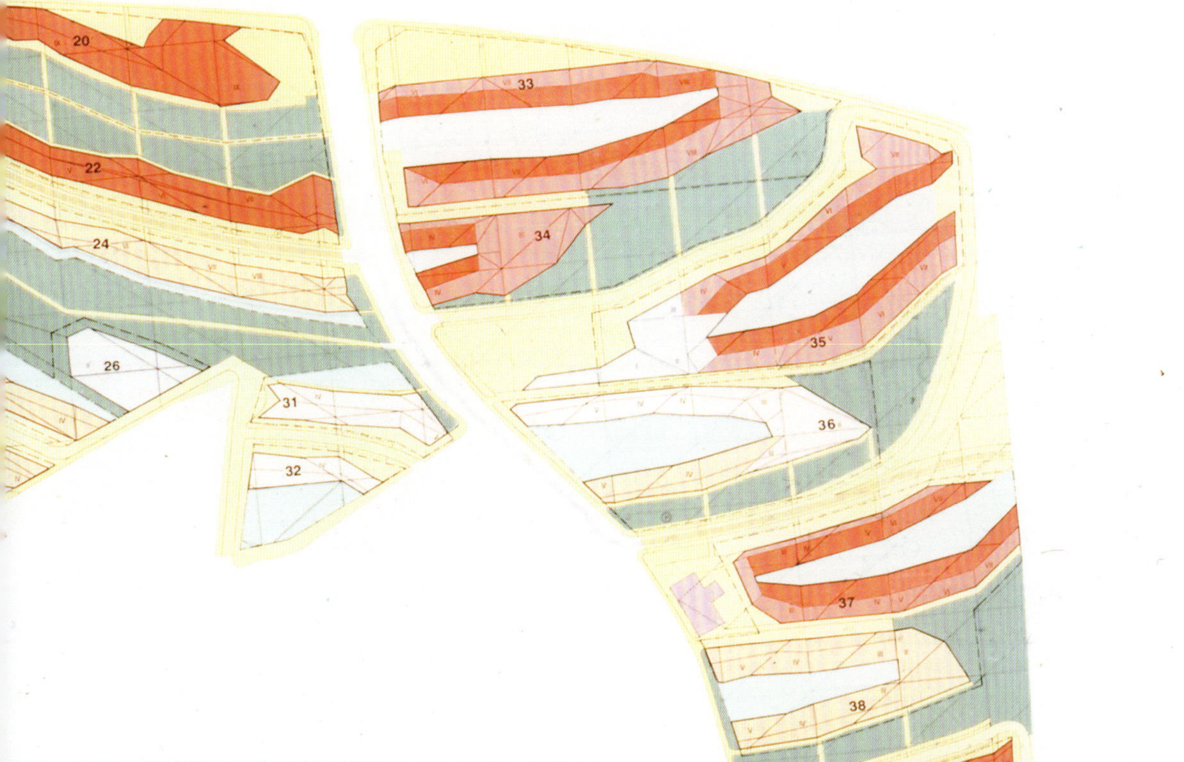

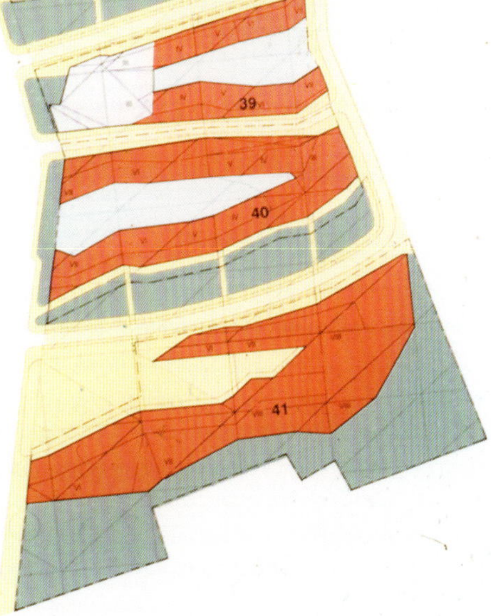

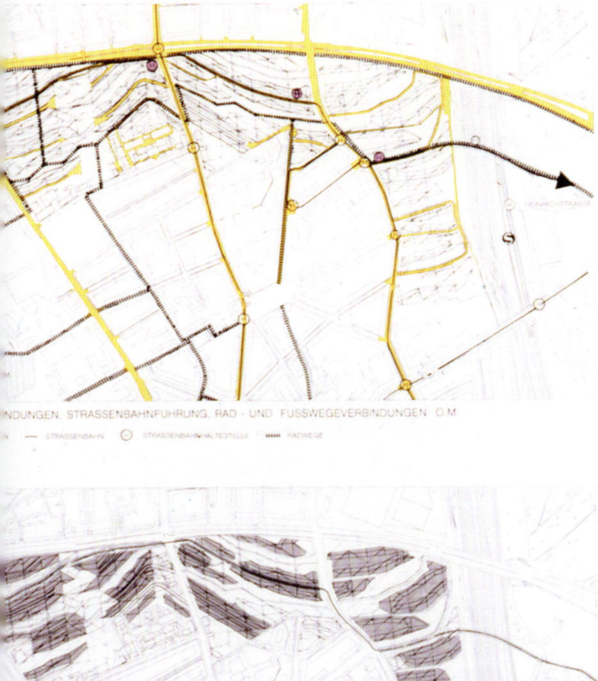

…NDUNGEN, STRASSENBAHNFUHRUNG, RAD- UND FUSSWEGEVERBINDUNGEN O.M.

— STRASSENBAHN ⊙ STRASSENBAHNHALTESTELLE ▪▪▪ RADWEGE

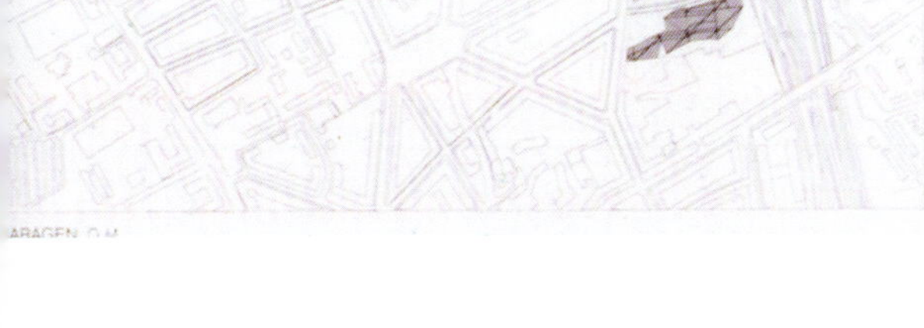

…ARAGEN O.M.

NUTZUNGSVERTEILUNG

- BUROFLACHEN
- GEWERBEFLACHEN
- WOHNFLACHEN - FREI FINANAZIERTE
- WOHNFLACHEN - SOZIALER WOHNUNGSBAU
- WOHNFLACHEN - STUDENTENWOHNEN
- BURO-/GESCHAFTSFLACHEN
- PRIVATE GRUNFLACHEN
- OFFENTLICHE GRUNFLACHEN
- JUGENDZENTRUM/KINDERGARTEN
- GESCHAFTSFLACHEN/RESTAURANTS
- OFFENTLICHE VERKEHRSFLACHEN
- PRIVATE VERKEHRSFLACHEN

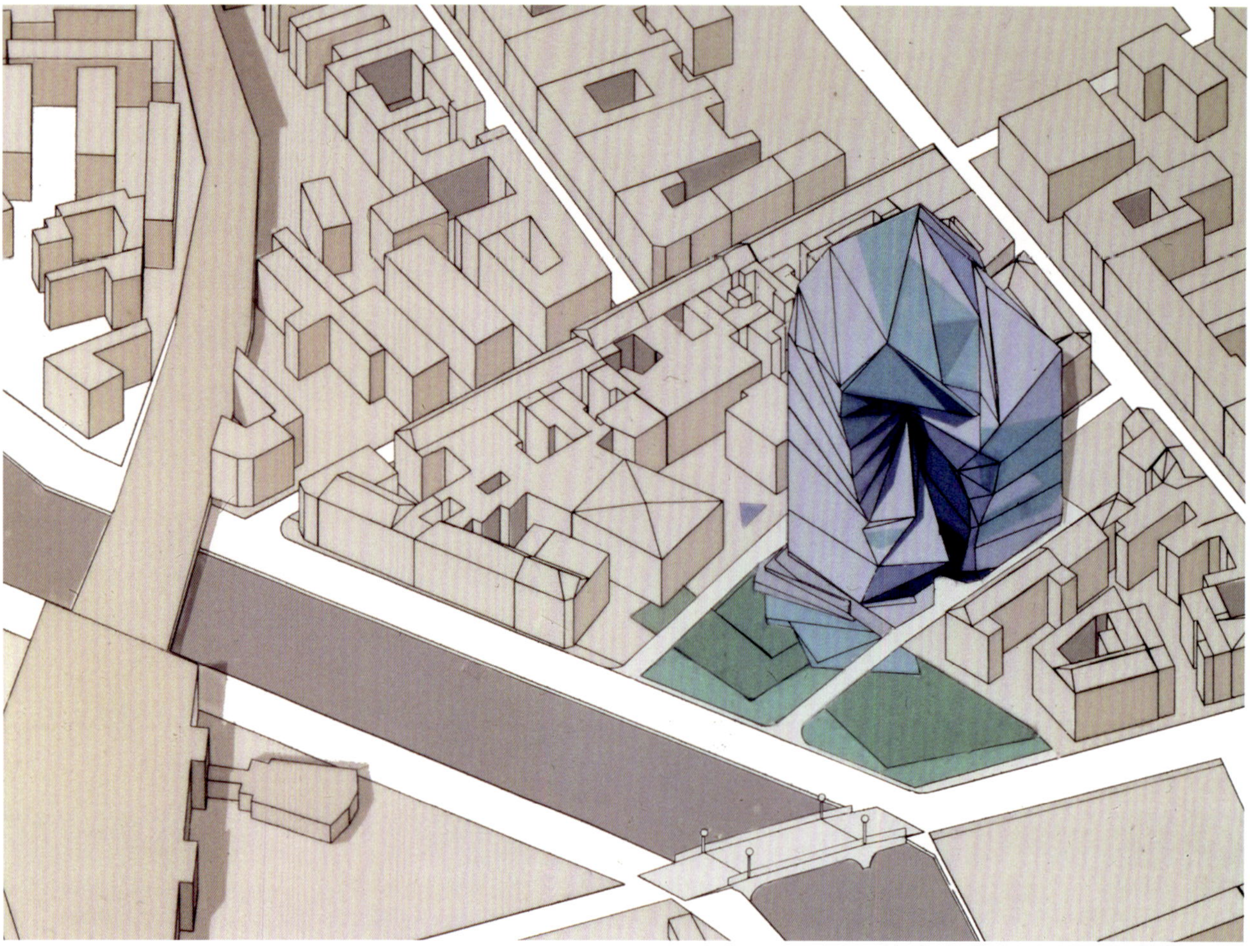

MAX REINHARDT HAUS

The thirty-four-story Max Reinhardt Haus emerges from the Berlin landscape as a landmark—a prismatic form that folds in on itself while simultaneously opening out to the infinite possibilities of its urban context. Named for the famous German theatrical entrepreneur, it occupies the site of his former Schauspielhaus adjacent to the Spree River and along the Friedrichstrasse.

This arched building of intersecting and overlapping forms presents a unified structure that separates, compresses, transforms, and then rejoins itself horizontally at the roof level. The origin of the form is the Möbius strip, a three-dimensional geometric form with a single unending surface that undergoes three iterative operations. In the first, planes are generated from the extension of vectors and the triangulation of surfaces; this triangulation permits the development of both a surface order for cladding and a trussed structure for vertical and lateral support. The second iteration inverts the strip, performs a similar operation to that of the first step, and then imprints these surfaces on the initial form, thereby creating a phantom form. The third step maps an element of Berlin's history onto the form itself by folding large public spaces between the grid and floor plates of an already folded structure—a reference to the cubic volumes of the German neoclassical architect Karl Friedrich Schinkel. These voids seem to occupy the layered spaces of the floors as aggregates in a matrix and without any apparent effect on their makeup. Olin continued the Möbius movement, downward in a spiral, an upside-down ziggurat of sorts that played with the open form of the building above.

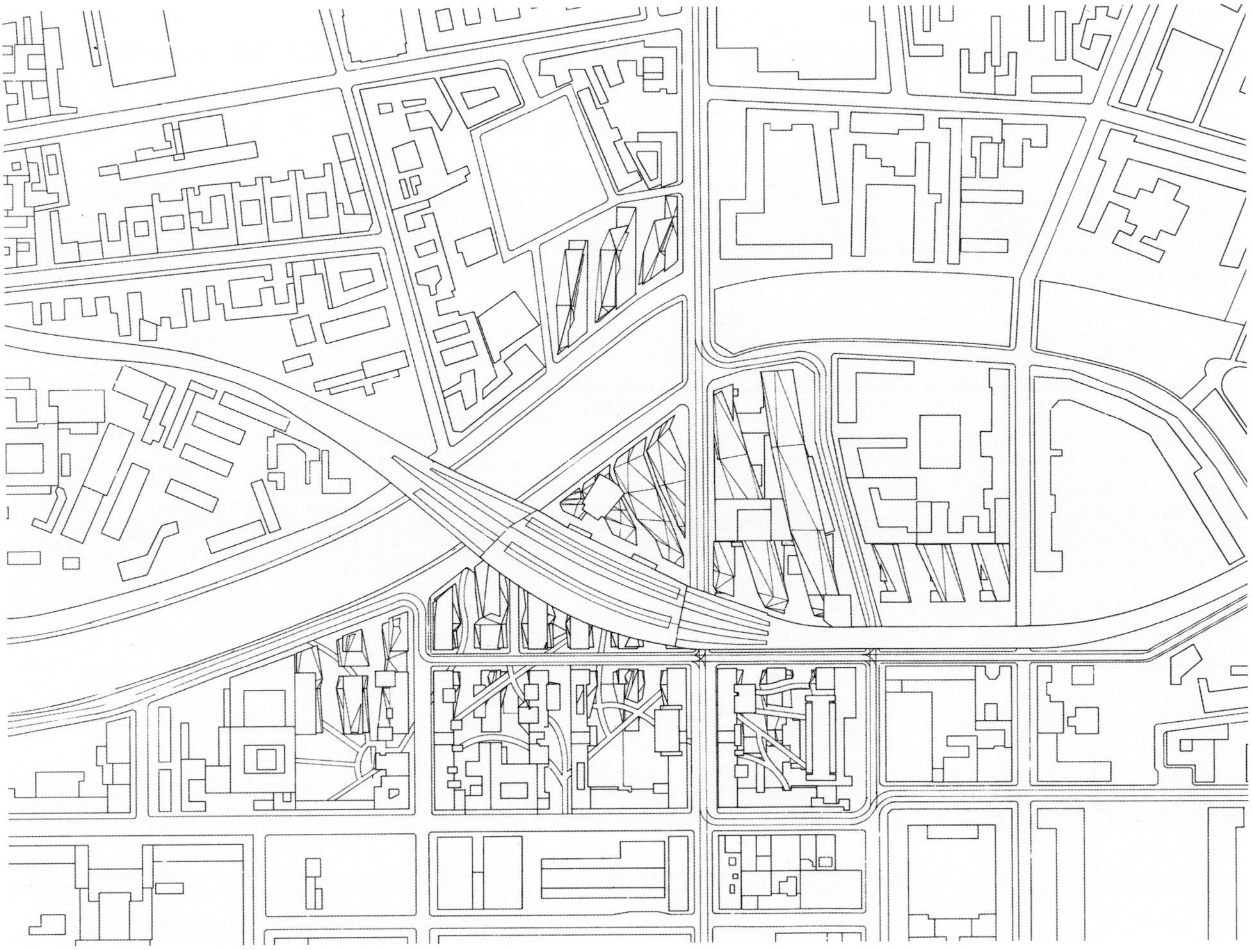

BANHOFF FRIEDRICHSTRASSE COMPETITION

The project begins from the major figural networks of the particular site: the Cardo and Decumanus of the Unter den Linden-Friedrichstrasse crossing; and the interlacing of the Spree and the S-Bahn. A multi-layered superposition of the histories of Berlin is transformed into a dynamic model for 21st-century urbanism. The scheme consisted of a large integrated landscape of interwoven circulation systems and spaces that sliced through a traditional pattern of Berlin blocks. Taking the larger regional patterns of rivers, railroads, streets, and open spaces, varying their size and orientation—in particular using the system of allées and drives that Peter Joseph Lenne employed in the Tiergarten—a series of braided spaces resulted in an urban vermicelli of paths, tree rows, buildings and absolutely unique places.

To the south, the project begins as a traditional perimeter block. Superposed onto this ideal form are the traces of the buildings of this area as they were when destroyed in 1945. Their former courtyard outlines become part of the new building blocks in a contemporary example of the figure-ground reversal. Then the ideal form of the Hilberseimer linear siedlung is put down as a matrix structure which transforms the courtyards of the perimeter blocks as extended U-shapes. This linear matrix is then transformed through the twining structure of river and railroad, becoming reoriented as the orthogonal structure of a new Berlin on the north side of the Spree.

Thus, the project proposes a conceptual framework that is transformed by the specific histories of the site and its particular formal context, into a dynamic mapping, an interplay of landscape and building, the past and the future, concept and reality—an intricate and eccentric ensemble of spaces and buildings.

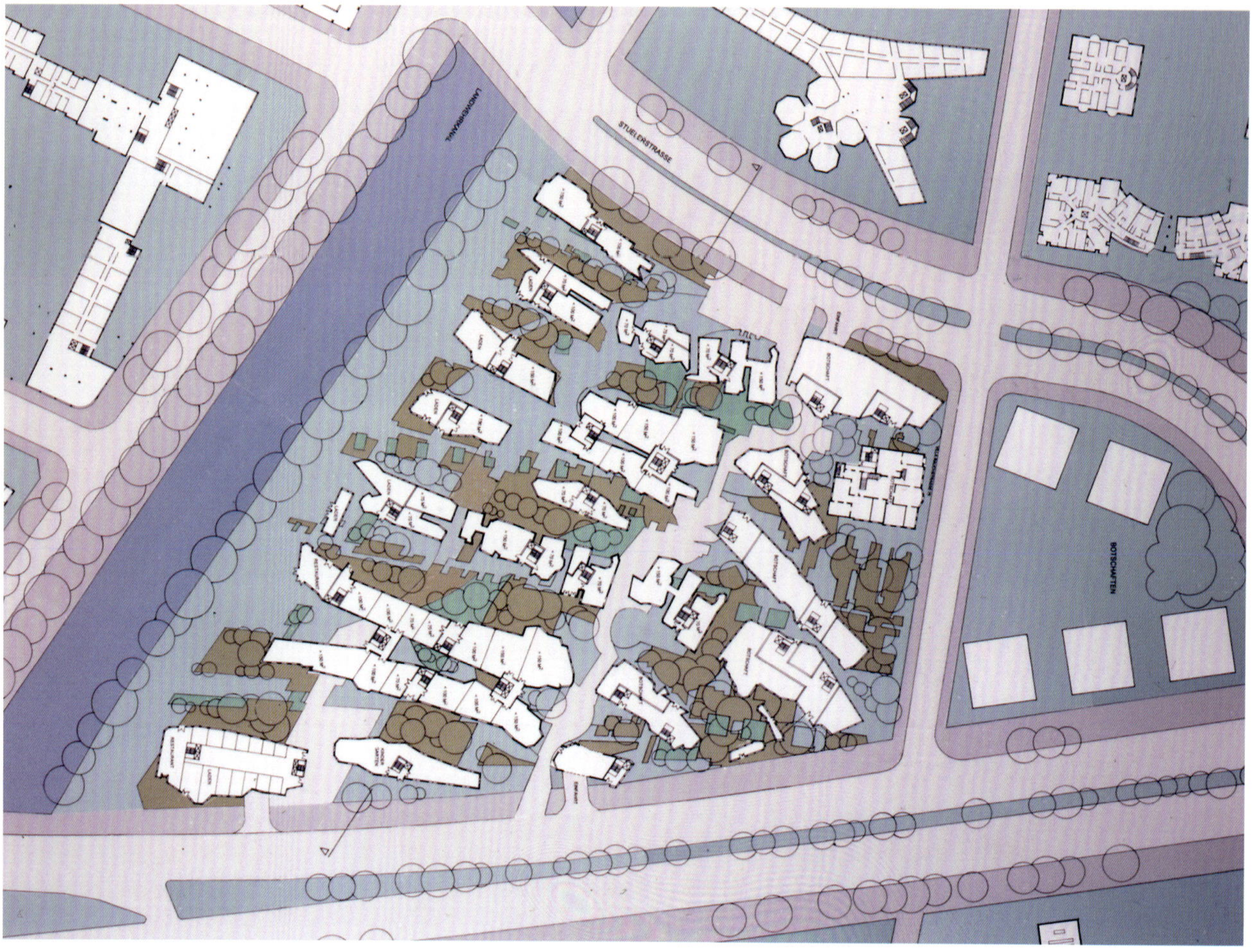

KLINGELHOFER DREIECK SÜD HOUSING

Using the transformational techniques seen in the common idea of morphing, popular in contemporary film, the architects superposed the analog figure of the watch mechanism and the digital process of the computer chip on the site to produce an intermediate, ungrounded figuration that formed a new pattern of urban living.

This pattern is derived from viewing the site at two scales. At the scale of the city, the morphing process conceptually resituates the site from its status on the periphery of the center, bringing it into a new urban relationship with the new Spreebogen government buildings and corporate headquarters on Potsdamer Platz. At the scale of the block itself, the housing and embassies propose a new living relationship through newly figured public space that belongs to everyone.

The project is seen as a performance landscape rather than as typical building envelopes. The figure/figure proposal is intended as a guide to building heights, spacing/density, program distribution and building appearance (transparency and solid) rather than specific building forms, in order to provide the maximum of flexibility in the actual development of the site.

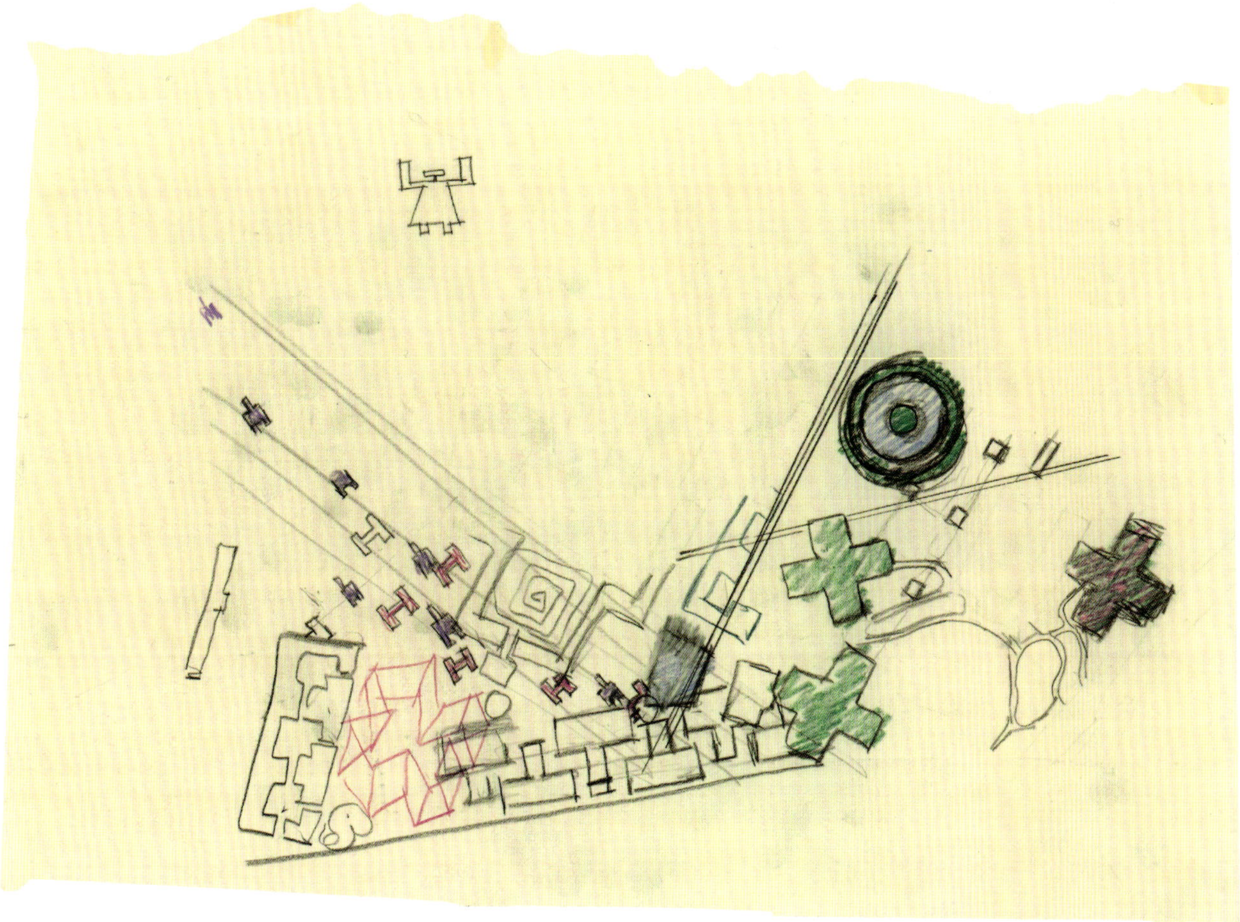

PLACE DES NATIONS MASTER PLAN

This master plan competition for the United Nations in Geneva acknowledges the important symbolic role of landscape in the development of architecture. A new series of facilities for the UN and various international agencies were desired for a site adjacent to the historic center of Geneva. The location incorporated the site of Le Corbusier's unrealized League of Nations, the traces of which provided an initial background for our project.

The UN project takes as its symbolic basis the history of this site both seen and unseen, active and passive, to formulate a new symbolic relationship between land and building. It attempts to weave these traces of past and present into a new fabric that is neither nostalgic nor hierarchical but rather attempts a new landscape mosaic in which repetitions and transformations blur the hierarchical categories of figure and ground, landscape and building, public and private, city and suburb.

Fundamentally, three conditions animate this scheme. First, traffic was pushed to the western edge of the site by aligning a main thoroughfare with the location of an existing underground communications services tunnel. Second, the precise location of the traces of Le Corbusier's second scheme for the Palais des Nations was connected to the underground conduit to produce a series of landscaped terraces to the east of the existing UN building, connecting the park back to the Place des Nations. In an attempt to reduce the isolated figural quality of the existing UN building, a series of landscape terraces was also developed on the western side of the building, again using a transformational process that moved from the form of the building to the line of the underground conduit. Third, introduction of the forms of Le Corbusier's Mundaneum project are rearranged on the site of the Sismondi College. This alternate strategy produced a non-totalizing site strategy to allow for different architects and many different styles to participate in the new UN project.

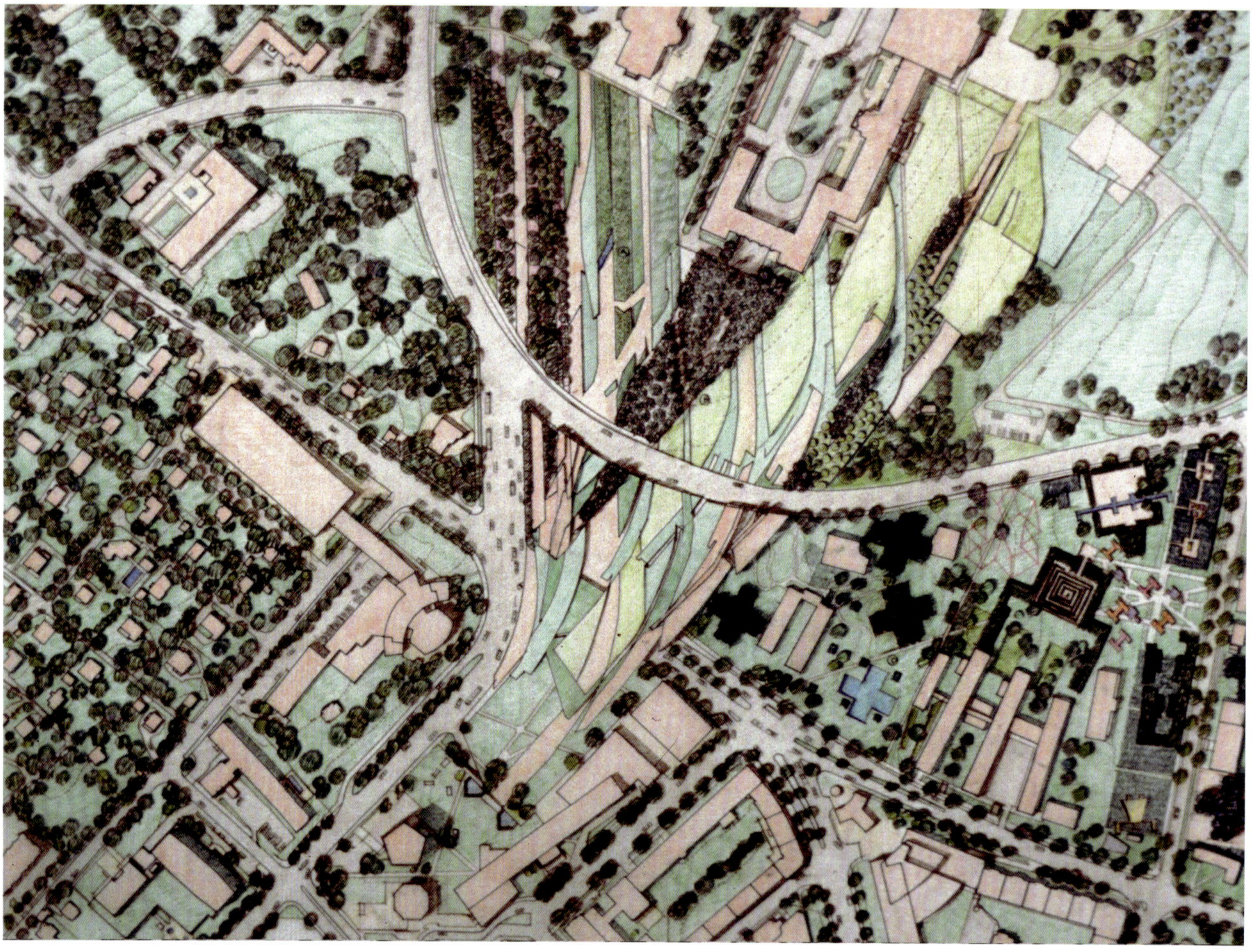

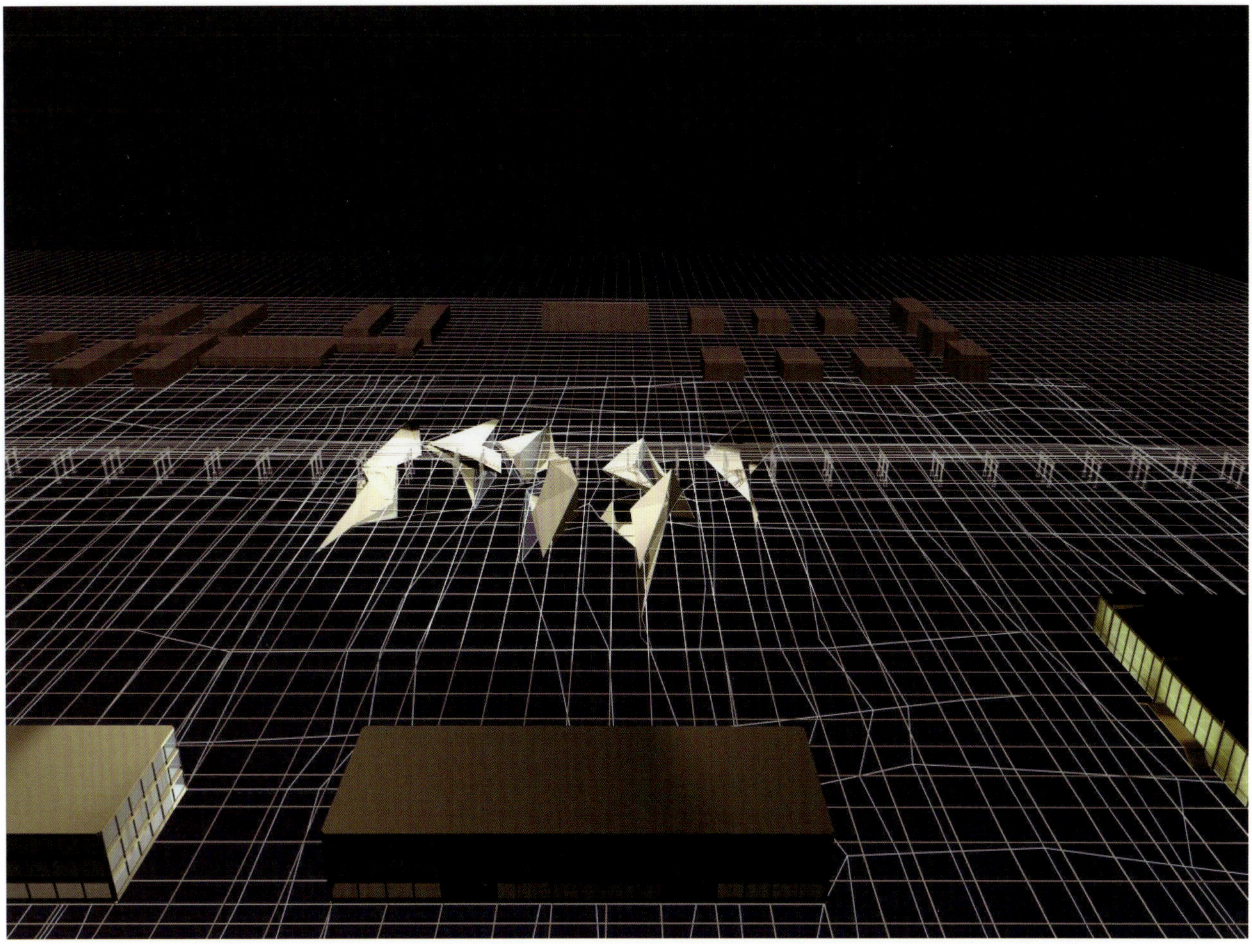

ILLINOIS INSTITUTE OF TECHNOLOGY STUDENT CENTER COMPETITION

Mies van der Rohe's canonical urban project, the IIT campus plan, radicalized and transgressed existing collegiate types—from the monastic enclosures of the Cambridge colleges to the axial great lawn of the University of Virginia—projecting an urban campus that set its own interior rhythms different from its urban context. At IIT, the individual is clearly symbolized in the free-standing object blocks and the flowing dynamic relationships of spaces, free of axial hierarchies. The separation of place for the collective is more subtle, achieved not with traditional physical boundaries such as encircling walls but with the absence of such boundaries, by a texture of building that marks the difference between civitas and universitas.

This is the context in which the IIT student center competition was seen. Occurring at both an urban seam and a campus edge in Mies's plan, it seemed to require a natural boundary, a frame for its objects. But this new, postmodern boundary is no longer the product of a clear-cut modern duality but rather derives from a blurring of the boundary between sameness and difference. The form of this blurring was the challenge of this project.

The Eisenman/Olin proposal blurred landscape and building, creating landforms on a previously flat plain that both denied the object quality of the new student center and reframed how one viewed the original Mies campus. The location, dimension, and amplitude of the landform/structure were defined by an extension of the spaces and sitings of Mies's campus buildings. A striped pattern of prairie grasses alternated with strips of suburban lawn out of which the glazed roofs of the building emerged.

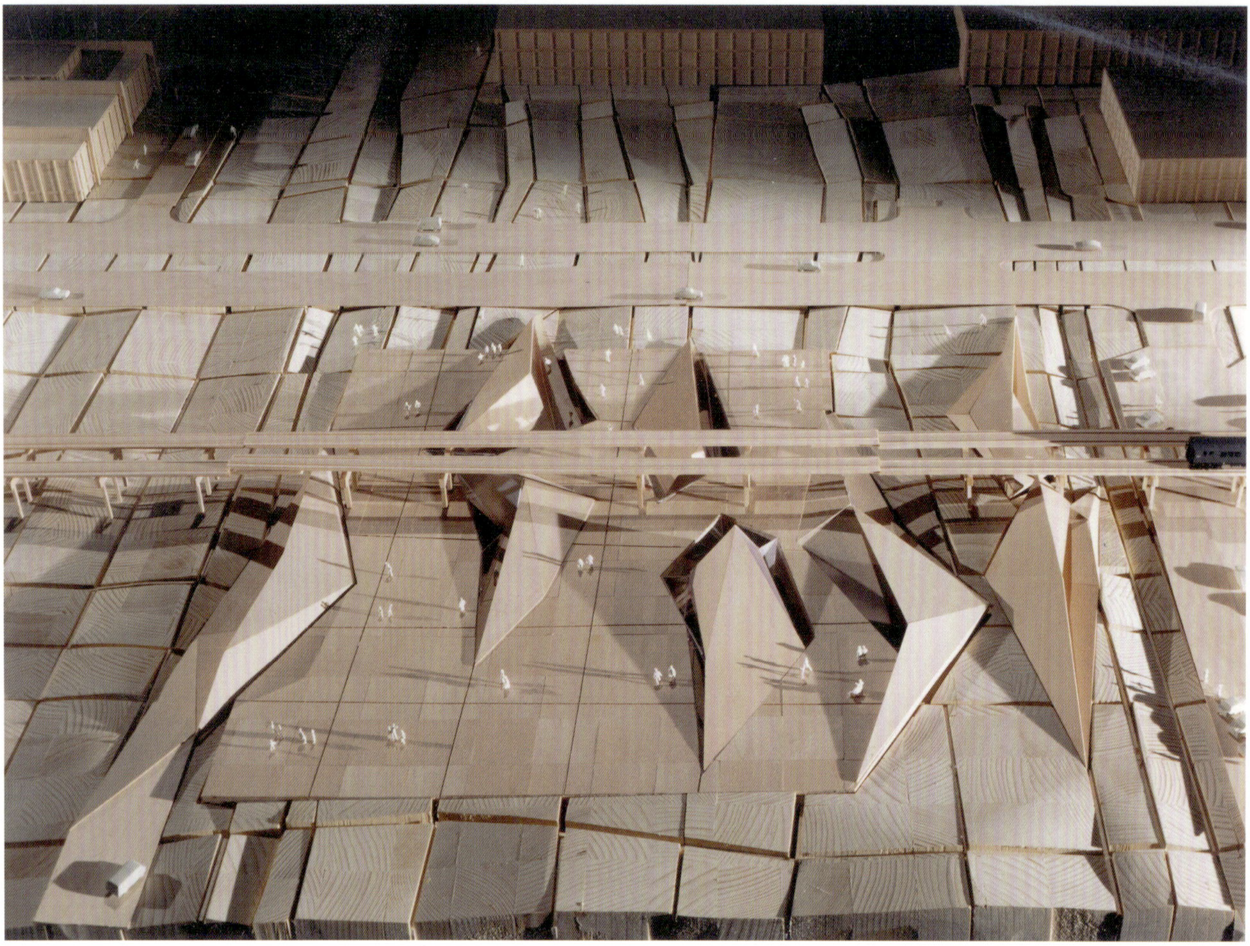

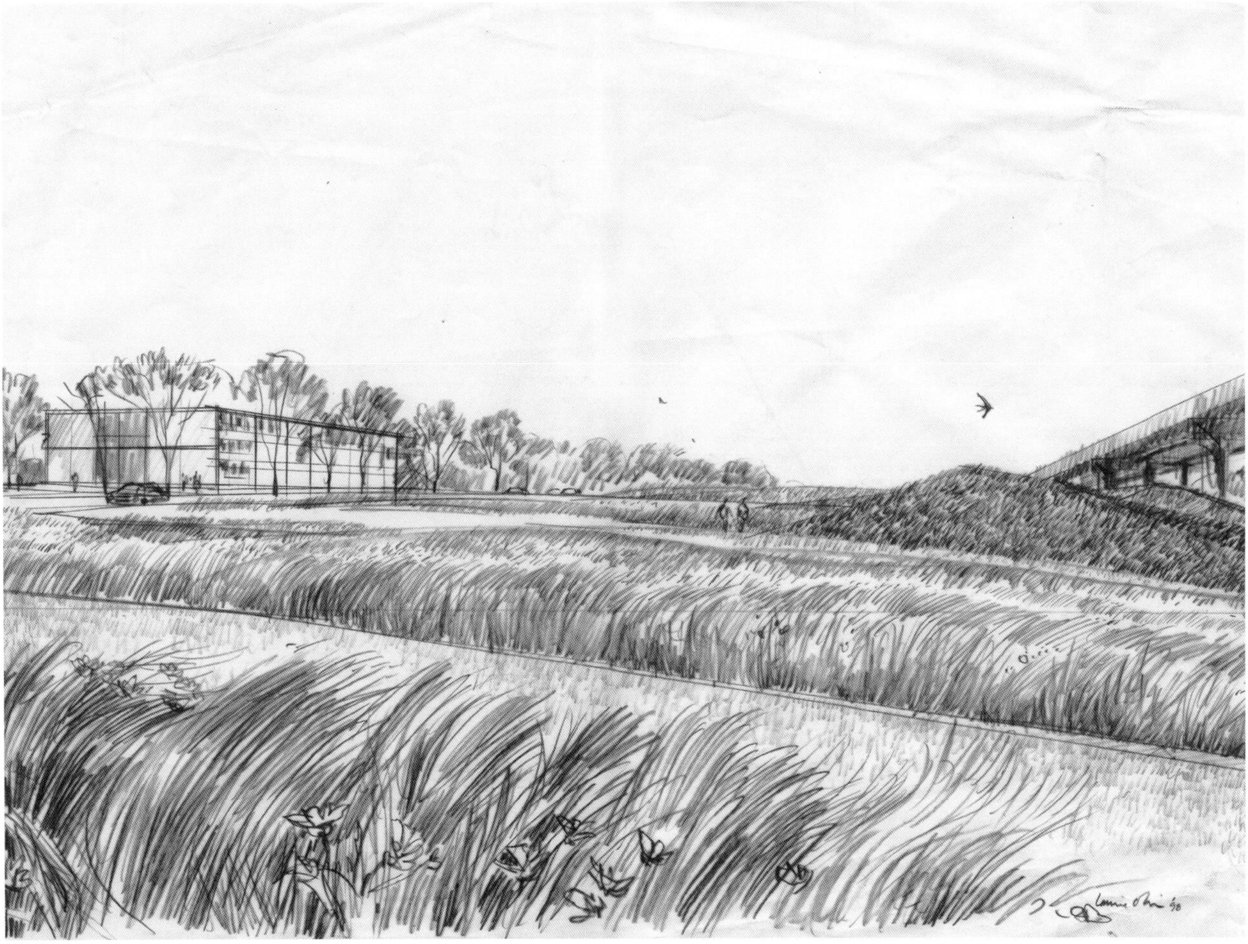

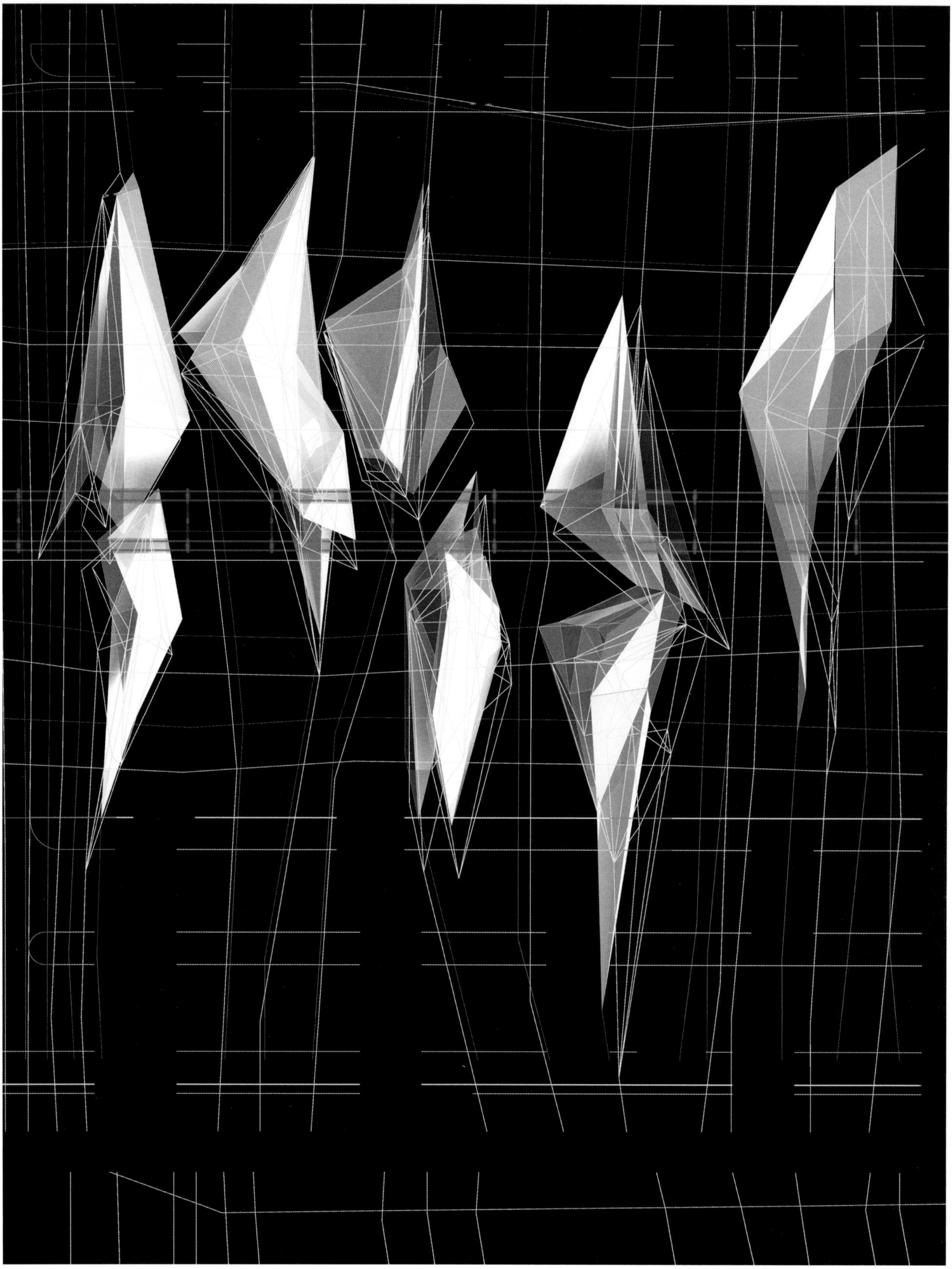

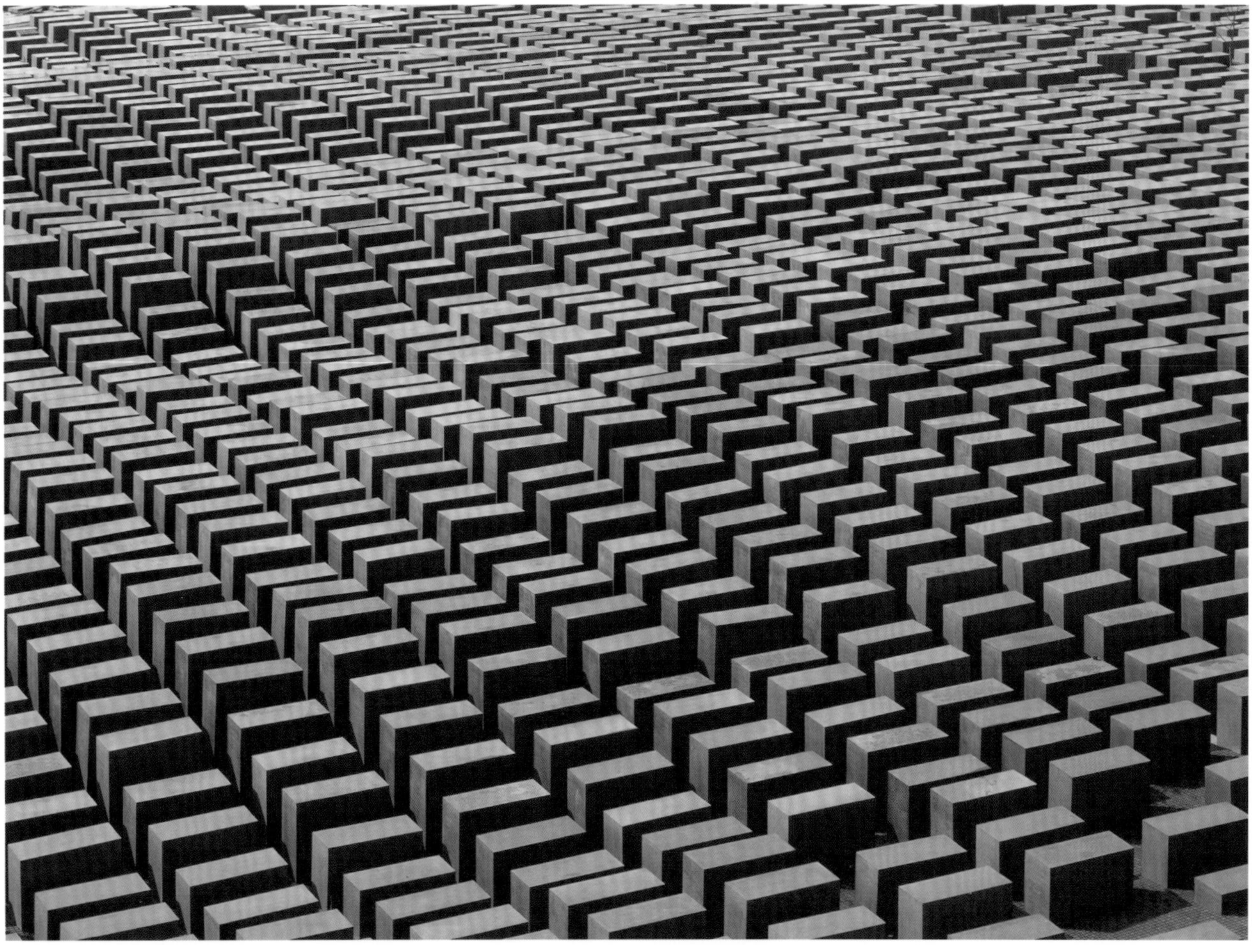

MEMORIAL TO THE MURDERED JEWS OF EUROPE

The Memorial to the Murdered Jews of Europe manifests the instability inherent in what seems to be a system, here a rational grid, and its potential for dissolution in time. It suggests that when a supposedly rational and ordered system grows too large and out of proportion to its intended purpose, it loses touch with human reason. It then begins to reveal the innate disturbances and potential for chaos in all systems of seeming order, the idea that all closed systems of a closed order are bound to fail.

In searching for the instability inherent in an apparently stable system, the design begins from a rigid grid structure composed of some 2,700 concrete pillars, or stelae, each 95 centimeters wide and 2.375 meters long, with heights varying from zero to 4 meters. The pillars are spaced 95 centimeters apart to allow only individual passage through the grid. Although the difference between the ground plane and the top plane of the pillars may appear to be random and arbitrary, a matter of pure expression, this is not the case. Each plane is determined by the intersections of the voids of the pillar grid and the gridlines of the larger site context of Berlin. In effect, a slippage in the grid structure occurs, causing indeterminate spaces to develop within the seemingly rigid order of the monument. These spaces condense, narrow, and deepen to provide a multi-layered experience from any point. The agitation of the field shatters any notions of absolute axiality and reveals instead an omnidirectional reality. The illusion of the order and security in the internal grid and the frame of the street grid are thus destroyed.

Olin joined the project to introduce landscape to the memorial, which is across the street from the Tiergarten, and to work with the architects on issues of pavings and surfaces. Through plantings at strategic moments, the Tiergarten appears to be knitted to the memorial. At the client's request, an underground Ort of information was designed to minimize any disturbance to the Memorial's field of pillars. Its mass, weight, and density seem to perceptibly bear down and close in on individuals. The stelae are manifested in the form of a coffered roof deck with rib spacing which matches that of the field above.

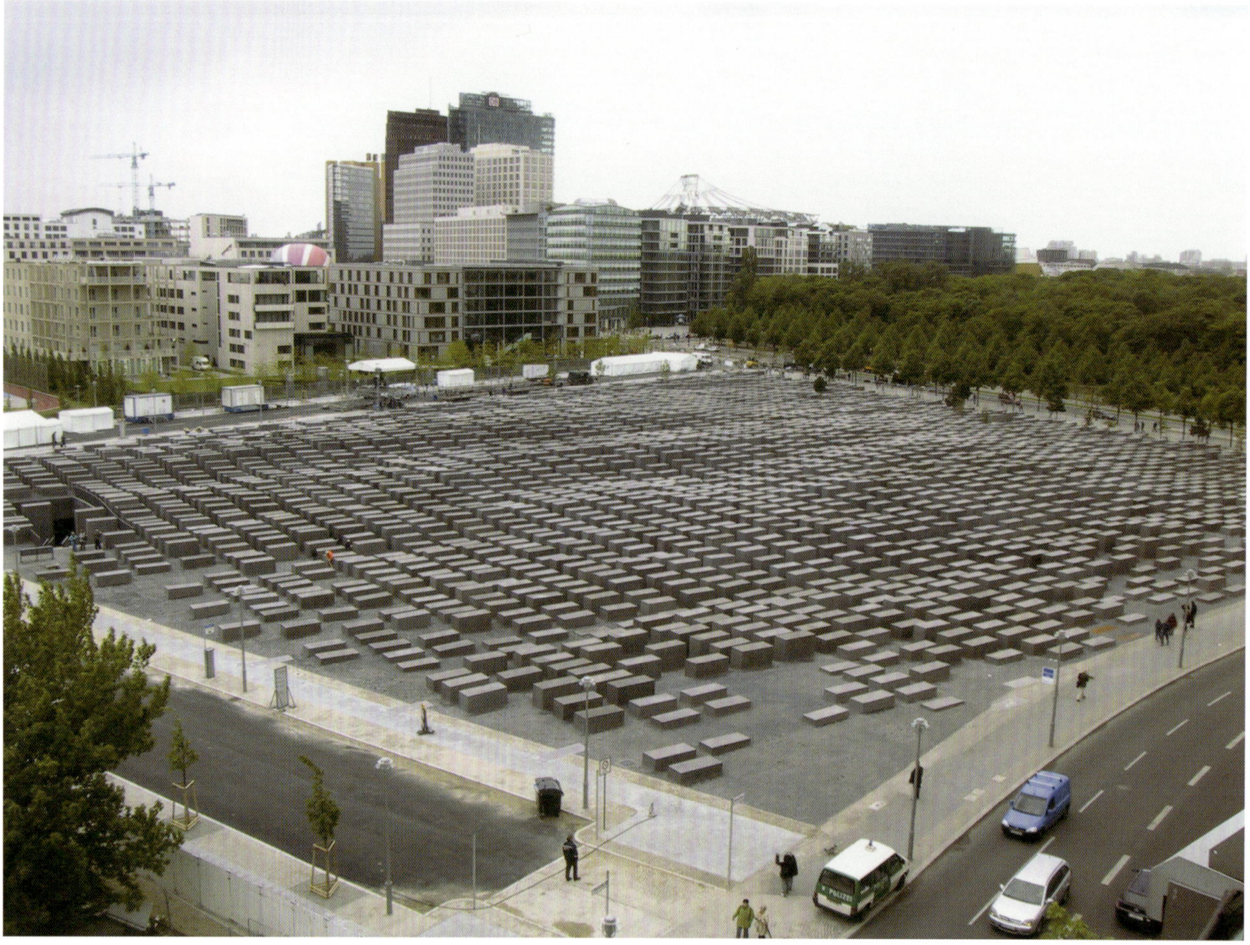

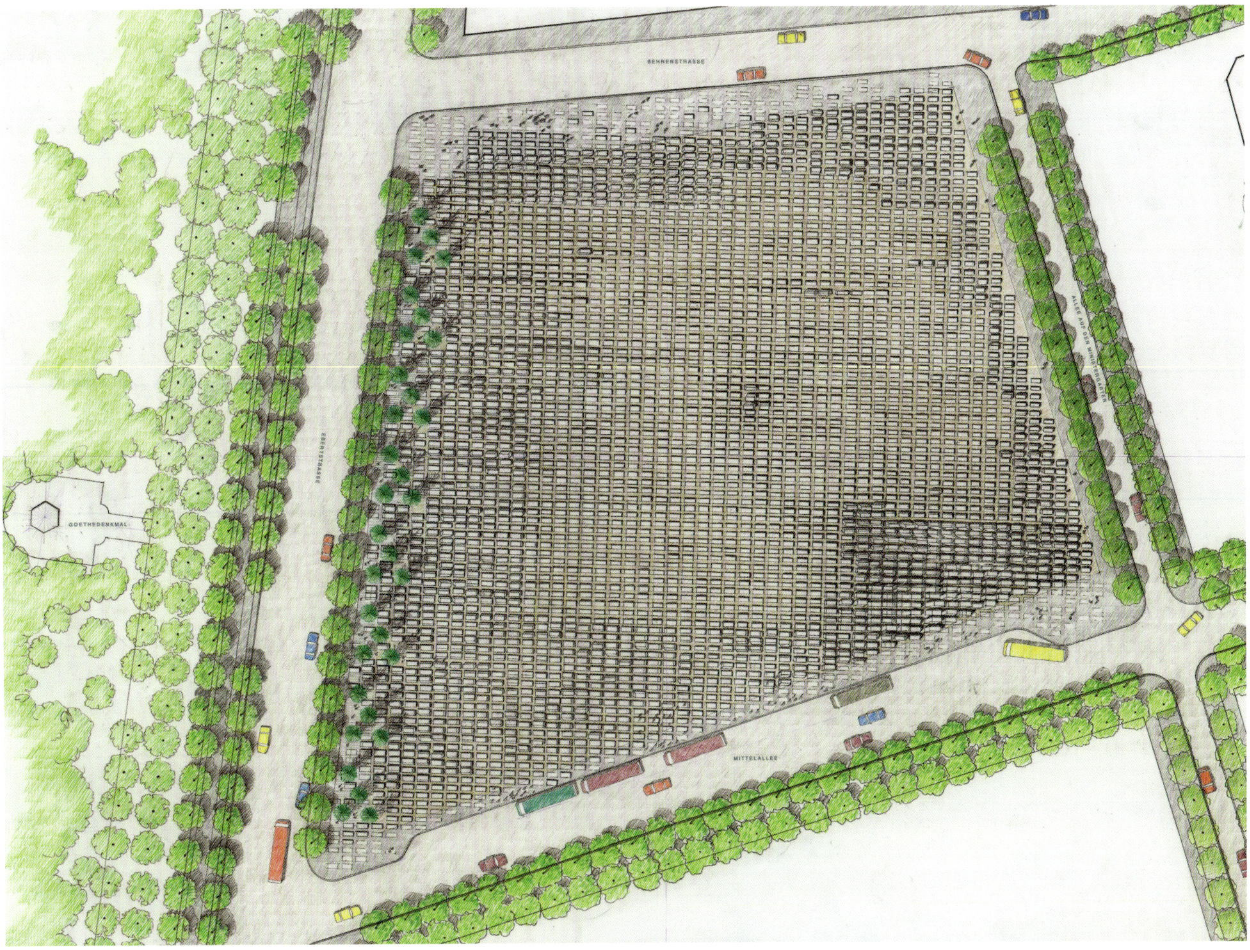
BEHRENSTRASSE
ALLEE AUF DEN MINISTERGARTEN
EBERTSTRASSE
GOETHEDENKMAL
MITTELALLEE

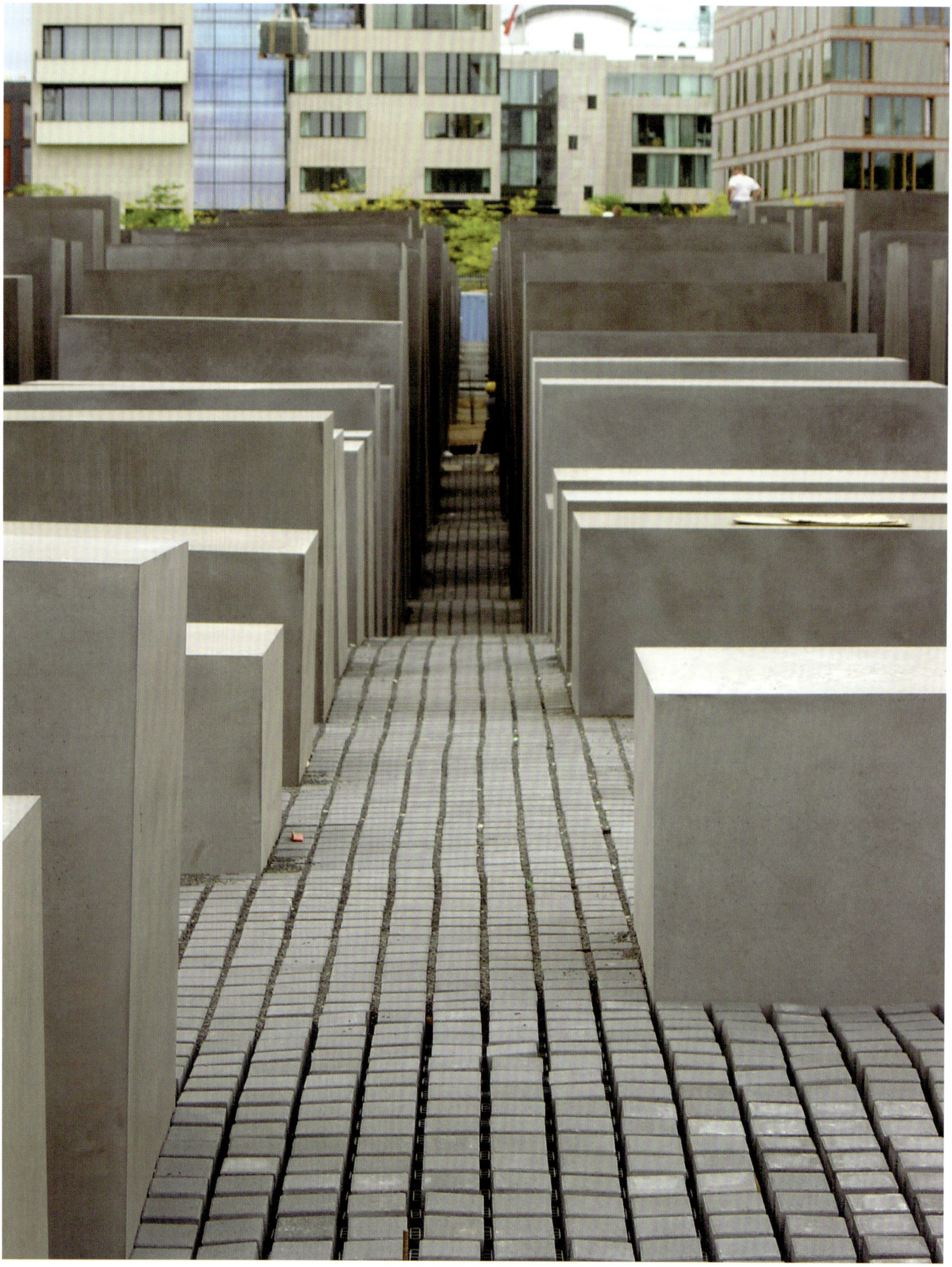

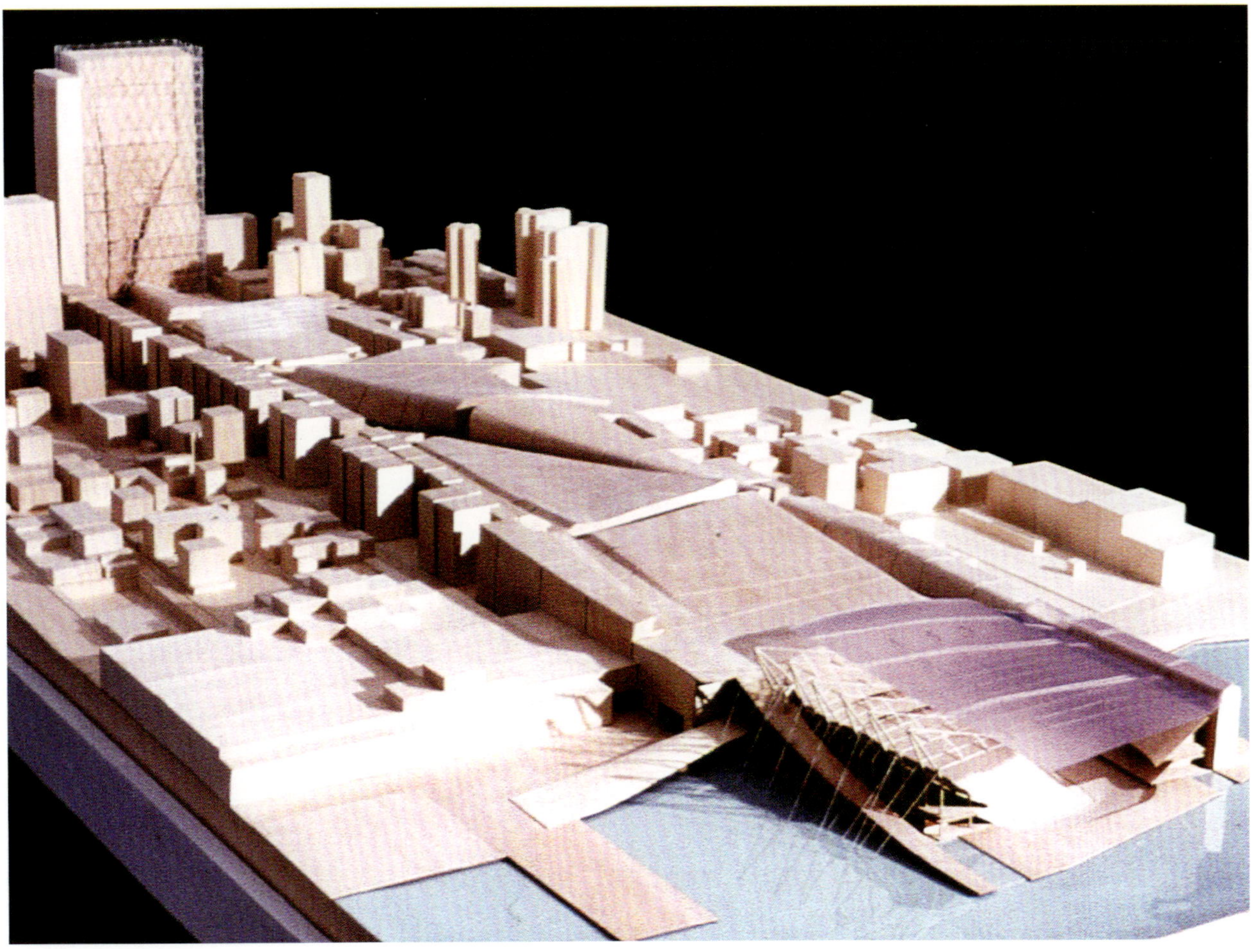

IFCCA MANHATTAN COMPETITION

With planning for the west side of Manhattan and the former Pennsylvania Railroad yards stalled at the time, the Canadian Center for Architecture sponsored a competition for this waterfront site. Eisenman and Olin's project is an amalgam of striated (existing gridded) space and a new smooth space introduced via the computer in order to blur the traditional figure/ground distinction between building and context. This strategy can be seen in the way three "buildings"—a stadium, a convention center, and a new Madison Square Garden arena—are integrated into a continuous fabric of public space.

The architectural idea for the West Side project is twofold. The first is to warp the ground—formerly a flat datum of gridded space—in order to make it figural. The warping process leads to a figure/figure ground condition and a second landscape. The second idea activates the section of the figure/figure condition by programming interstitial spaces generally seen as residual. Spanning Eighth, Ninth, and Tenth Avenues and the West Side Highway was a proposed park that climbed gradually to a height overlooking the new stadium and public waterfront areas.

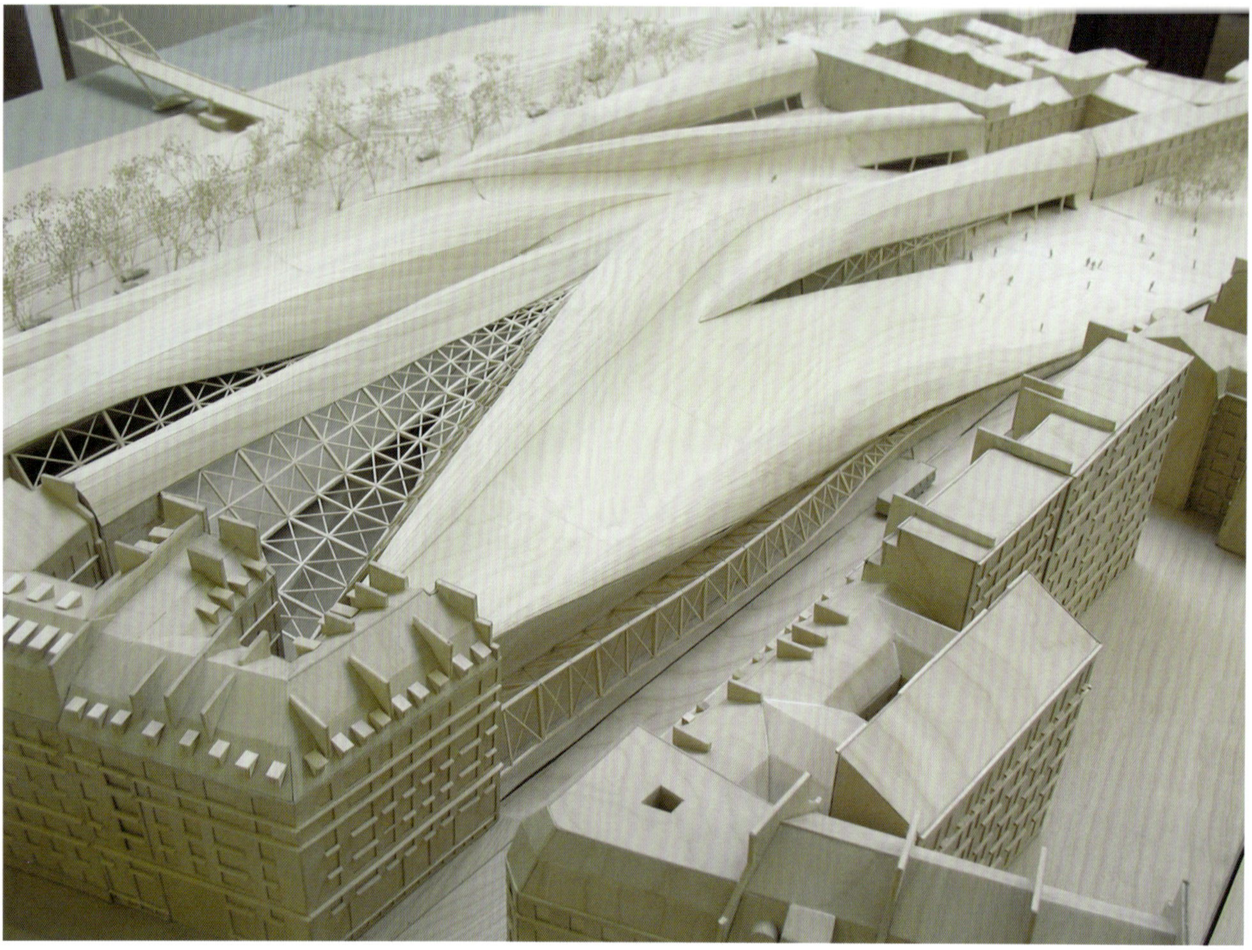

MUSÉE DU QUAI BRANLY COMPETITION

Roland Barthes said that the view from the Eiffel Tower condenses the city of Paris into a new cognitive map. Eisenman and Olin's project extends this idea and makes the roof of the Musée du Quai Branly the major facade when seen both from the Eiffel Tower and from within. Thus the view from the Eiffel Tower is of a building-scape where landscaped gardens that respond to the distant geography of the museum's contents flow into the building volume, blurring the cognitive mapping of figure and ground. As the sinews and tendons of this urban biological anatomy split apart they reveal a mirror image of the Eiffel Tower. The roof forms speak of a new coding of the two different end typologies of the site, the public courtyard and the private residence. From the origins of qualitative science in Darwin to the sinewy musculature of Leonardo's art as science, this project proposes a new template that, while different from the Eiffel Tower or the Parisian arcades, shares some of their genetic code.

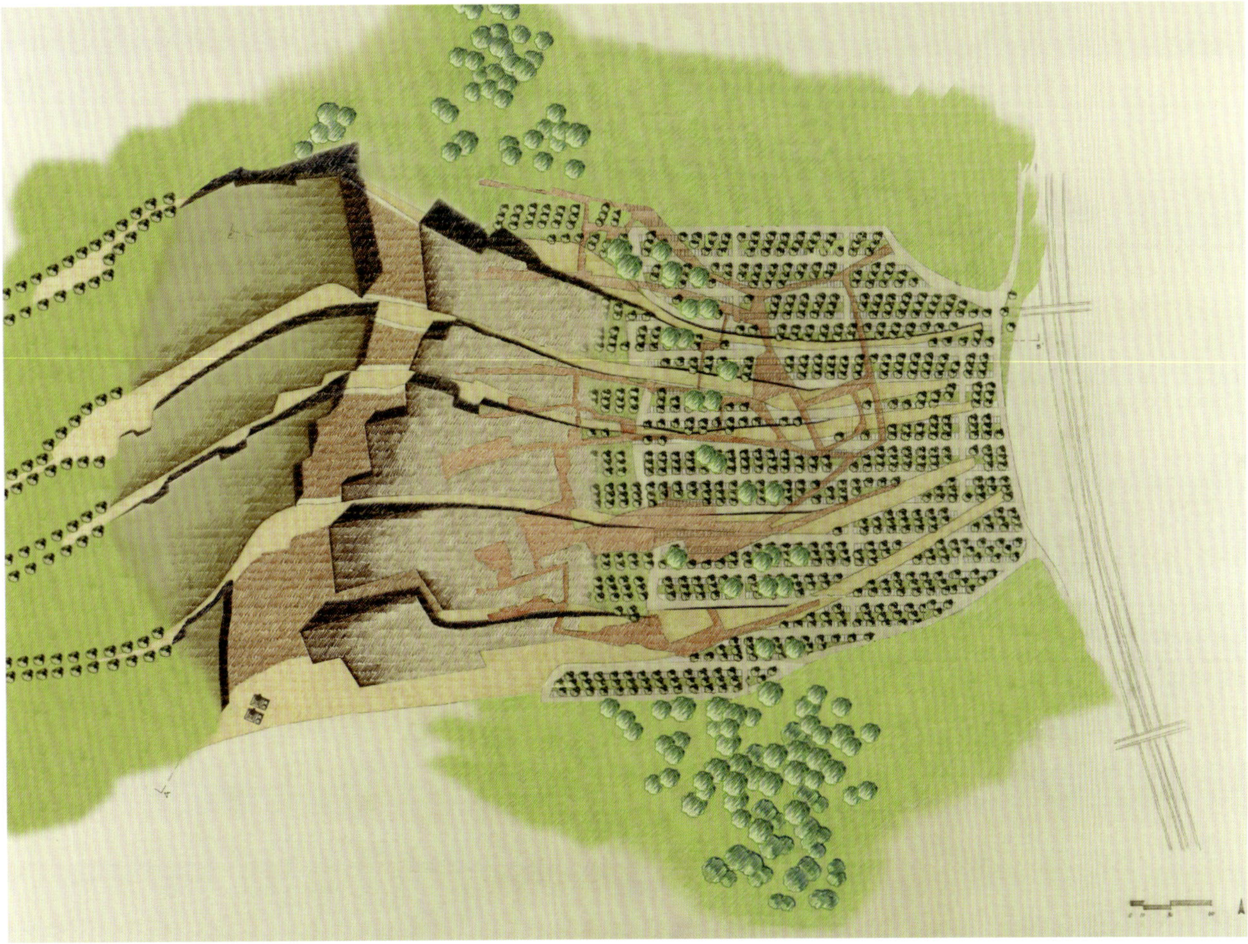

CITY OF CULTURE OF GALICIA

The design of the hilltop City of Culture evolves from the superposition of three sets of traces. First, the plan of the medieval center of Santiago is placed on the hillside site, which overlooks the city. Second, a Cartesian grid is laid over these medieval routes. Third, the topography of the hillside is allowed to distort the two flat geometries, thus generating a topological surface that superposes old and new in a simultaneous matrix.

The original center of Santiago conforms to a figure/ground urbanism. The buildings are figural and the streets, residual. Through the transformative mapping operation, the City of Culture emerges as a warped surface that is neither figure nor ground but both a figured ground and a figured figure that supercede the figure-ground urbanism of the old city. In place of what had been an agricultural hilltop will be a set of canyons and ravines created by the rising and falling building volumes, themselves clad in stone and seeming to comprise a new hilltop when seen from a distance.

The six buildings of the project are conceived as three pairs: the Museum of Galician History and the New Technologies Center; the Music Theater and Central Services building; and the Galician Library and Periodicals Archive. Visitor experiences of any given building will be affected by its relationship to its immediate partner. An arboretum is also proposed for the site.

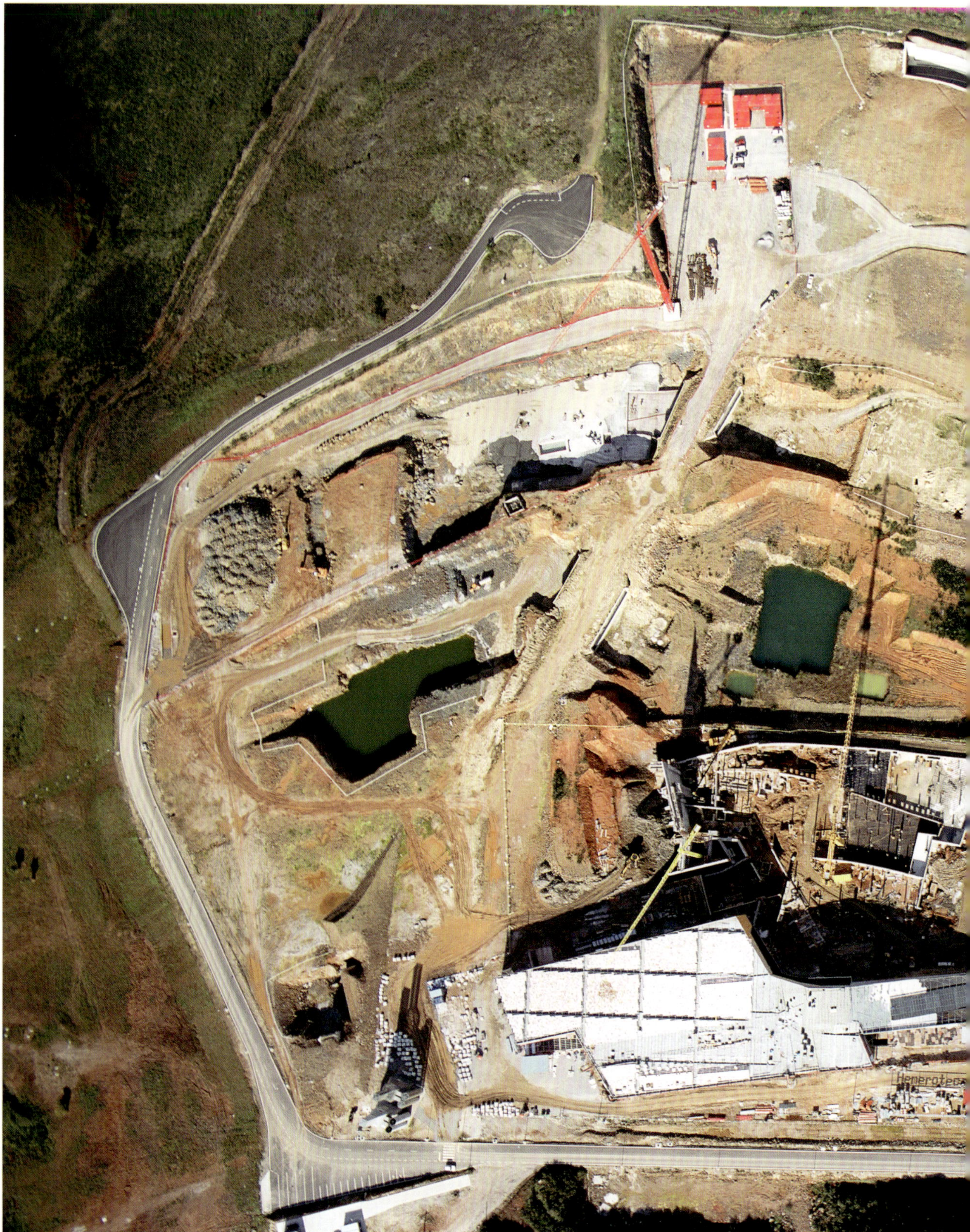

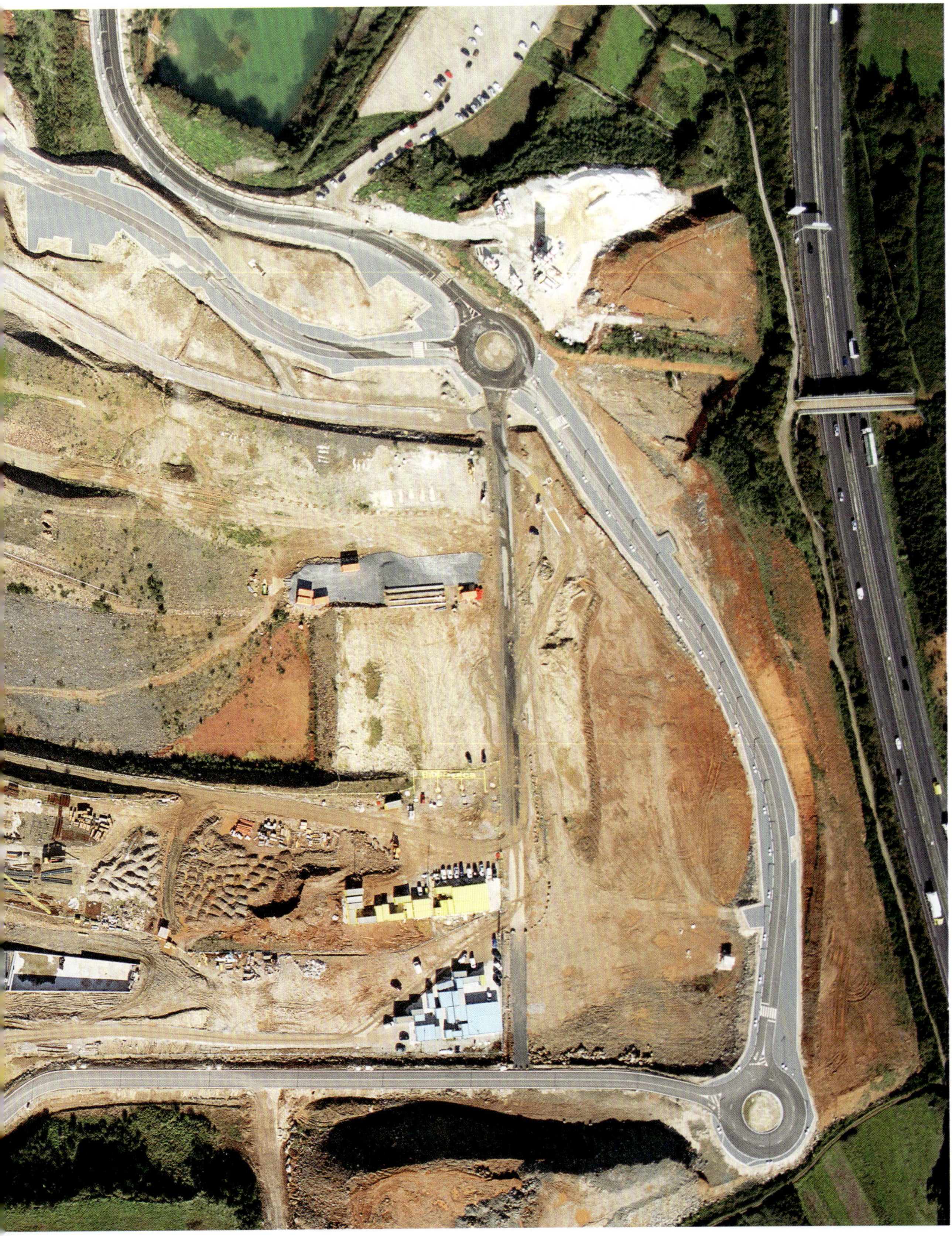

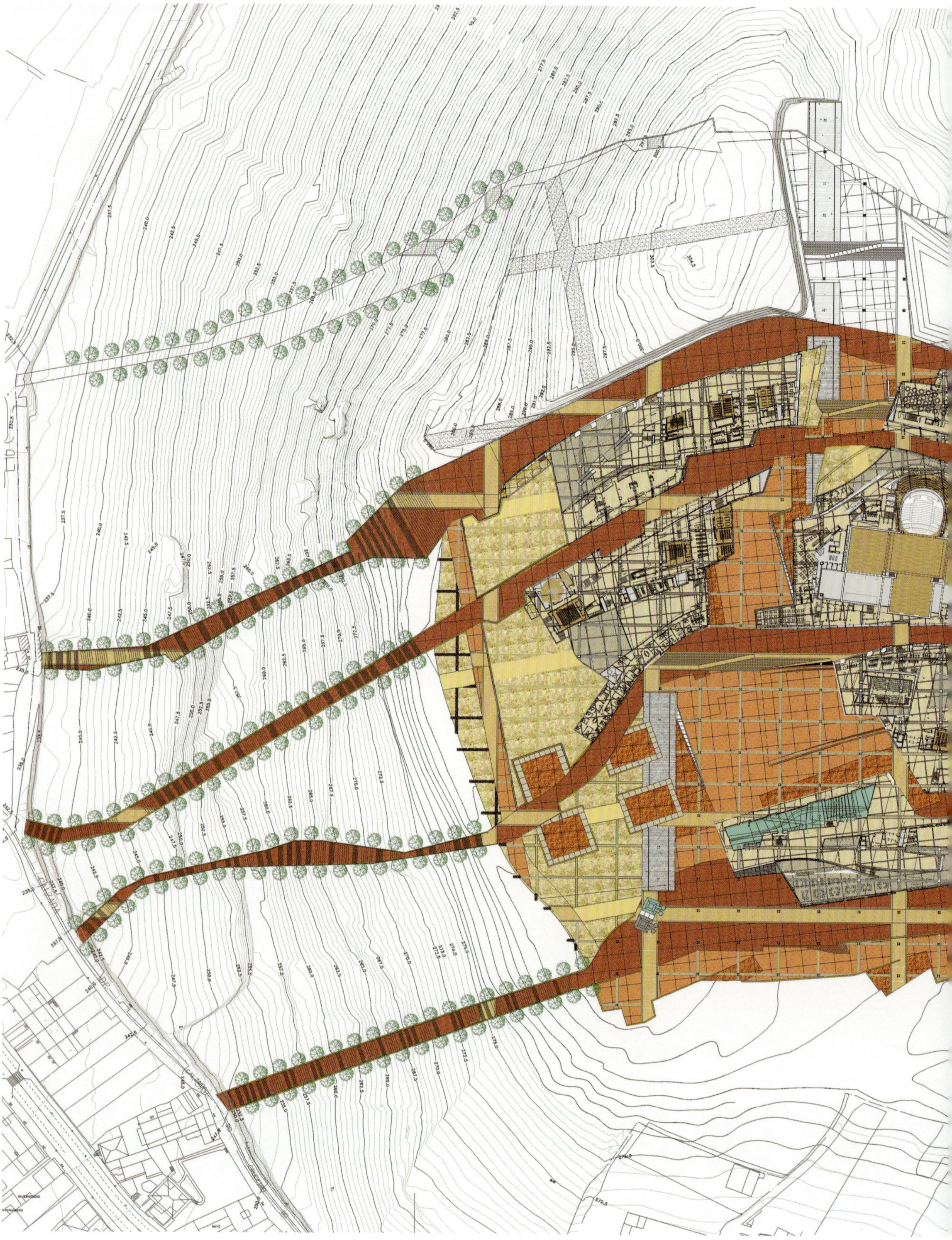

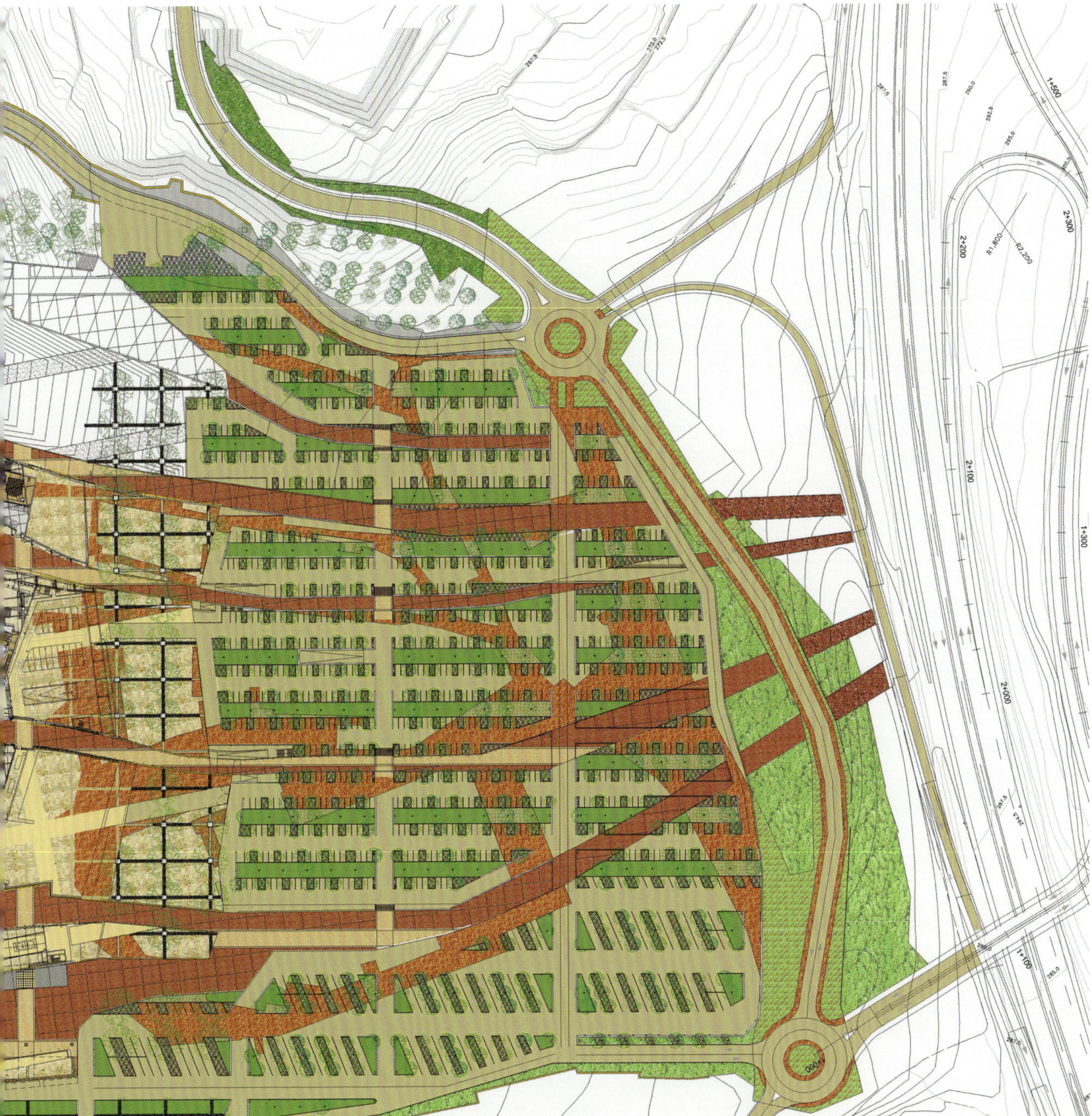
1+500
2+300
2+200
R1,800
R2,200
2+100
1+300
2+000
1+100
0+000

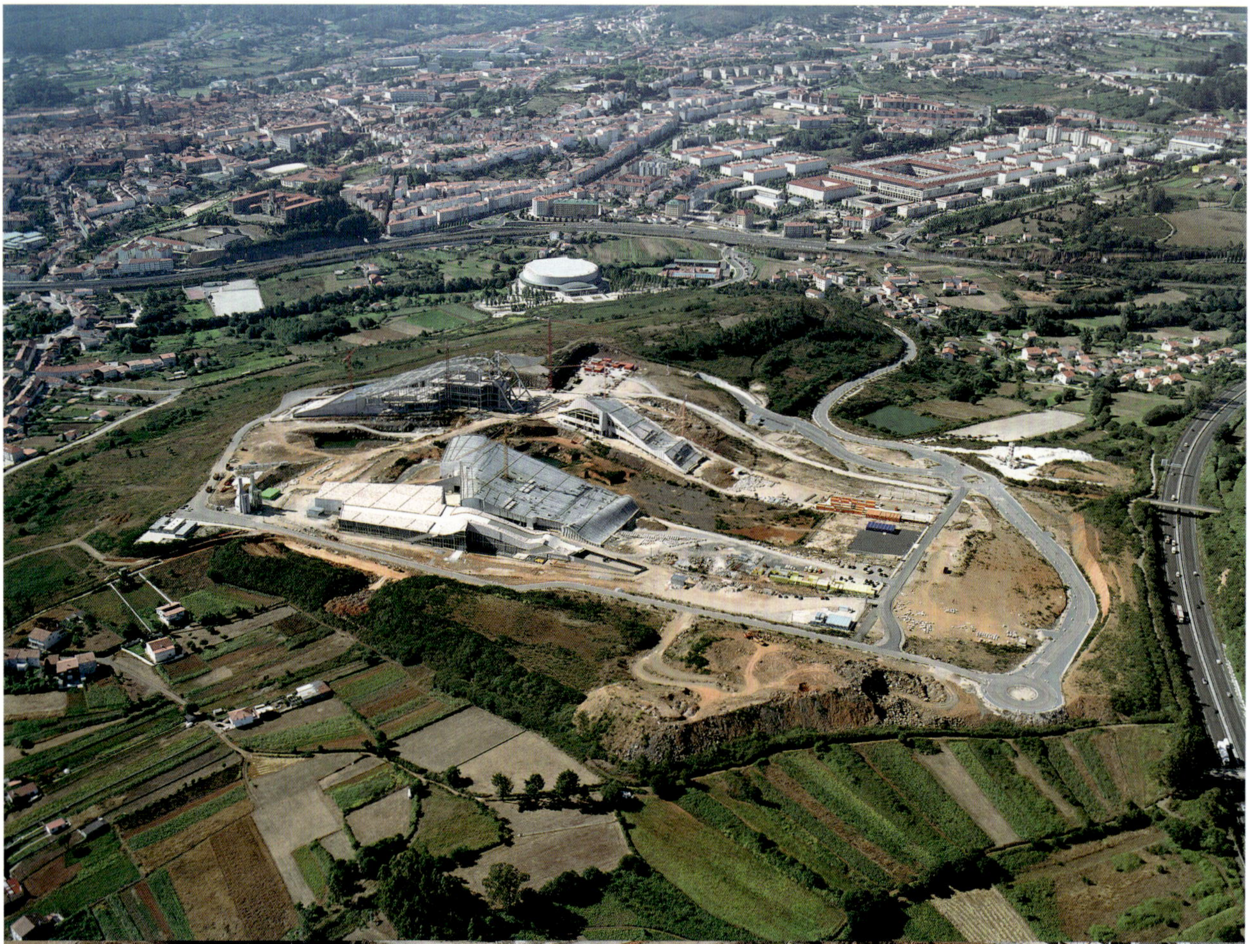

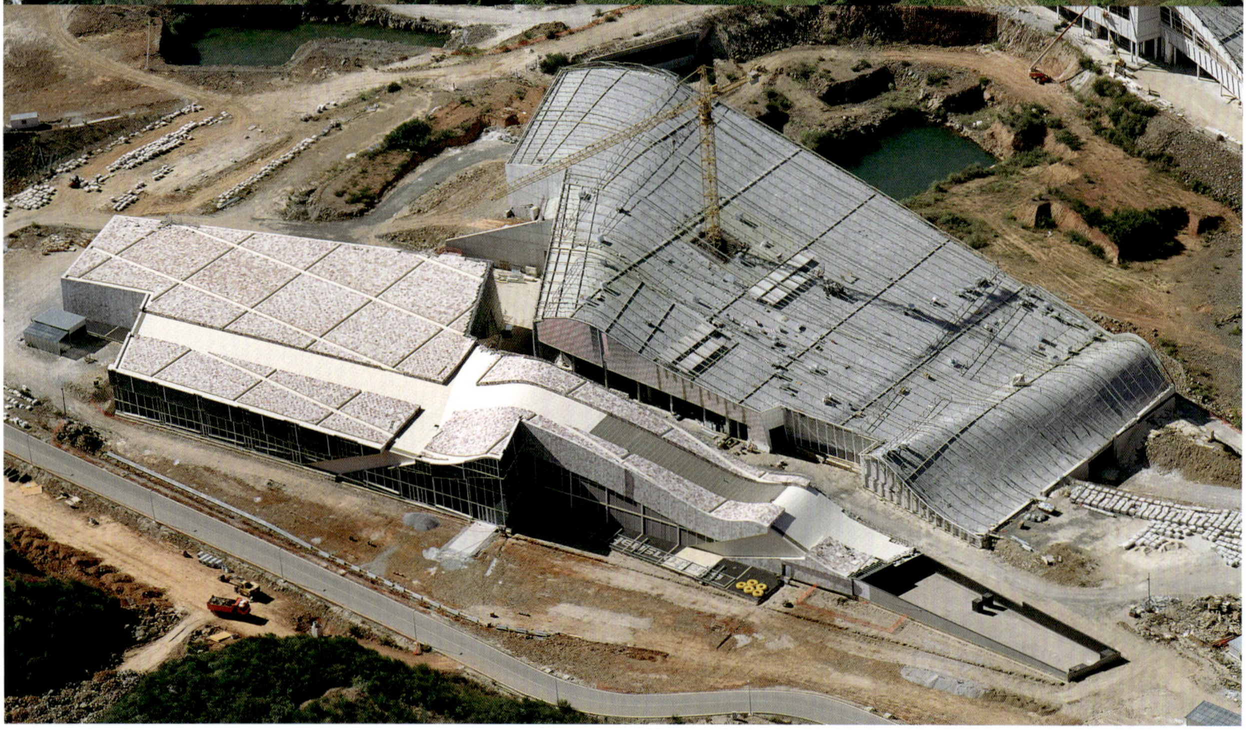

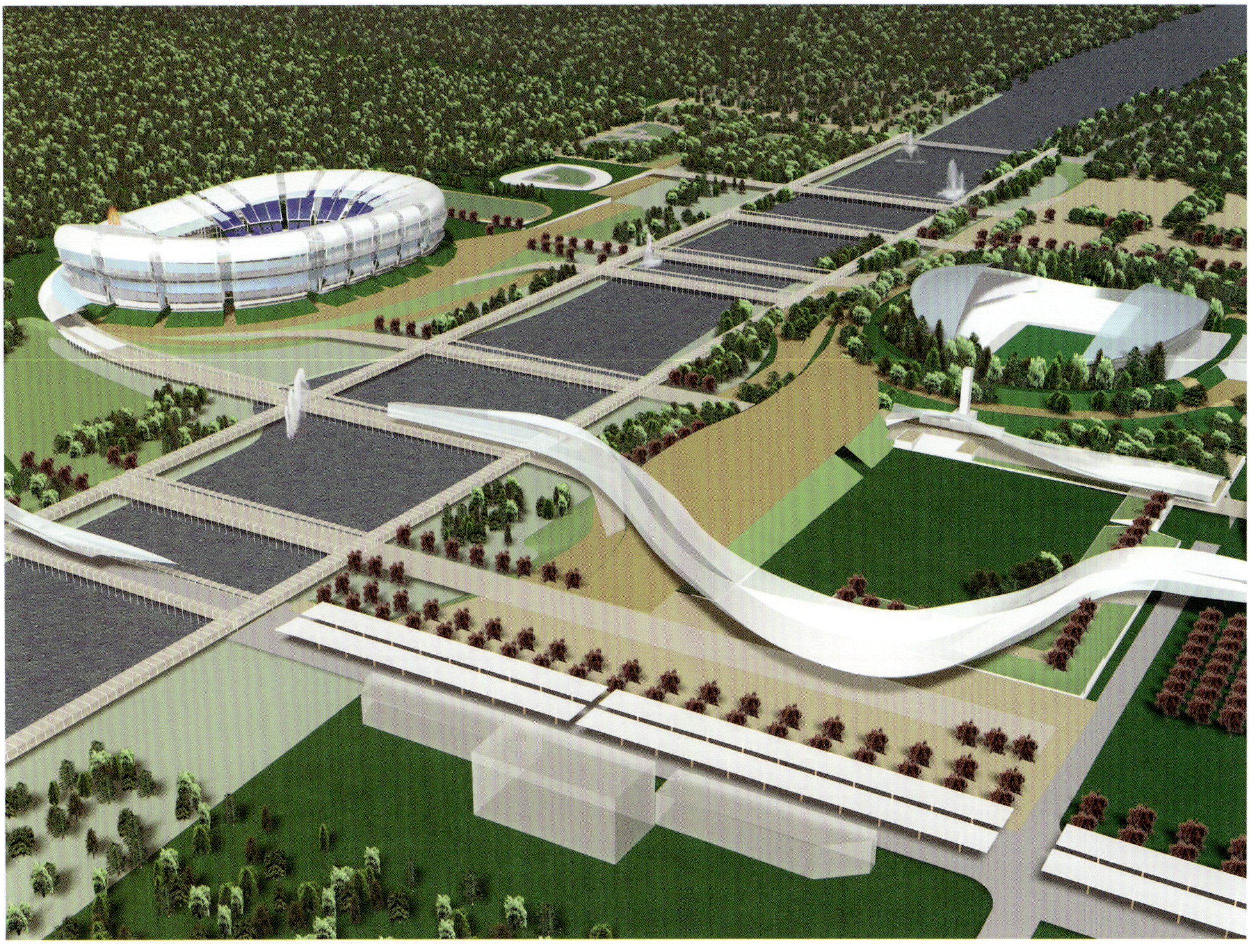

LEIPZIG OLYMPIC GAMES 2012

The proposal for the Leipzig Olympic Games site focuses on the Elsterbecken Canal and features a bold new constructional idea for a stadium. Because the canal divides the site in two, it initially seems to present circulation problems. Rather than design a single, signature bridge to cross the waterway, the canal is integrated in a lattice of bridges that creates a new central axis running north/south along either side of the canal and east/west across it. This makes the canal a unique and integral figure in the massive circulation requirements of the Games.

This treatment of the canal and surrounding landscape is designed to sustain the natural environment after the Games are over. The long axis of the waterside bridges terminates at the northern end of the site with a splashing water feature, and dredging the center of the canal produces a new aquatic ecology. Circulation throughout the site is contained and controlled by landscaped earthworks. These extend from the earthen berm at the soccer stadium to the tram station and, crossing over and under the east/west bridge connections, to the swimming and basketball venues. The two east-west bridges connecting the new stadium with the soccer stadium, basketball arena, and swimming venue will remain after the 84,000-seat Olympic stadium has been returned to its 20,000-seat legacy mode.

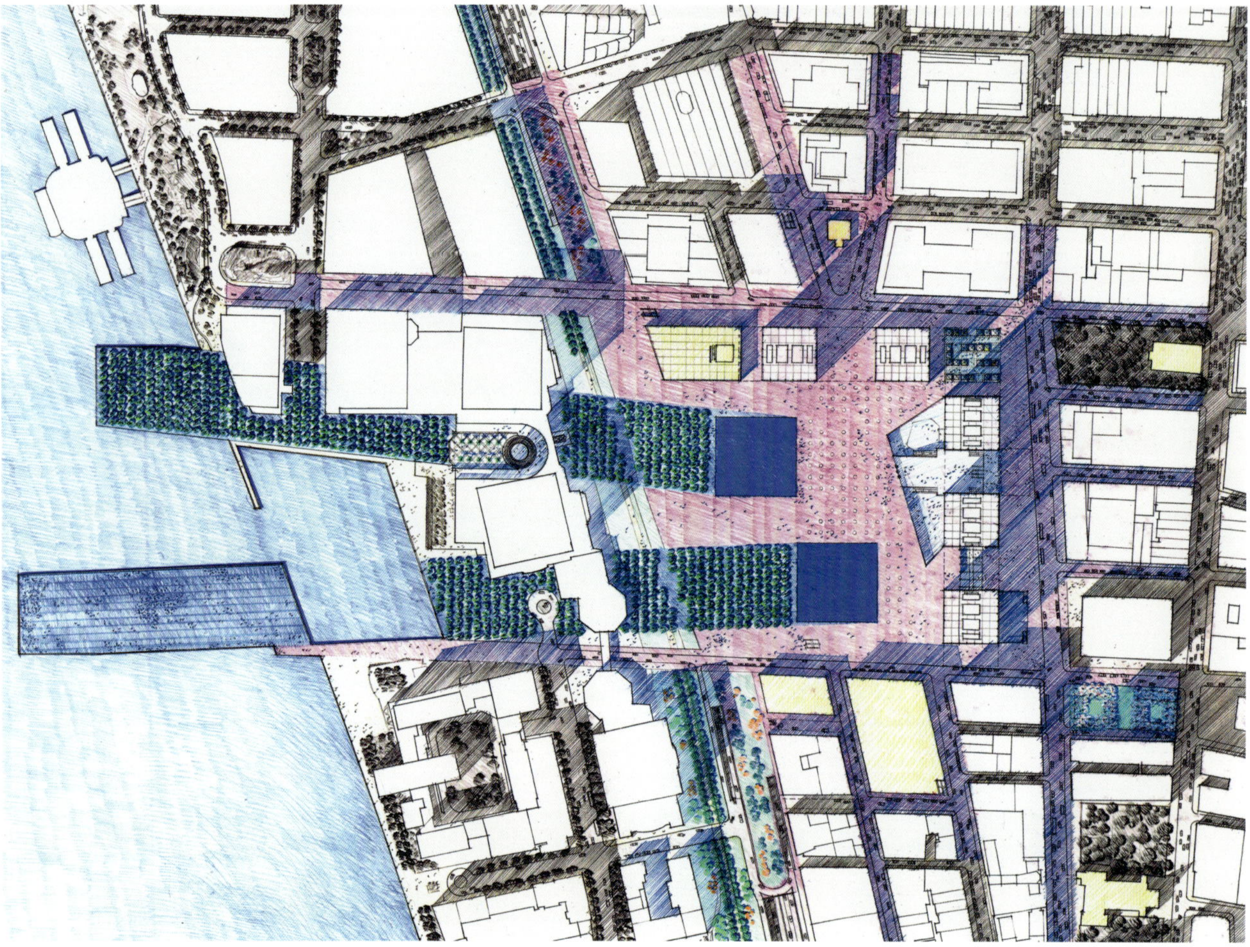

WORLD TRADE CENTER PROPOSAL

In October 2002, Laurie Olin joined Peter Eisenman, Richard Meier, Charles Gwathmey, and Stephen Holl on their competition entry for the prominent, controversial site in lower Manhattan following the events of September 11, 2001. The team's proposal, called Memorial Square, differs from the 19th- and 20th-century precedents for urban plazas such as Rockefeller Center; it is both contained and extended, symbolizing connections to the community, the city, and the world. A series of red granite "fingers" that extend from the site facilitate pedestrian connections between Memorial Square and greater Lower Manhattan while serving as reminders that the magnitude of what happened here was felt far beyond the immediate site.

The most visible sign of renewal are the proposed hybrid buildings, rising 1,111 feet to restore the Manhattan skyline with geometric clarity in glowing white glass. Composed of five vertical sections and interconnecting horizontal elements, the two buildings represent a new typology in skyscraper design. At ground level, these forms become ceremonial gateways into the site. In their quiet abstraction of solids and voids, the buildings appear as screens, suggesting both presence and absence, and inspiring reflection and imagination. Their cantilevered ends extend outward, like the fingers of the ground plan, reaching toward the city and each other. Nearly touching at the northeast corner of the site, they resemble the interlaced fingers of protective hands.

The footprints of the original towers remained as empty pools in a large public piazza or forum-like space. The pools also overlooked two memorial groves, or allées, of shade trees, planted to mark the final shadows cast by the World Trade Center towers before each fell. The groves extend over the West Street Tunnel to the Winter Garden and then continue west of the World Financial Center. The peaks of the shadows are marked by piers on the Hudson River. Within the high-rise buildings, a series of aerial gardens were proposed for the upper levels of the horizontal interconnecting elements and for large openings cut within the vertical members.

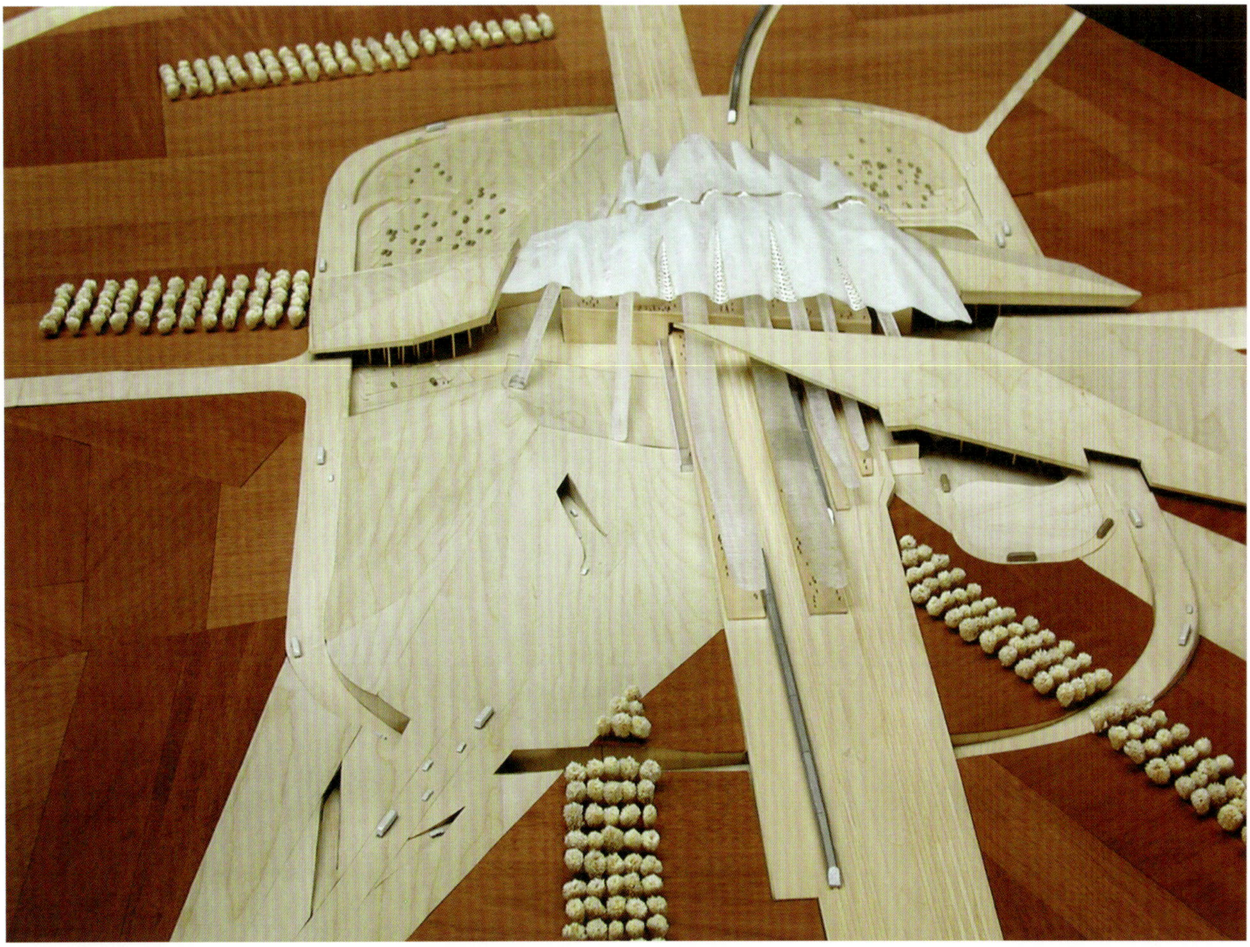

AFRAGOLA TAV STATION COMPETITION

The high-speed rail station serving greater Naples erupts from the flat Pianura Campana, seemingly heaving back the fields and orchards of the valley. Working with a series of overlaid patterns of ancient Roman aqueducts, medieval agricultural fields, geological faults, lava flows, and contemporary circulation routes, Olin developed a landscape that at times forms unusual relationships to the roads and buildings. The station structure is rational and fluid. Trains and automobiles glide between and under a system of great tubes, which frames a commanding view of Vesuvius to the south. A unique and recognizable image on the landscape, the station both mirrors and complements the linear nature of the high-speed train (which requires the station to be comprehended in an instant) and the figural nature of Vesuvius. These elements, combined with the lyrical, translucent main roof and the structural tubes, produce a contemporary sense of the veil and the figure in all their ambiguity and translucency.

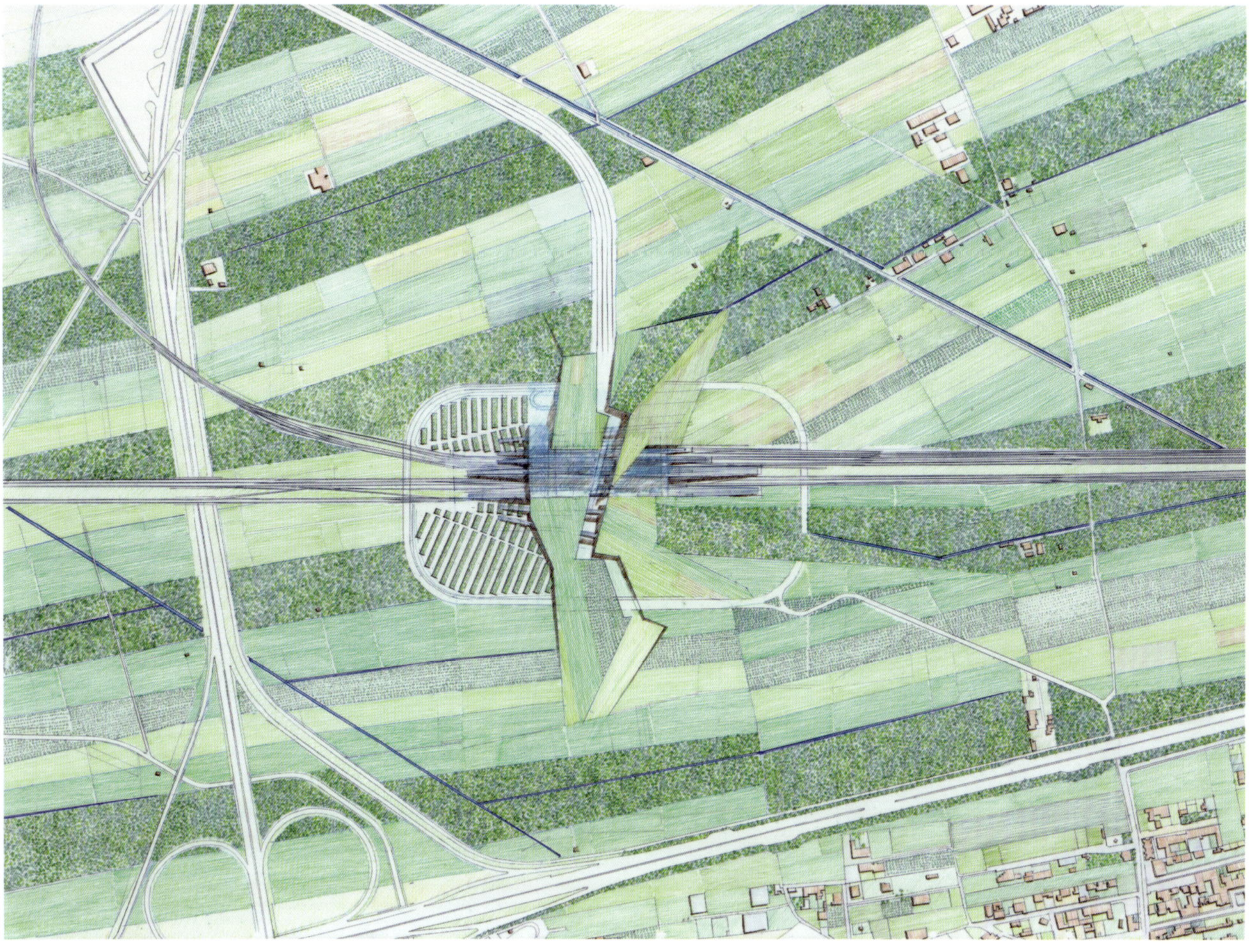

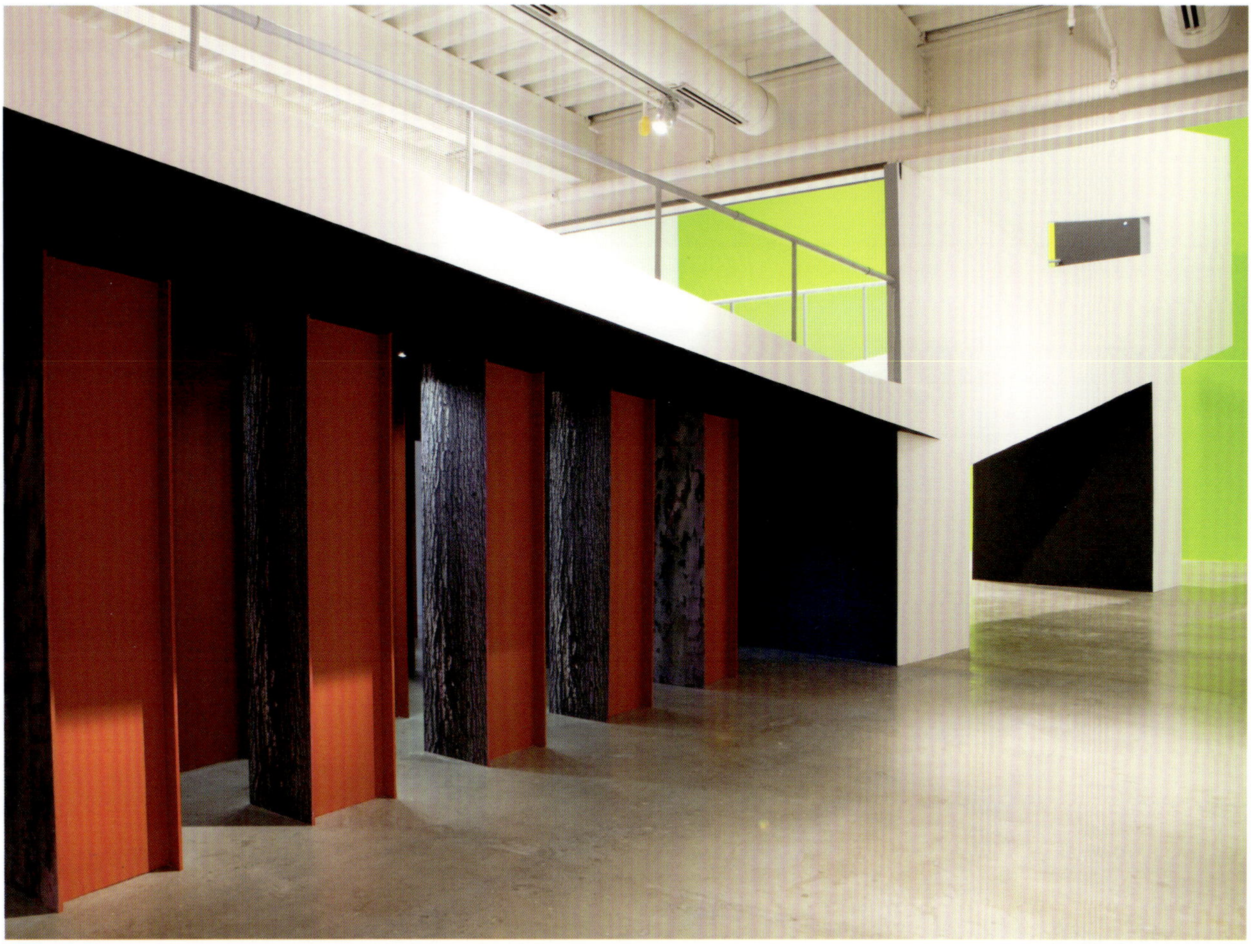

FERTILIZERS, INSTITUTE OF CONTEMPORARY ART

Although confined to an installation inside a building, this commissioned project represents several concerns and strategies that have long been present in Eisenman and Olin's collaborative work. The first of these is an interest in landforms that are also structures, a condition that provides the kinds of physical and sensual experiences that lie at the heart of both landscape and architecture. These include a concern for ground, or surface, and one's shifting relationship to it. Because it was impossible to dig in the ground of the gallery itself (as the project is sited on the second floor), early thoughts focused on building a new floor above the existing one—a floor that could operate independently of the gallery and lead to the possibility of moving away from it. At the same time, ambiguity about the nature of a structure that would allow upward movement suggested several possibilities—dislocation, discomfort, curiosity, and stimulus. Ideas of extension, amplitude and seriality have persisted in Olin and Eisenman's joint work, as have notions of spaces that are full or empty, contradicting expectations or normative processes. The ICA project, as in so much of the work they have proposed, questions the privilege given to particular forms in either architecture or landscape. Finally, their interest in movement, sequence, and the multiple experiences and possibilities of any given set of paths, or forms, is manifested in the finished project.

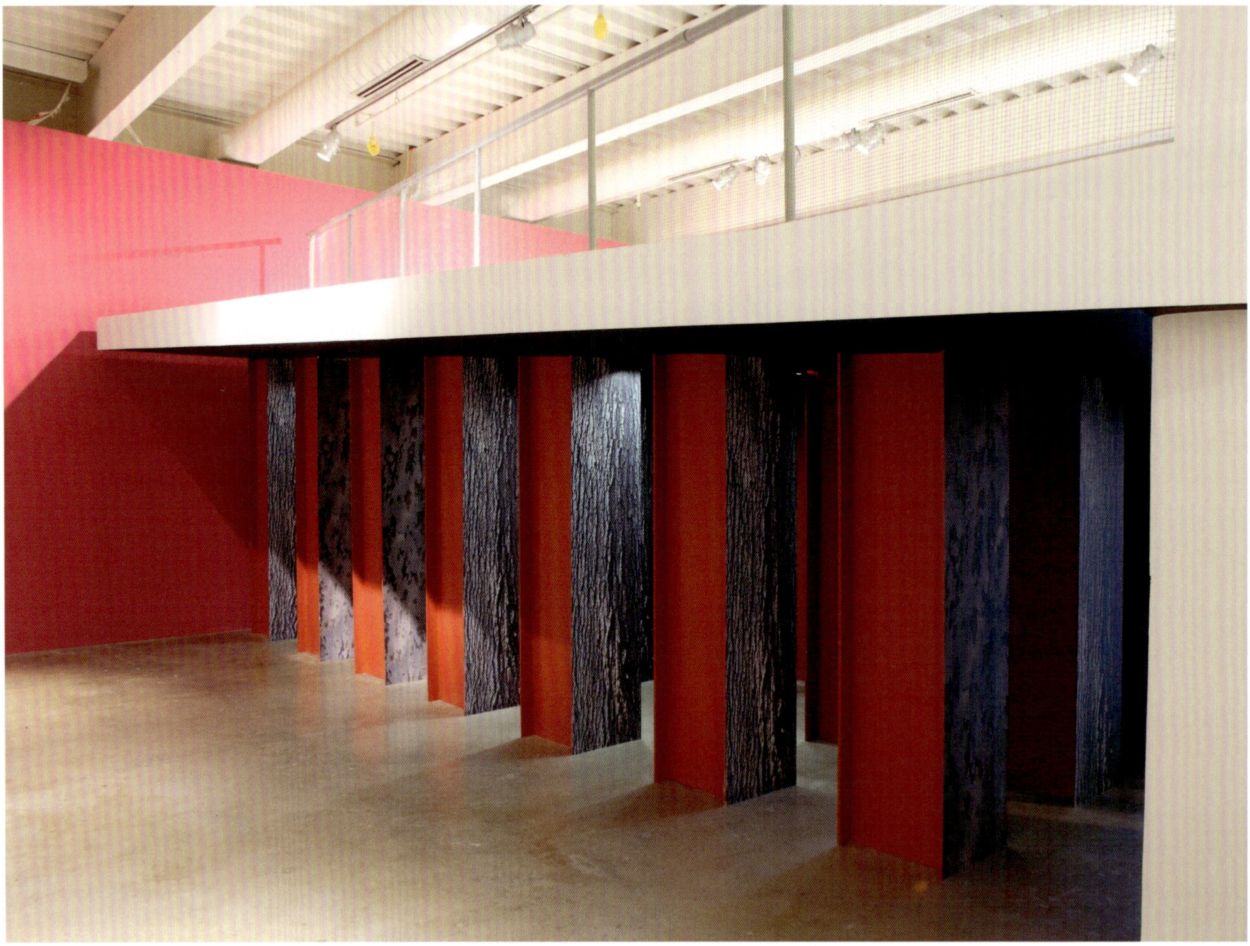

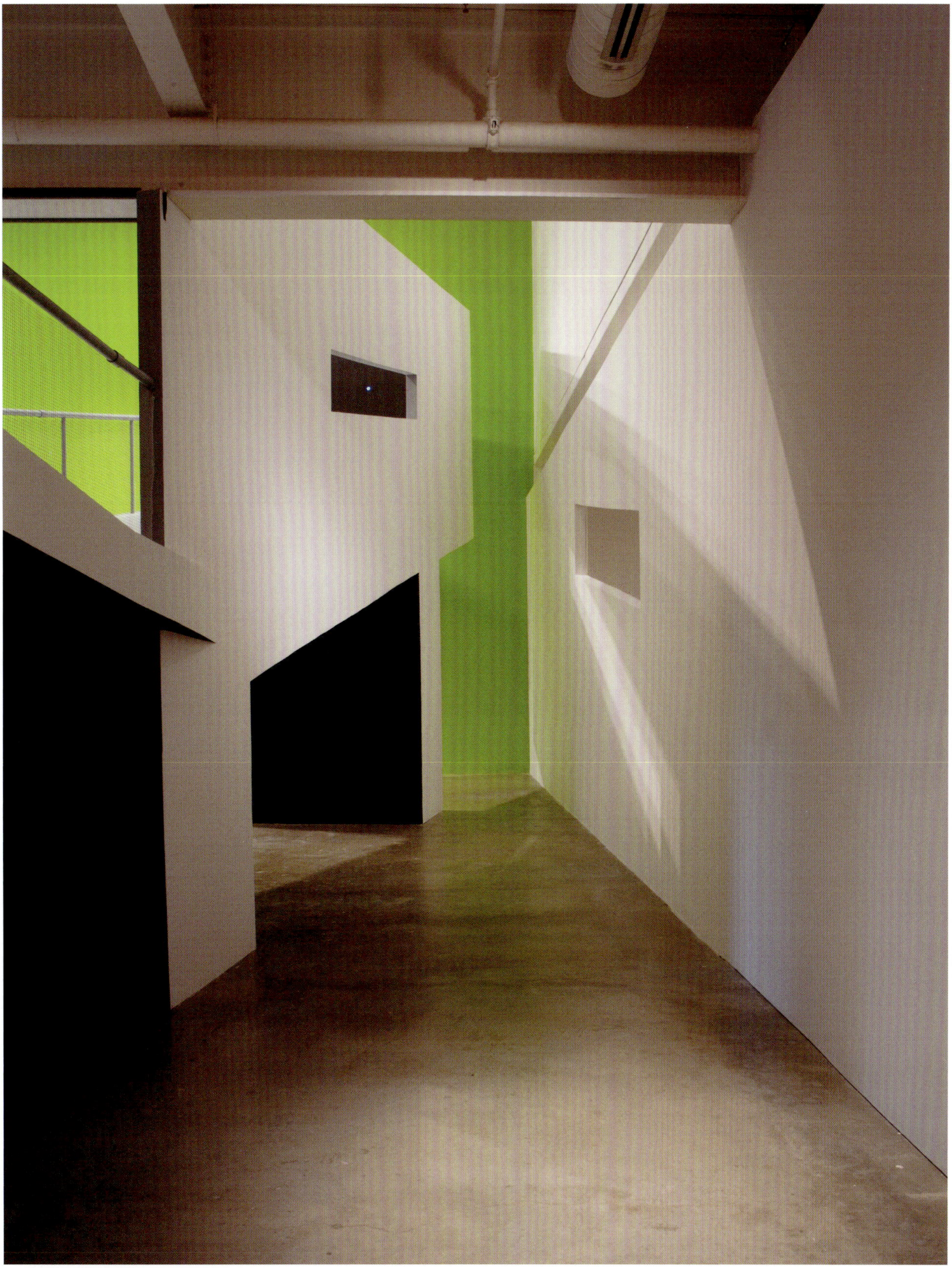

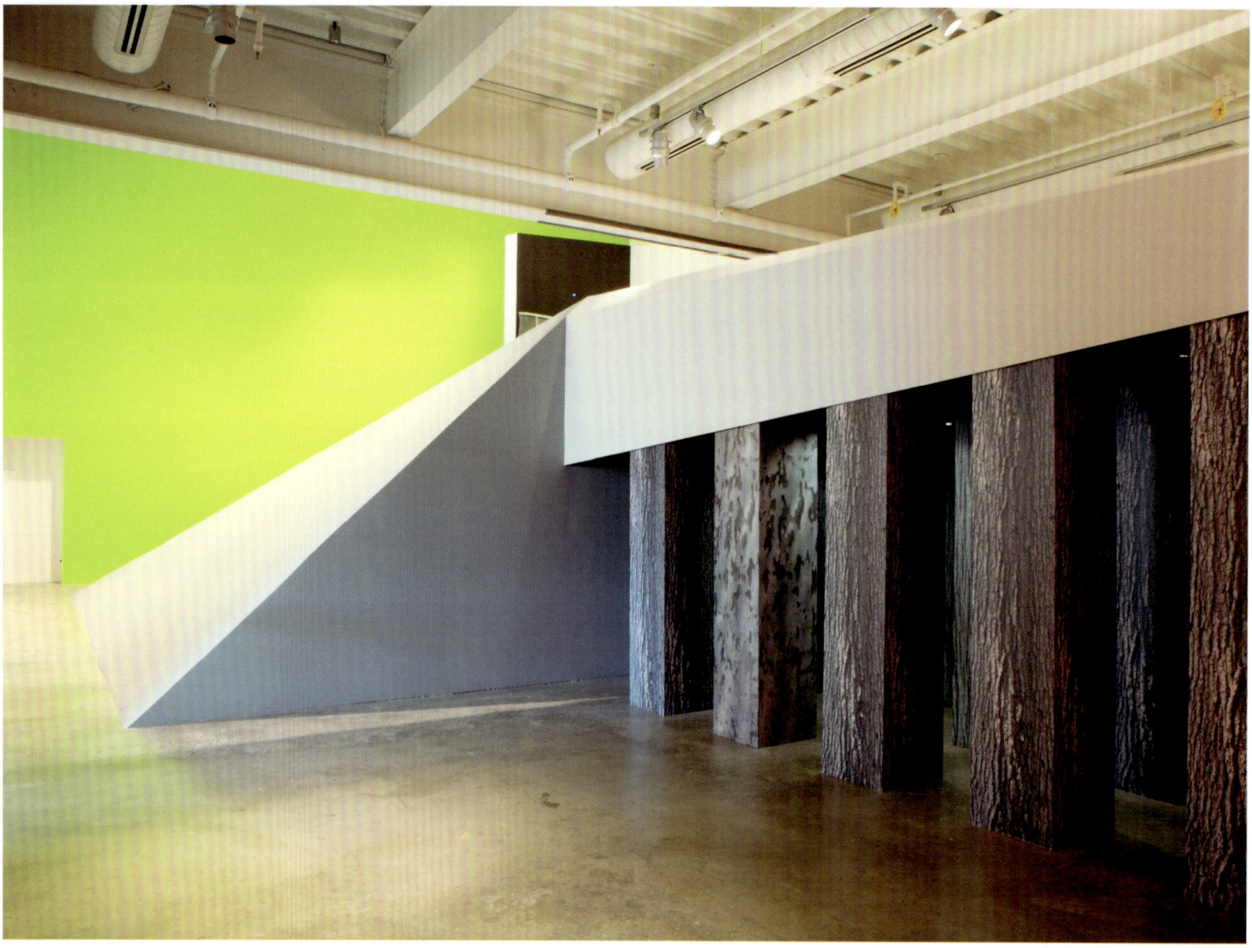

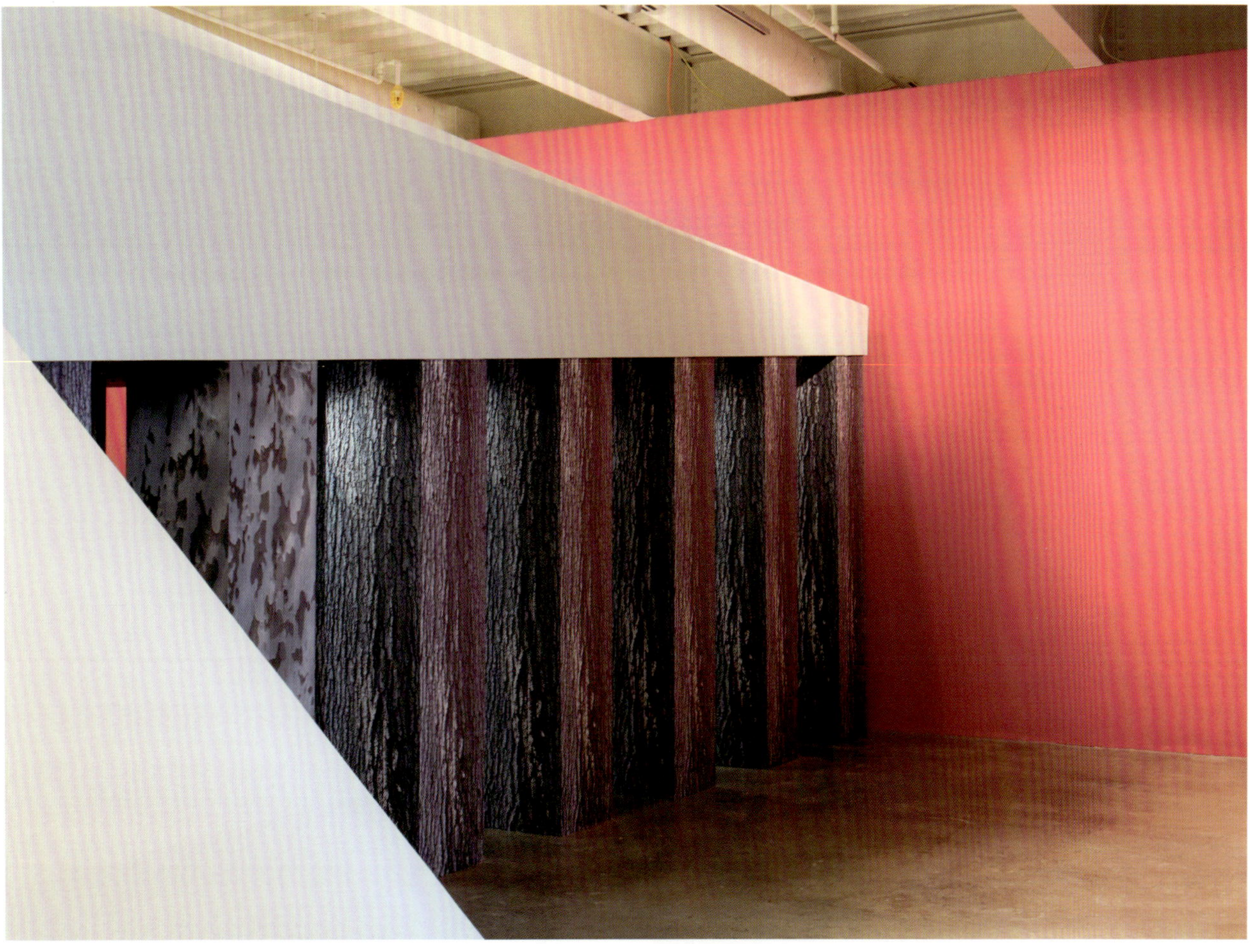

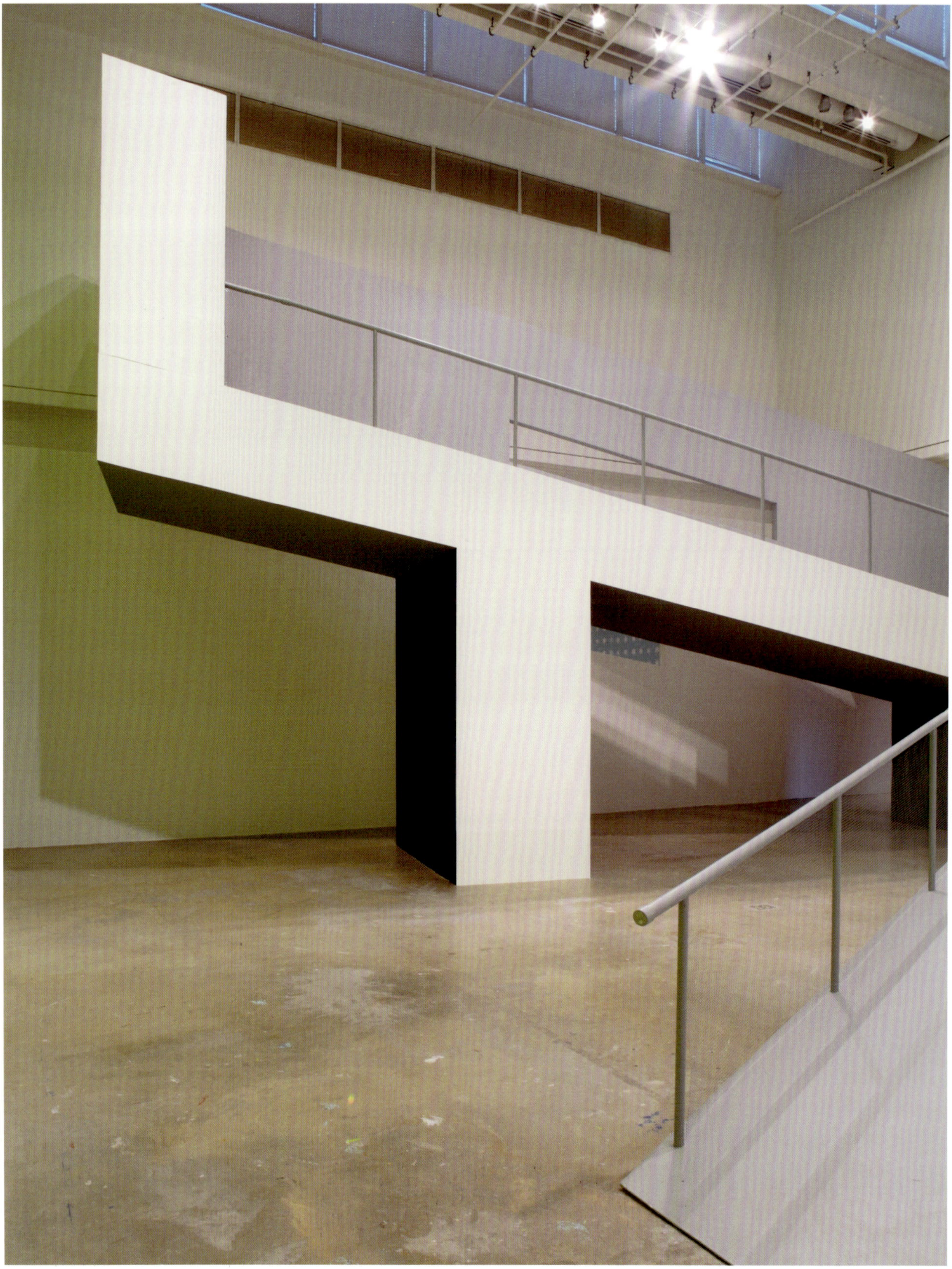

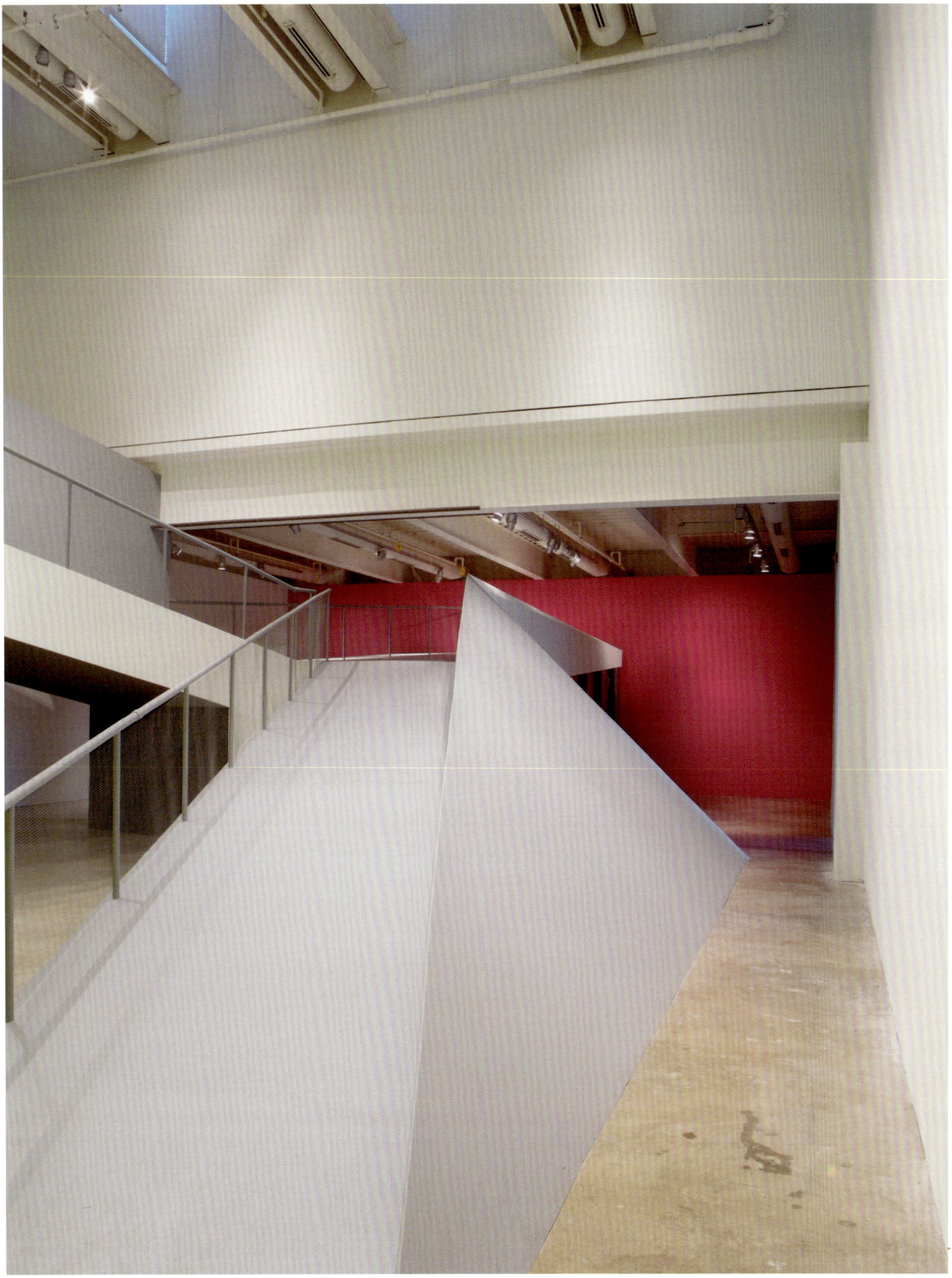

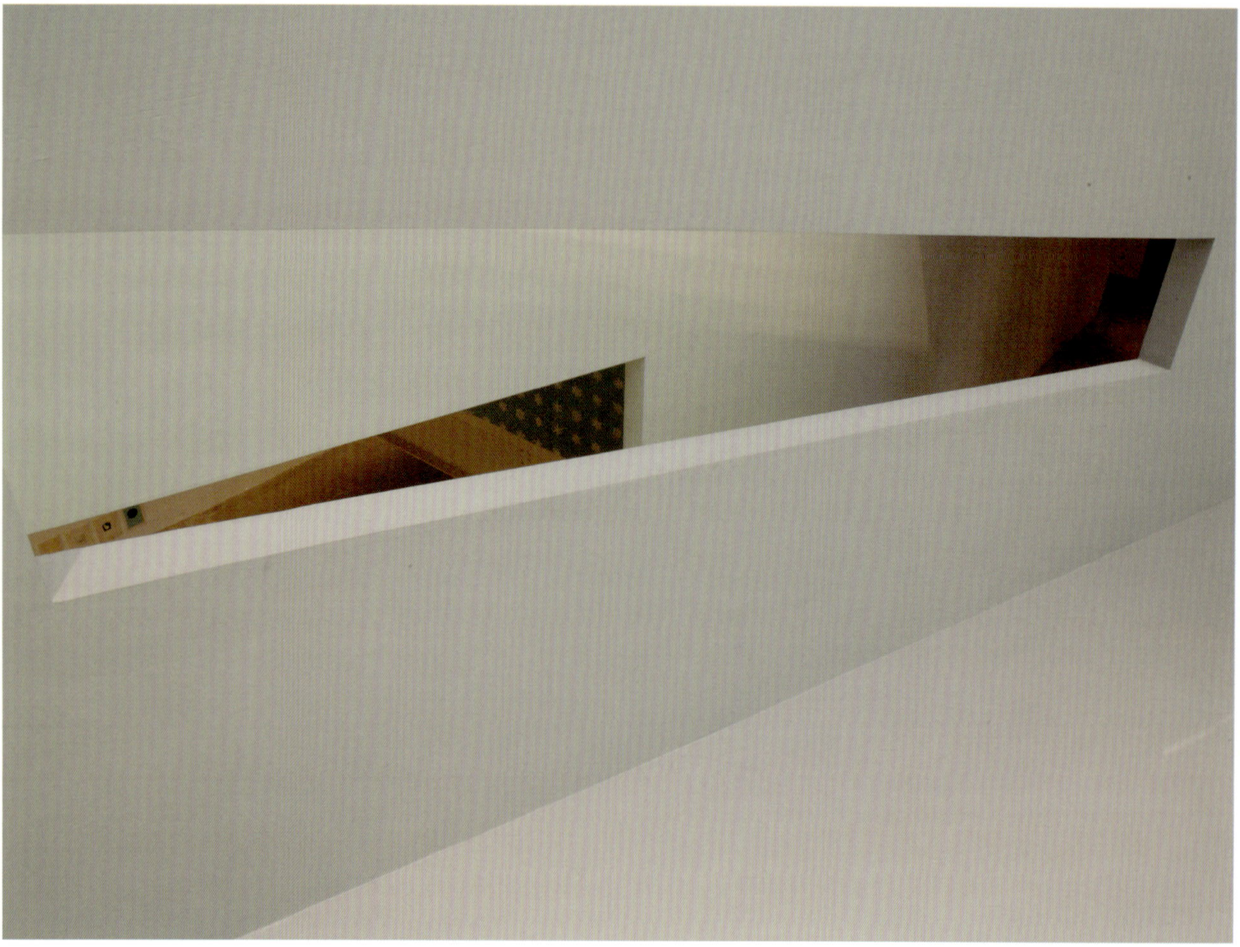

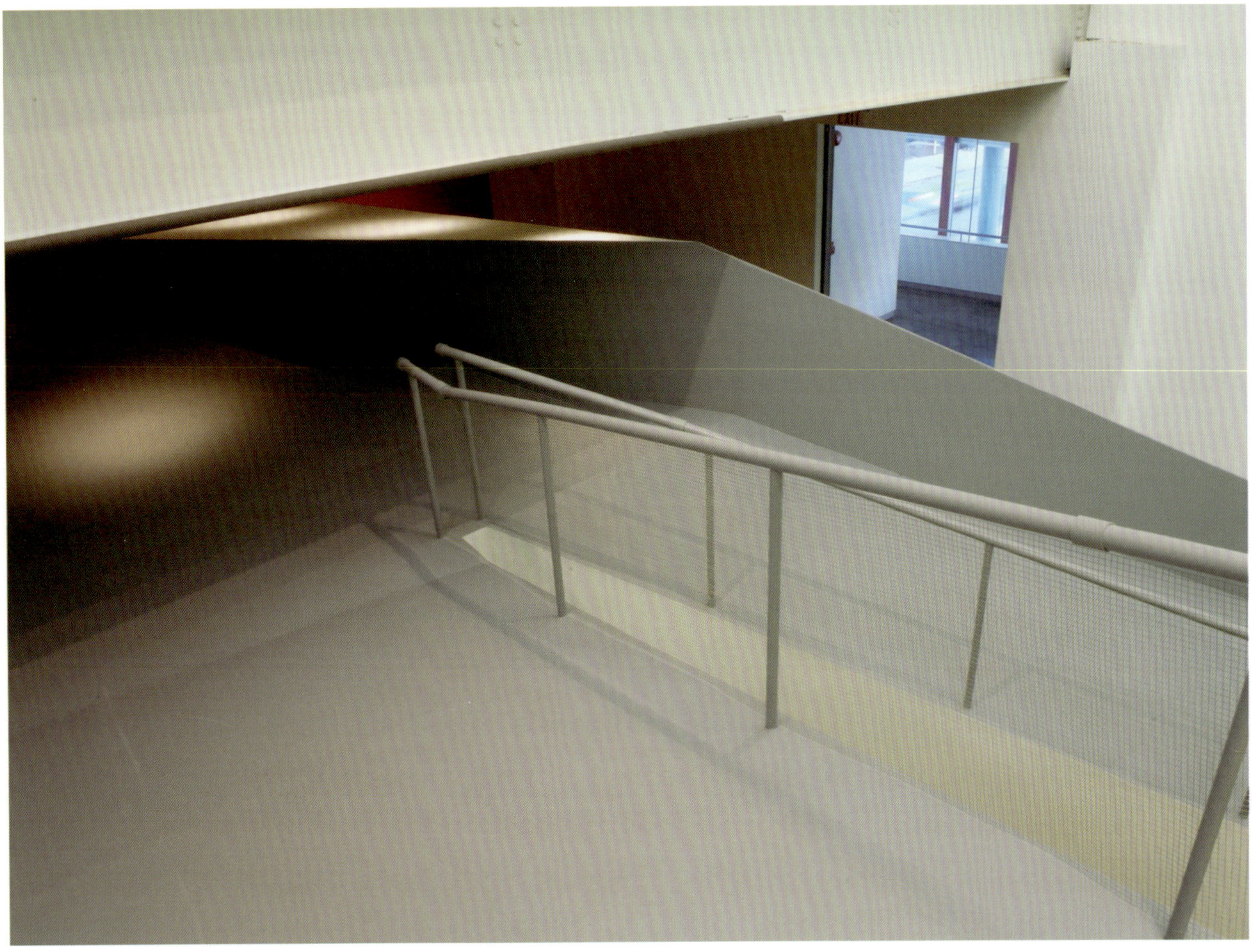

LAURIE OLIN AND PETER EISENMAN
INTERVIEWED BY CLAUDIA GOULD
AUGUST 2006

G: The beginning of your collaborative relationship was a competition you did for a city park in Portland, Oregon. Who brought you together and why?

O: The Portland competition was the first time I ever met Peter. I knew of him when I lived in New York in the 1960s because of a group called CASE. I was at Edward Larrabee Barnes's office with Jaquelin Robertson, who was part of CASE. In 1967 there was a show at the Museum of Modern Art that we did a project for, and Peter and Michael Graves also did a project, so I knew Peter's work.

E: The show was on new city architecture and urban renewal in December 1967. I had started the Institute [for Architecture and Urban Studies] in September. I said to Jaque, why don't you come join me at the Institute, and he said, "I'm going to do urban design for Mayor Lindsey, why don't you work with us?" And I said, "Why don't you give us projects to do for you?" These became the first projects we did at the Institute, housing projects. And Laurie was floating around.

O: I had left Ed's office and was doing some freelance work for Jaque and Richard Weinstein.

G: So did Peter invite you to work with him?

O: I think Jaque called me, because it was a project in the Pacific Northwest. By now, Peter and Jaque had a firm, Eisenman Robertson. It was an open RFP [request for proposal], so we put together a team that made the interview cut and then the competition.

O: The Wexner competition was interesting because we knew who our competitors were, and we knew what the site was. Peter asked me a series of questions in the following order: he said, "How big is the program?" I said, "It's this big." He said, "Could we put it here in the oval?" I said, "You could put it there but we'd lose the competition." Then he said, "Well, could we put it all in this area between the buildings where the street is?" And I said, "You could, but we'd lose." So Peter said, "Would it all fit behind?" And I said, "Yes, but we'd lose because there's no visibility." So Peter said, "Then we have to put it on both sides," and I said, "Yes, we have to use the whole site." So he and I decided we would use the whole site somehow. We didn't know how, we just knew we had to occupy the whole territory.

G: That's interesting, because every side is different.

E: I'll tell you why we won. We were not allowed to bring models to the jury, but you were allowed to take photographs of the model. What we did, which was really against the rules, was make a beautiful, big model, and we took it secretly to Ohio State. We asked if we could bring in visual material to show the jury, and they said yes. So when everybody else was gone, we walked in with the model and put it in front of the jury and they wouldn't let us take it away...

O: The thing about competitions is you have to figure out which rules to break. In the course of doing the Wexner, Peter and I really did have fun. It was kind of terrifying when we were trying to figure out how to build it.

E: For the first time we defined a way of working together.

O: A way of working together and a way of thinking about a site.

G: Working together in a way that no one else has done since.

E: No, just not up to that moment. No one had done that. I mean, that landscape...

O: It was pretty radical.... I remember the day we were talking about building up and cutting down, and we did a section that showed stuff going up and stuff going down, and we were trying to figure out how to have a person experience both. That's what we're still interested in.

E: That's where this show comes in. "Fertilizers" is exactly that.

G: How do you feel about reviews at the time the Wexner was built that describe it as the building that theory built? How did that description strike you then, and what does it mean to you both now?

E: People love to say those things, but what does it mean? What architecture that's worth its soul isn't built with ideas? The Wexner doesn't have some theory. We were flying by the seat of our pants. It was a one shot, that moment. I think critics said that because they wanted to say something derogatory. Theory is a dirty word. Like formal. Formal and theory are the worst words. And then they started calling it deconstructive. I didn't know anything about deconstruction in 1982.

O: Form and formalism are totally useless words because everything that exists has form, even gas clouds.

E: There's a big argument today about form and shape. Form means something other than what you see. Form means some interior organizing principal, and this gets people a little bit wacky. They think that the organizing principal should be the function, the structure, the shelter, the experience, right? And, of course, this is where Laurie and I move apart a little, this is where there would be, if anything, a difference.

O: I've always been more overtly interested in figural composition in terms of expressing an interest in what something might look like.

G: The notion of a continuum in building and landscape is one of the main and most successful aspects of the Wexner Center. It continues at IIT, Long Beach, the Disney Hotel, and many of your projects. Can you talk about where the grid meets the organic with the abstraction you've inherited?

E: Well, first of all I don't think the terms narrative and abstraction or figure and grid have anything to do with any one specific aspect of our work. In other words, all of the projects have all of those elements at the same time. There's not one that you can say is purely figural or purely abstract.

G: But one aspect comes from one of you and something comes from the other, and for some reason it gets joined together.

E: No, I don't think that's true.

O: On our best projects what would usually happen is that Peter would invite me to do something. He would call me when he was starting to think about it and ask if I wanted to work on it, and I'd say sure, sounds like fun. I would come to New York and we would have an extended conversation about what might be possible, what might be ideas, what the content might be. Sometimes we would have two or three of these conversations as things began to start, and they would go from one to four hours, and would ramble around, and all sorts of stuff would come up.

E: And he'd start drawing.

G: I have some questions about Santiago de Compostela. I read that it is culturally and psychologically important for the region, but I also see that it's been important for both of you on an emotional level. Will you speak to that?

E: The difference in this project for me is that we used stone for the first time.

O: We've used stone before but not this way.

E: The site is stone, but now the buildings are stone. I had never thought of using stone, so it wasn't so much emotional as it was certainly getting over an inhibition and saying, let's try it.

G: And you pushed yourself with it?

O: Well, think of it this way. In many of the projects I've done with Peter there's a monolithic aspect to them, there's a tectonic that really comes out of thinking about geology. And in this project, the buildings now achieve that to a degree. The site and architecture are unified in a geologic conception which achieves something we've been drawing and thinking about.

EXHIBITION WALKTHROUGH
INSTITUTE OF CONTEMPORARY ART
SEPTEMBER 8, 2006

Claudia Gould: "Fertilizers" is a celebration of Peter Eisenman and Laurie Olin's twenty-five-year collaboration of built and unbuilt projects. This says a lot about the profession. There are a lot of architects and landscape architects and architecture students here tonight, and many of you know that even such a long collaboration as this one can produce very little built work. In this way, it's a difficult profession. We thought here at Penn it would be interesting to celebrate the professions in some way, while at the same time, offer a glimpse of what it's like to be an architect and how hard it is—the disappointment and the great joy of actually being able to build. Fertilizers. Can you tell me how you came up with that name and what does it mean?

Peter Eisenman: This is basically a celebration of landscape's relationship to architecture. The focus is on Laurie and his collaboration with my office, not us and our collaboration with Laurie. So we thought "Fertilizers" had something to do with making things grow, but also something to do with making things explode. We are always looking for hidden meanings and that's why it's not "Fertilizer," but "Fertilizers"—both growing and exploding, which are both part of what you see here.

Laurie Olin: My wife actually wondered if it had something to do with what people think of our work on occasion.

G: Peter, will you talk about how this project embodies a lot of the ideas that you and Laurie have been playing with for the last twenty-five years? And, what's successful about the project, and what's not?

E: What is successful about it is that we thought it together, and then Laurie drew it and built it.

O: That's very generous of Peter, but I'll say a couple of other things. For a long time, Peter and I have tried to conceive of the things that are common to both the art of architecture and the art of landscape. We have never been really interested in objects, so when Claudia asked us to do something in a room indoors we thought, "Ugh, how do you do that?" It's sort of the antithesis of what we have tried to do in our collaborations. So we could only think that we might be able to employ some of the strategies we've used in our other work, which has to do with how to move through and experience the full possible range of a place. In this case we couldn't dig a hole, which we did in several of our other projects—we've done some pretty good holes—so we tried to figure out how to use the holes in the building, like that door. And then we made some other holes so that we could look down into other layers.

E: When Laurie is not working with us, for me he is a different guy. And what I like is that when he works with us he becomes Dr. Jekyll, or Mr. Hyde, one of the two....

O: I think this is the Hyde side.

E: He produces work that forces me to think about landscape in a way that I wouldn't do without him. I think that together we produce work that is not landscape added to building, but building as landscape, or landscape as building. We would like to think of "Fertilizers" as this crossover, as between ideas of "is this a building that's really a landscape that you can walk on?" or, "is it a landscape that is a building?" I think that edge is what we tried to get here.

G: The disorientation here in "Fertilizers" is also found at the Wexner Center, whether in the plinths and the experience of moving around the outside of the building, or inside, traveling up the ramps that go nowhere, visiting galleries that are odd sizes and shapes. I remember the University was very much against those plinths because they thought students would get hurt. Do you remember that discussion?

E: One of the things you find here that is also in the Wexner is a series of three small staircases that went up a series of different levels. You would get used to walking up the first staircase and coming to a gallery, then walking up the second staircase and arriving at a gallery, then you walked up the third staircase and you banged your head on the ceiling. The first time somebody banged their head they fell off the end of the stair, so they had to install glass to prevent it from happening again.

O: People just don't pay attention.

G: The view from the top of "Fertilizers," down through the slit in the wall, is actually a wonderful way to look at John Armleder's show on the first floor. It's a beautiful glimpse. And then up at the top there's our own little *Étant Donnes*—a secret about nothing.

E: But there is something to see when you get up there, though for anyone who has vertigo, you'll feel it.

G: But there's also a sense of vertigo in the forest of columns. The forest reminds me of the columns at the Wexner, the non-structural columns. It's a beautiful metaphor of that building and the landscape, and for that, well, I'm really delighted.

E: Well, both of us are very grateful to have a chance to do an exhibition here. This is what the Italians would call a *percorso*, a sort of walk through the woods. There are the woods and the city, the different feelings. You stand down here on the gallery floor, but when you're up there you get a very different feeling of the space, and I think that's what landscape and architecture are supposed to do.

G: I just want to give you a glimpse of how these two really think very differently. I learned that there was a discussion about how to make the bark on the trees. Laurie said immediately, "Oh, I'm going to draw the bark." And Peter looks at Laurie and says, "Just photograph a tree—just use a camera and photograph it." So each has a very different sensibility regarding mathematics, science, art and poetry.

O: We started with real trees. Peter said too literal, I said okay, so I drew a grid. Peter said great, they should be this shape, and I said fine. And then I said, let's put bark on them, and he said okay. So it was more like a ping-pong game, it went back and forth.

G: So, finish this ping-pong match please.

O: Well we've been doing it for twenty-four years—we don't want to finish.

CONVERSATION: PETER EISENMAN AND LAURIE OLIN
INSTITUTE OF CONTEMPORARY ART
SEPTEMBER 20, 2006

EXCERPTS FROM AN INFORMAL DISCUSSION WITH EISENMAN AND OLIN, INTRODUCED AND MODERATED BY JULIA CZERNIAK. THE FORMAT WAS LARGELY QUESTION-AND-ANSWER FROM THE LARGE AUDIENCE OF PENN STUDENTS AND FACULTY.

Audience (James Corner): I am wondering about the place of theory in your respective work and in your common work. How do Laurie's pragmatism and Peter's philosophy dialogue?

E: First of all, you're trying to make a dialectic out of this. Nothing is white and black. Jacques [Derrida] taught me a great lesson when I worked with him. He said, "You know Peter, architects need not be good philosophers." I'm a really bad philosopher and architecture is bad philosophy. Okay, it's probably also bad theory. When I say a discipline is made up of problems, I'm not talking about solving problems, I'm proposing to open up those problems to inspection, whereas Laurie says that he is interested in problem solving. You can sit here and say that, but you can't build a building just on air, or theory.

O: I will confess, maybe I am a pragmatist. As far as philosophy goes, I'm closer to a Zen attitude about how to do things, and I'm much more interested in the physical property of stuff than Peter is. Let me put it this way: I have a problem with the way ideas and concepts are portrayed by a lot of my colleagues in academia. Take, for instance, the concept of a cube. A cube—now there's an idea. Imagine these lines with corners, but with no scale and no properties, it's just a concept, an abstract idea as a cube. Now if I said to you, a six-foot cube, that's very different from a two-foot cube. So it's starting to become something. And then if I said a six-foot cube of shaving cream, you'd say, a six-foot cube of shaving cream, Jesus! Now, imagine that as opposed to a six-foot cube of black granite. They're not the same thing; they're such completely different concepts that the notion of the physical materiality has everything to do with the theoretical idea of those cubes. So, yeah, I'm a pragmatist.

E: The question I would ask you is, in what way would either of those cubes—even though they are different and even though you might prefer black granite—solve the problem that we were working on?

O: They usually don't. But they end up being the expression of what we are proposing. Everything ends up with the problem of expression.

Audience (Helene Furjan): One of the things that intrigues me about "Fertilizers" is the idea of a tactile vision that has been a part of landscape since at least the picturesque, if not before. It's something that operates differently in architecture, it comes and goes. I'm interested in the way in which that might be a part of your work. In this piece, as with other work you've done, you're really confronted by certain things: with the steepness of the gradient of the ramp; the fact that you've deliberately made everyone almost walk into the ceiling beam not once, but twice; and so on. The second question is, we're in Philadelphia, and you make us go up to a peephole. I'm wondering if there's also an important reference to a Duchamp's iconic piece of work at the Philadelphia Museum of Art?

E: I think your question is very good. You know, I go to my buildings a lot and I say, wow, I really like this, and yet they seem almost like happy accidents. For example, I couldn't have predetermined what it would be like in Berlin [at the Memorial to the Murdered Jews of Europe] to watch people move around in the piece, to disappear and then come out of this gridded space. And it's pure accident, I didn't think about it.

O: It's not an accident, Peter.

E: As for the peephole. The peephole is an iconic Philadelphia destination. You're seeing the street through the peephole, which you've already experienced and seen walking up. I have a problem with heights, and I didn't think the ramp was going to be as steep and as problematic as it is. At a certain point I said, "I can't go any

further." I've done rooms in buildings that have made people sick. Heinrich Heine said that you can kill a person as quickly with a room as with an axe, and I truly believe that. I think there are a lot of haptic qualities in the work, but I don't need a theoretician like Deleuze to tell me so. I believe that when you work as an architect you develop an eye. I can only look at real models. I can't look at computer screens because anybody can manipulate that. You've got to look at the physical model and assume what it would be like to be in and around the space, and still you can never get all the corners.
You miss things, bad things and good things. Now, I can tell you what I don't like about the project because I missed it. And I told Laurie, I missed it.

O: I agree with him. The truth is that we drew it, we built a little model, we thought we knew what we were doing, and then it got built, and I thought, oops.

E: So, I'm not worried about the haptic because it will always come up and bite you.

O: But that physical experience is obviously something we both care deeply about.

Audience: Do you feel that the architect reacts to, or promotes, changes in our culture?

E: The only changes that architecture can provoke are changes within the discipline of architecture. They cannot change culture. And that's a categoric statement.

Founded in 1963, the Institute of Contemporary Art at the University of Pennsylvania is a leader in the presentation and documentation of contemporary art. Through exhibitions, commissions, educational programs, and publications, ICA invites the public to share in the experience, interpretation and understanding of the work of established and emerging artists.

*Peter Eisenman and Laurie Olin would like to especially thank Shannon Bowser, Robert Chaney, and the entire ICA installation crew for making "Fertilizers" a built project.

ICA IS GRATEFUL FOR THE GENEROUS SUPPORT OF THE PHILADELPHIA EXHIBITIONS INITIATIVE, A GRANTING PROGRAM OF THE PHILADELPHIA CENTER FOR ARTS AND HERITAGE, FUNDED BY THE PEW CHARITABLE TRUSTS AND ADMINISTERED BY THE UNIVERSITY OF THE ARTS, PHILADELPHIA. WE ARE ALSO GRATEFUL FOR FUNDING FROM ELISE JAFFE + JEFFREY BROWN AND THE GOLDBERG FOUNDATION, INC. ICA ACKNOWLEDGES SUPPORT FROM THE ARCHITECTURAL AND DESIGN COMMUNITY: AMUNEAL MANUFACTURING CORP.; THE ACCENT ON ARCHITECTURE GRANTS PROGRAM, SUPPORTED BY GRANTS FROM THE AMERICAN ARCHITECTURAL FOUNDATION, CNA INSURANCE COMPANIES AND VICTOR O. SCHINNERER & COMPANY, INC.; ATKIN OLSHIN LAWSON-BELL ARCHITECTS; BALLINGER; KIERANTIMBERLAKE ASSOCIATES LLP; MGA PARTNERS, ARCHITECTS; AND MINIMA INC. ADDITIONAL FUNDING HAS BEEN PROVIDED BY THE HORACE W. GOLDSMITH FOUNDATION, THE COMMONWEALTH OF PENNSYLVANIA COUNCIL ON THE ARTS, THE DIETRICH FOUNDATION, INC., THE OVERSEERS BOARD FOR THE INSTITUTE OF CONTEMPORARY ART, FRIENDS AND MEMBERS OF ICA, AND THE UNIVERSITY OF PENNSYLVANIA. ICA IS ALSO GRATEFUL FOR IN-KIND SUPPORT FROM LOEWS PHILADELPHIA HOTEL.